T0157739

# RIEN
## IMPOSSIBLE
# EN
## MAURITANIE

## MOHAMED
## HAIDARA

authorHOUSE®

*AuthorHouse*™
*1663 Liberty Drive*
*Bloomington, IN 47403*
*www.authorhouse.com*
*Phone: 1-800-839-8640*

© *2012 by Mohamed Haidara. All rights reserved.*

*No part of this book may be reproduced, stored in a retrieval system, or transmitted by any means without the written permission of the author.*

*Published by AuthorHouse    03/08/2012*

*ISBN: 978-1-4678-9061-8 (sc)*
*ISBN: 978-1-4678-9082-3 (e)*

*This book is printed on acid-free paper.*

*Because of the dynamic nature of the Internet, any web addresses or links contained in this book may have changed since publication and may no longer be valid. The views expressed in this work are solely those of the author and do not necessarily reflect the views of the publisher, and the publisher hereby disclaims any responsibility for them.*

*Photographs copyright by Anders Graver.*

# CONTENTS

This book is dedicated to Mariem and Mwoiny.

The latter, my guard dog, companion and fellow shepherd, the former, the formidable and beautiful woman, who has now chosen to walk by my side.

## CHAPTER ONE

# BEGINNINGS

E VERY STORY HAS a beginning, and mine no less bizarre than anyone else's. I had been living a nightmare that was divorce. Harassed by my soon-to-be ex and abetted by the Family Court System, which allowed her to contrive evidence of an unsavoury nature. What for all the other tiers of law in England is perjury, in the case of family law is evidence. Armed with facetious on-going criminal proceedings, she and her legal team ripped from me from my son and left me out to dry. I was being arrested weekly/two weekly under Section 5 of The Public Order Act, for simply walking in the direction of my ex's house, though a few miles away there was a market town in between! Normally I'd be released around 0300 hrs 25 miles from home. Raids on my house at all hours but mostly after midnight. From moment of contact they'd get abuse. I'd use the floor rather than the toilet and went on hunger-strike. I'd sign everything Mickey Mouse and screw up my copy into a ball and throw in the face of the desk sergeant. After a year and a half of abuse and being constantly ignored, treated like a leper, being threatened with 18 month's imprisonment for releasing details of the case, I pointed out that I would only be releasing details of the mechanics of the legal system, which allow perjury and hearsay to be used as evidence. That I would immediately go on hunger strike at the point of arrest. Naturally friends and neighbours became distant and there'd be red zones in my home town. Letters to Tony Blair and my MP came to fuck all, marches, canvasing and bitching, publishing details of the mechanics of a legal system that were abhorrent in a supposed civilised country, hoping I'd be arrested and take it to the next level. On top of the shit being shovelled copiously in my direction, I got some bad news. A divorced man I had met on a Fathers-4-Justice march, had had enough. One day he went for a walk, filled his pockets full of stones and took a swim. Men were dumped in prison for following the dictates of their betters, held without trial, men criminalised for being simply divorced fathers. What is the state of play after ten years? Same old same old.

Since living in Mauritania, I've met a great many people who have taken off; leaving jobs, home and security, to trek off into the sunset, some with their families and some without. Some are borne by dreams and others, are fuelled by alcohol. A case in point is the six members of a Parisians brass band who decided to travel to Mali on La Poste mobylettes, to attend the Tuareg Festival . . . my beginning, was born out of sarcasm. Also, it was difficult to recollect the exact phrase when being asked if I remembered what I had said years later, when perhaps 10 000 or more sarcastic comments have passed my lips since. When asked by my son then aged seven; at an inopportune moment, what I'd do when he left home, because I may have been busy at the time and would never actually say, "Fuck off I'm busy!"

But instead I said: "I'll buy a camel and walk the Sahara!"

So, several years later after being reunited with my sarcasm, it gnawed away at me for two months, until I finally decided upon a new life. Lesson number one; never discount anything as being done and dusted. It'll always come back and bite your ass later. It would be seven years later that I could finally put the ghost of my divorce experience behind me. This ass-biting would be poetic justice and allow me to finally take control of my life.

My story begins in June/July 2005, just as a military coup d'etat (The Islamic Republic of Mauritania's ninth since independence in 1960) was taking place in my future country of residence. I began by filling my ass, arm and mouth with every vaccination I thought I'd need to survive the rigours of Africa. (It's a pity they don't have one for the White Maure!) My next plan of action was to sell off my possessions and give those that I couldn't, to Save The Children, which amounted to a small fortune. I have since seen the many new and expensive Toyota LandCruisers of that charity here in Nouakchott and the insincerity and complete disregard that the resident NGO's have for their work, considering the extent to which famine has struck R.I.M., is sickening in the extreme. This done, I said goodbye to those people that mattered, left my will with friends and left the UK in early September by Atlas Blue, when I should have been at a going away party. I don't like these at all.

I had worked with a Saharawi nurse, we'll call Fatima, in the UK for two years. When I told her that I was travelling overland to R.I.M. from Marrakech to acclimatise, before heading off into the Sahara, she became very excited. It would have been very easy to fly direct but stupid, to leave the fridge of the UK and walk straight into the furnace of the Sahara. She asked if I would take some photographs, phone numbers and email addresses to a cousin, if indeed he were still where he was last reported to be. If not there was another and another. She had made and lost contact with various members of her family throughout the years in exile. But with family in prison in Laayoune, exiled at Tindouf or moved abroad or had died as in the case of her uncle and aunt only recently, it was difficult to keep in touch. He lived on the coast, south of Laayoune. Later, I would pass Dakhla and would I do the same for a friend of Fatima's, Khadi, who lives in London. During our time together she had told me everything about the struggle of her people for The Saharawi Arab Democratic Republic (SADR) and I knew that it would be difficult and perhaps dangerous, but being a Scot, we don't know difficult or dangerous. We are stubborn in the extreme where human rights are involved. We've had to contend with our southern neighbours' continued harassment over hundreds of years, and we're still here, a proverbial pain in their ass! I touched down in Marrakech and stayed two and a half days doing the tourist thing and had 400 Dirham taken from my pockets as I traversed Djemaa El Fna on the second night, always a sucker for those pretty girls, imbecile! (This would be minor in comparison to what I would later experience in R.I.M.) I took the Supratours bus to Agadir and was instantly struck by its Britishness and of course it's full of English tourists. Here again, I stayed two days and played with the English tourists that has since become a habit with me. Indeed, on my last visit to my sister Lesley, I met the local Lenzie Tory candidate out canvassing and illustrates nicely the game that I like to play with the English abroad. I immediately shake their hands in turn wishing them a good day in French and continue to speak French when it is abundantly apparent that they don't understand a fuckin' word I'm saying. I don't insult them; as such, and finish off by shaking their hands in turn, which a great many don't like. This morning, the three Tories hadn't a clue what was about to hit them. I began by shaking their hands vigorously, wishing them good morning and when I knew the game was afoot I laid in . . .

"It's a waste of your time trying to get my vote as I am not a local and furthermore, you are a complete, waste of space and you have no chance around here but as this is a democratic country, you have the right to try and garner a vote or two. But it will only be a vote or two!"

I finished off by wishing them luck and throughout it was all I could do to stop pissing myself. I declined to kiss the young woman as I thought they have me arrested for sexual assault. Anyhoo, she wasn't that pretty. So, this is what I do with English tourists anywhere I encounter them in the French-speaking world, especially those who adopt the shout and point method of communication. As for not saying good day, thank you or good-bye, that just bugs the hell out of me. The English language is peppered with French. There's no excuse for bad manners.

Leaving Agadir in the early evening, Supratours took me onwards to Laayoune. On reaching Tan Tan the mood on the bus changed, everyone on guard. mp3's switched off, phone calls abruptly finished and everyone reaching for their ID cards or passports. This is the border between Morocco and The Western Sahara, the most sparsely inhabited region in the world, comprising of desert flatlands and enormous reserves in fish, petrol, minerals and mines. Lots of them. Twenty million anti-personnel and a comparative number of anti-tank mines I believe. Simple and effective control of a population, where the victims are mainly livestock and children. The reception from the Surete officer was as if I was an escaped criminal. He walked straight up to me and demanded to know my country of birth, my profession and my reason for being on the bus. It occurred to me that perhaps Scottish sarcasm wasn't appropriate here and I smiled a stupid smile being as courteous as I could; given that I didn't like his attitude towards me or the Saharawi, told him I was en route for Mauritania. As I was the only Westerner on the bus and only two Saharawi's sitting nearby, our passage wasn't impeded too long and we trundled onwards to Laayoune.

Laayoune, a huge, huge military base and the capital of SADR, the Moroccan flag draped everywhere. Laayoune, the capital of an independent state, which is a member of the African Union and recognised by forty-four nations. In 1975 the Moroccan King Hassan II led 350 000 Moroccans 4 km over the border into The Spanish Sahara, The Green March. He later claimed it was 40!! The Spanish later withdrew in 1976 when General

Franco died. The Spanish troops wouldn't have stood a chance against the Polisario, Moroccans or the Mauritanian's as they were undernourished, poorly equipped and poorly motivated. If it weren't for the Saharawi many would have simply died of starvation. The Polisario Front then took on both the Moroccans and the Mauritanians who withdrew from the fight soon after. It is interesting to note that at the outset of war between The Polisario and Mauritania, 10 000 Mauritanians defected to them. They are in effect cousins and look very similar. A UN inspired cease-fire and agreement in 1991 between the Polisario and Morocco to abide by a referendum that would determine once and for all if the Saharawi's wanted independence finally brought hostilities to an end. To this day that referendum hasn't been held or is likely to be, given the wealth of SADR and the despotic nature of King Mohammed VI as he and his thugs continue to abuse . . . sorry I do apologise for the error, his governor, military and gendarmes continue to administer the 'Saharan Province.'

It was late afternoon when the bus pulled up outside its office and the capital was mostly deserted but for the many military and police going to wherever they were going to and a group of boys playing football behind me across the road from the Supratours office, in a huge hot and dusty square. The few passengers left on the bus were picked up by friends and relatives and driven off, leaving me all alone. Across the road I could see a café, which sold camel milk. There were three Saharawi men sharing a small pot of tea and one glass and two Moroccans with short leather jackets drinking coffee, smoking cigarettes and very interested in me. I decided to have some milk and find a taxi to take me out to the coast. The owner gave me the nod on the two flick (police) and I winked in acknowledgement. On asking for camel milk and the whereabouts of the camel market I became an instant friend. He found me a car to take me out of town and through the next two weeks I was in and out of the café, meeting Saharawi, two of which, later escorted me to the camel market. It was here I saw my first Mauritanians, camel thieves who had brought stock through the minefield north of Zouerat. This is the Mauritanian version of The Wild West, where Polisario, Moroccan, Mauritanian military and Customs, along with whores and bandits from all over the Sahara live and trade with whatever it is they have to, in order to get by. At Laayoune camel market, the camels will be sold for perhaps 1500 euros each, whereas in Mauritania a little under 300. A simple matter of economics, and losing a few to mines matters little when they have been stolen in the first place. I came across two of the brands I would later see in my neck of the woods. It gave me some satisfaction to know that their camels had been stolen, as they had belonged to complete and utter bastards. One day, I might just steal more of their camels and do the same. I have an invitation to do so. It would make an interesting video for YouTube.

On the drive out to the coast, we passed the huge hotel filled with a couple of dozen pristine UN Toyota LandCruisers (Toyota do very well from world misery). My driver told me that the UN officials rarely leave the hotel but for taking their Saharawi mistresses out shopping or to party at the beach. In fact, as I travelled in and out of Laayoune the majority were parked up as I had first seen them. I have an eye for such things and have introduced a café game here in Nouakchott. Road watch. Sitting on the terrace of Café Tunis drinking coffee and smoking a sheesha with my Arab friends, we watch the nightly parade of cars and 4x4's trundle past, starting around 21.00 hrs. Perhaps you will see the same seven or eight 4x4's drive past four, five or six times. It's a very small capital and there's not much to do, apparently. They move from fast food joint to fast food joint feeding the faces of their fat wives or themselves, rendezvous-ing at the vast expanses of spare ground such as at Stade Olympique or Palais de Congress with friends or girl-friends to drive off somewhere else in a hurry going, nowhere.

I arrived at the seaside café after negotiating three police checkpoints and a visit to register at the local Gendarmerie Royaume. The driver had to obtain written permission to come and go to collect me. He took off and I introduced myself to the young man running the café, with the code Fatima had given me, her family name and the gate at which her family had last lived near in a Moroccan city. The recognition slowly arrived along with a burst of frenzied Arabic and I instantly became a family member. My bag was grabbed from my shoulder and I was gently thrust at a table and sat down. Whereupon, tagine, tea and sheesha appeared almost instantaneously. The café was full of Saharawi watching the gyrating Arab gazelles (a Senegalese word for a petty girl—a tall girl would be called a giraffe) on the huge satellite TV sharing a coffee or pot of mint tea and smoking profusely. Fatima's cousin asked me dozens of questions as I handed over her photographs, phone numbers and email addresses. I knew I had to give him the bad news as soon as possible. As I was about to do so, his younger brother arrived and they burst into Arabic talking non-stop, looking at the photographs, phone numbers and addresses I had given them. I was kissed many times by them both and an endless supply of coffee came my way, all the time I still had this news to give them. At last a silence descended upon the table and I put my hands on theirs.

"Your uncle died five months ago from cancer, your aunt died two months later from injuries she received in a car accident."

This is still hard to take and tears are running down my face as I type. Here I was a stranger who had arrived with messages of hope from long lost family and also a message of despair. We were crying from joy and sadness. Sorry to say but sadness is a way of life for the Saharawi interspersed by moments of sheer joy. They are a remarkable people. It's a tragedy that the world stands by and does nothing to help.

I learned much from my new family and was in and out of cyber cafes in Laayoune talking with anyone who made my acquaintance, though discreetly as the ever-present secret police are everywhere. As curfew approached Saharawi youth would and still do, congregate opposite the parked up vans of the police and military, to then engage them in fights. The crews simply change shift but not the aspect of the vehicle. Here they eat and sleep, spending twelve hours a day, waiting for trouble to kick off. I managed to take photographs of riots and its after effects on the local population. Namely the injuries received by them from the military and gendarmes. Students in the main and some disturbing sights of elderly people with swollen faces and broken limbs. These I passed onto the BBC and wrote reports. Also a photograph of a huge Saharawi flag draped outside a block of flats. I thought I had wiped all the photographs I had taken but was to find out almost two years later that I hadn't, six of them to my cost at the Moroccan/ Mauritanian border. Instantly branded a terrorist and friend of the Polisario, I was eventually given one day to enter and exit Morocco after three hours of good cop/bad cop, which they don't do very well. In fact, piss poor.

"You know when the photographs were taken, you know that I haven't been back since, so why don't you simply wipe the disc and let me go!" I had the phone numbers of five Saharawi contacts which they noted down. I phoned everyone on leaving the interrogation, using the mobile of a French driver I knew who sold cars on his way south to Mali, to tell everyone to lose their numbers. Give me 24 hours, an empty room, a hose with a water supply (no water boarding necessary) and a radio. I'd have them sign a piece of paper saying that they alone were responsible for the Holocaust and that they were the love children of Mickey and

Shiva. I signed nothing. Not that I would have anyway. It's that Scottish thing again. Indeed, on my last day in Laayoune, to illustrate the insane madness, the police had gone into the university and had brutally beaten a 17-year-old Saharawi girl, ripping her mehlefah and breaking her collarbone for no apparent reason. That night for the first time, Moroccan students were seen on the streets with Saharawi youth battling with the police and military.

I had secured a lift from a Mauritanian at the café and waited for another three days past my intended departure date before he arrived, and therefore had extra time with my two Saharawi girl friends that had teased and taunted me beyond all reason to stay with them. I was driven directly to Dakhla to then contact and hopefully meet the family of Khadi. Dakhla is now considered as the Hawaii of West Africa and visited by surfers of every persuasion. Then it was a depressing backwater. On my second night, I eventually made contact with Khadi's family and was being taken to dinner by three younger brothers. As evening approached, we rounded the corner to be confronted by a wall of riot police and almost simultaneously a group of stone wielding youths appeared and laid into them. All hell broke loose and we split up as the police gave chase. Of course wearing a turban; as instructed by my guides, two policemen chose to run after me. I took off and soon found myself lost and being hunted like a rabid dog, my pursuers screaming at me to stop. A phrase from my distant past arrived in my head; a grandfather in a hospital waiting room had shouted at his two errant grandsons, "Sit beside me so I can slap you!"

I burst out laughing which only incensed the riot police further as they screamed at me to stop. All the time I was looking for a way out and seeing a flight of stairs directly ahead of me, heading towards a roof, so I took off up them, hoping to further exhaust my pursuers. I ran out across the roof and taking the roof to my left as being the easier to jump, did so and it was quite a gap! The next again to my left and I managed to clear a larger gap which deterred the police, who still in riot gear but minus their shields had given up exhausted or had bottled the jump or both. At the next roof, in the dying moments of the day's sun I gave them the finger and kept going, roof to roof and began a slow descent back onto ground level to find a hidey-hole, stinking of cat's piss to catch my breath.

Darkness descended and the sounds of sirens began to slowly move off and I resurfaced some thirty minutes later, when all had gone quiet, very quiet, eerily quiet. I phoned the number of my contact from a small shop and was met fifteen minutes later, to be taken around the back streets to dinner. It would be a year or so later in the chambre de guides at the Auberge Sahara that I would meet a Mauritanian, Baba. He had heard of my story from Sidi, the owner of the auberge and Baba verified it as he had actually seen me in action. He was with friends on a terrace that night, and had watched my 'graceful' flight from the riot police, who really weren't up to such antics.

"You Scots can run!" he said.

"Good." I said adding, "I thought it was all a dream, a bad dream. I didn't imagine it!"

"No, it's all true, and you're still a good runner." He said.

"Thank you for the complement sir." Baba's still a bandit; a big bandit and I wouldn't trust him as far as I could throw him.

My hosts took me to the border after a further three days of talking, eating, drinking tea and staying out of sight of the nightly battles waged on the streets. I arrived at the Moroccan Surete office and handed over my passport and filled in the form. I waited for hours in the sun and eventually was called.

"Registration of your car?" the Surete officer asked me.

"I don't have one!" I replied.

"You need a registration number!" He said to me, sternly.

I took the form and his pen and walked out to the first car, took its number and handed it back to him.

"C'est bon?"

He looks at it and smiles. "Oui."

He stamps and signs my passport and I leave The Western Sahara, sad but relieved and take off across no-man's land on foot.

The piste is clearly marked by car tracks and I wind this way and that, surveying the many cars that had come to grief on mines. I feel no fear as you can jump on the bastards all day quite safely. Still, there are A-P's and the A-T's in quick retrospect, are very, very old! My inner eye advice is to keep to the car tracks, no shortcuts; even if looks as if you could. Up ahead I see a car parked up, baggage everywhere with two figures crouched at the rear offside wheel. I stop and help the two elderly Mauritanian men to change their wheel, under the hot sun as the hard stony ground had burst their treadless tyre. At least the spare had some kilometres left on it, though not many! (This is the normal state of affairs here in R.I.M.) This done, I move on to leave them to sort out their baggage.

On arrival at the Mauritanian Poste Gendarmerie, then a simple shack, I encountered the same idiocy as across the border. "Where's your car?" He asks in French.

"No French. I don't have one." I said.

"How cross no-man's land?" He asks in English.

Smiling a stupid smile to camouflage my sarcasm, which in the case in dealing with idiotic border officials is always a good idea.

"On foot." I reply as I pointed to my feet.

"No car?" He asks in English and mimics driving a car.

"No car." I said, waving my hand side to side, barely managing to keep from laughing.

"Serious." He says in English.

"You speak English?" I ask.

"Little only." He replies.

"Why serious?" I ask.

I immediately hold up my hand to stop the lunacy that I feel is about to go on day if I let it . . .

I very slowly ask in English, "Why don't you, copy last registration number, then, paperwork's finished."

Just like my fuckin' patience. He smiles, talks to his counterpart in Hassaniya and they write it down. He gives me my passport and sends me on my way.

Round Two, the Surete. "Passport, visa." Passport I hand over, "Visa I don't have." I said.

He begins telling me how difficult it will be and blah blah blah. In my frustration I remembered that I was to refuse to speak French as instructed by the Mauritanian who gave me a lift to Dakhla because he said the officials would make life difficult in order to extract baksheesh.

"No French." I said.

He tells me he needs to pray to think about it.

"No French." I said.

He talks in Hassaniya to another officer who looks at me and I smile a stupid smile.

"No Arabic." I said.

"Pas Francais, pas Hassaniya." He said.

"No French and no Arabic." I replied.

Hassaniya is a dialect of Arabic only spoken in R.I.M., why would I be able to speak it? I continue to smile, and a little rhyme goes through my head. 'The farmer's wife she had a pig, and could not stop it grunting, so she took it round the back, and kicked it's little c*** in! Even though the sergeant is supposed to be praying he's also watching me, as I apparently take little or no interest in anything or anyone around me, squatting down on the floor, near the door. I smile the smile of an imbecile lost in his own thoughts, rhyming rhymes of a blue nature. He stops and slowly sits at his desk, takes a glass of tea offered to him by a young boy, who then offers the other sergeant a glass but not me and he studies my passport long and hard.

"Quel pays?" He asks.

I look at him all confused and not understanding French.

"Country?" The other asks in English.

I smile a wider smile.

"Ah, you speak English?" I ask.

"Pas Anglais." He replies.

"Britain." I reply.

"Ah English." He said.

"No Scottish." I reply.

He speaks to his counterpart in Hassaniya, and then asks, "Where Scottish?"

"Britain." I reply.

"Kilt." I add and I model the kilt for them in a Highland fling sort of way. A smile of recognition arrives on the face of the second sergeant and he tells his counterpart where I'm from.

"Ecosse." He says.

"Scotland." I reply.

The first sergeant nods, signs his big book, stamps the visa into my passport and signs it. I pay the going rate and move onto . . .

Round Three, Customs.

"How much money do you have?" The sergeant asks me in French.

"No French." I reply.

"Dollars, Euros?" He asks abruptly.

"No dollars, no euros." I reply.

If he looks in my bag, I'm done for.

"Only Dirham." I say.

He shakes his head and says in French, "Bloody toilet paper."

I manage to keep a straight face and smile the smile of an imbecile.

"Sorti de ici."

"No French." I reply.

He waves his hand to dismiss me. I nod acceptance of his order and leave, with a small fortune in Dirham, Euros and Dollars as I knew I would. The reprieve from the banditry is only short-lived but it is a minor victory in the scale of things. And one that continues to cheer me up when things go wrong, as they continually do here in R.I.M. Along with the 500 000 ougiya (UM) I arrived with, I was to lose another 2 500 000 UM or a little over £6000 over the next two years to the bandit Maure, through loss of equipment and legal fees trying to recover that which was stolen from me.

I then take off towards the road that will cut the railway line from Choum to Nouadibou and take me south to Nouakchott. It's as I walk along that the two elderly Mauritanian men stop and ask me where I'm going.

"Nouakchott." I reply.

"Where in Nouakchott?" The driver asks.

"I don't know, an auberge perhaps." I tell him.

"Get in, there's the Sahara, lots of European go there. It's good, I know the boss there, Sidi Mohamed." He tells me.

My Good Samaritan deed has paid off and we arrive there five hours later. They take me straight to the door. The auberge is empty and Khalifa the night security man and future friend, leads me to a small tent on the terrace. He enters my name and description in the book, as White Muslim. I am dressed in a woollen djellabah with my turban around my neck. I of course don't know this until at least a year later.

On my first morning, I take an early stroll around the auberge searching to buy and make breakfast and I see a beautiful Senegalese girl majestically walk by. She hacks and spits a huge mouthful of sputum, taking no break in her stride. It's the horniest thing I've seen in my life. I am instantly smitten by her. Love at first sight. Later after breakfast, I meet my future mentor and guide to all things Maure and Mauritanian, Isabel. A Portuguese artist; and girl friend of Hermann, a third part French owner of the Auberge Sahara, who had lived there for three years and speaks, Portuguese, French, Spanish, English, Italian and Hassaniya, with some Arabic. She immediately took me under her wing and introduced me left, right and centre to all and sundry.

My introduction is fast and instant. First stop the Auberge Menata, owned by Olivia and her then huband Maloum. Olivia is a strong willed, determined and beautiful French woman and her maison d'hote, Jeloua is luxurious tranquillity. I cannot recommend any finer. I am found a resident's visa within days and introduced to Isa's view of the White Maure's life, which sadly differs from mine and everyone else's experience. Her vast experience and knowledge is of the desert, the place I am heading for and I soak up everything she has to say. She takes off for months on end and meets with the women of various regions, sketches and paints and gets involved in their projects. She has the knack of bypassing the knowledge and acceptance of that strain of malevolent behaviour genetically embedded in the Maure. His capacity for lying, stealing from you, lying about stealing from you and finally erupting into childish violence when confronted and chased down by the legal or tribal system in order for you to rightfully reclaim what has been stolen from you, knows no bounds. She has a fondness for them that transgresses all reason.

None of us are perfect, me least of all. If I steal from you, it means that you are dead and have no use for what was yours. If you steal from me, you are no longer my friend. Sad to say, Hermann and I fell out, as he had in my opinion, gone native. He believed I was 'stealing' a customer from his auberge. All I was doing was getting some hashish from a friend who stopped at the roadside to give me a lift. He has become the thing he hated most, a lying conniving Bidan, whose newfound or re-established aggressive childishness knows no bounds when I am in his vicinity. I have no idea what he thinks he can do in this department, as he has no use of his left arm, damaged in a bike crash in the desert. He wanted to kill me, really wanted to kill me. Thankfully, as I write all is well between us. A littel strained but okay. I'm happy enough.

Though I am no longer welcome at the Sahara, the other third part owner Sidi Mohamad and I remain friends. The other third part owner is the ex-girlfriend's of Hermann and now wife of Sidi Mohamad, Kanya. She is of Algerian/French blood and a dangerous and spiteful union it is. She has sided with Hermann in his intense hatred of me because she could never control me and this gives a rightful claim to her intense hatred of me. She is obsessive about control and dislikes Isabel with a vengeance simply because she is the girlfriend of Hermann. I have no room for either of their spiteful outbursts and it belittles their intelligence to spend so much time hating me for other reason that they have nothing else to occupy their time. I suppose it gives someone else a rest. Sidi once apologised on her behalf but I said that was unnecessary as it made little difference to our friendship.

"Such is life." I said. "Here's a Scottish saying . . . Life's a bitch, you marry one, and then you die!" He appreciates Scottish sarcasm.

Approximately 5 days after I arrived at the auberge, Sidi took me to the camel market at Teinweich. Here, I selected a camel and with the help of a berger; after Sidi has chased everyone away, start to move away from the crowd. Sidi is worried.

"Why don't you leave the camel here and come back to the auberge?" He says.

"Why?" I ask.

"It's dangerous, the desert is dangerous, and there are snakes, scorpions and bandits!" He replies.

"It's the reason I came here today to buy and camel and walk the desert or at least a small part of it." I reply.

"Yes but . . ." He starts.

"But what Sidi? I keep this camel here as a pet and live at the auberge?"

He shakes his head knowing I am stubborn and on my way to doing as I said I would. I shake his hand and wish him good luck and head off with the berger, for a quiet spot around the back of the market to learn to handle my camel.

It's at this time that I make a connection with Ol Loli, an old soldier who fought against the Moroccans and Polisario. I later find out he's well respected amongst his peers at the market with an unwritten and unspoken authority. He immediately takes to me as I do him; an unspoken bond develops after he gazed intensely into my eyes for what seemed minutes.

"You know death my friend." He says.

I nod. From this moment he offers me his hand and his support and friendship, which has continued to this day. It is without condition and he is my lifeline to leaving here if the country goes belly up. It was a prediction he made that day which has now become a distinct possibility, given that the tenth coup d'etat has arrived and the madness continues.

With only forty-five minutes experience with handling a huge disagreeable animal, my last experience with animals was a hamster; I pack up under the ever-watchful gaze of Ol Loli. It was his berger that was instructing me. Mohamad constantly checks and monitors my packing and rope skills, constantly shaking his head and tutting like an old mother hen, wanting to pull me aside and do it all for me. He is restrained by Ol Loli, who is more measured in his teaching methods.

"Officer?" I ask him.

"No, warrant officer." He replies.

I nod. I'm finished and it's time to go and Mohamad takes my camel's (Wahad—Arabic for one) cord attached to a nose ring and I'm walked to the road by Ol Loli, who gives the berger his orders. We stop at the roadside as Mohamad walks Wahad across the road and Ol Loli gives me his orders.

"He will take you onto the piste opposite and send you off in the direction of the nearest water hole, which is two days and a half day's walk from here. Take careful note of where he sends you, it's important. There's a family there, give them my name, they'll look after you."

I simply nod and shake his hand. Our eyes meet and there's nothing more to be said. He turns and walks back to the market, in no particular hurry. It's good advice for the Sahara, no particular hurry.

I have forty litres of water in two twenty-litre rubber water sacks; eight days water, which my camel can lie on or you can drive an armoured Land Rover over without bursting. 40kgs of dried foodstuffs, two copies of Chekhov's short stories, two mess tins, a wooden spoon and fork, three snares, fire steel, sleeping bag, kukri, map, compass, GPS, a goodly supply of batteries and an mp3 loaded with eight hundred songs: Pink Floyd, Super Rail Band, Todd Rundgren, Gong, Kandle Mouyata, Frank Zappa, Tshala Muaria, Camel, Youssou N'Dour, The Yes, Mozart, Joni Mitchell, The Grateful Dead, Thione Seck, Led Zeppelin, Thandiswa Sawei, Steve Hackett, The Doors, Ali Farke Toure, Neil Young and Little Feat but to mention a few. I love African music in the morning, there's a primeval energy to it and it's great for jogging to before the sun gets hot! There's a little over 80kg of weight for Wahad to carry but as we're only doing 3-5 km/hr and he's under by 40 kg or so, there's nothing to worry about, except missing the water hole! Things often said in jest . . . have a habit of arriving, when you least need them or expect them.

Gong's Shamal in the Sahara is something else too, especially at the gallop! After prayers, Led Zep's Kashmir, just as the sun goes down. What more does a man need? A little luck and the ability to be able to put one foot in front of the other. March or die, the maxim of The French Foreign Legion. It's that simple here. You march with your head, not your feet. If it's one hundred and twenty-five kilometres, three hundred and two metres to walk, then it's one hundred and twenty-five kilometres, three hundred and two metres and no amount of bitchin's gonna make it any less. It's the last twenty that are the worst. Without Wahad I can do them in two and a half hours, with him four, with a little jogging a little under two easy. If you're going to bitch, then what the fuck are you doing wandering around in the Sahara? And what are you in a hurry for anyway? Whenever you take shortcuts there are consequences and in the desert those shortcuts can cost you your life as one I took two years later, almost did. My advice to you is in that case is, do it on Google Earth, watch a National Geographic DVD, or read Michael Palin's book, much much safer but not nearly half as much fun!

Mohamad stopped after an hour. We had been hemmed in by dunes to the south and north and the walking done in total silence, except for once when I told him that his back was covered in flies.

"Toi aussi, imbecile!" He replied.

I could feel that smile of an imbecile slowly widen across my face, thankfully underneath my turban. I instantly closed my mouth and continued to breathe through my nose. It's mid-morning and the sun was just getting hot but already difficult to breathe. Thankfully I had the sense to come out in the cold season.

After what seemed an eternity, he stopped and dropping Wahad's rope and beckoned me forward. He motioned with his right hand the direction I was to take, very precisely. Mohamad made me stand in the same spot and make the same motion with my hand. Correcting it once he stood back and nodded. I took another look at the horizon, taking out my compass and setting my heading and bearing, focusing about two kilometres away on a bush and two wind blown trees. I had it registered in my head. We shook hands and he turned back. I didn't watch him for more than a few seconds, picked up Wahad's cord to then take my own path. He'd be back at the camel market in a little over half an hour drinking tea with Ol Loli no doubt speculating on whether they'd see me again. Funnily enough, the same conversation was going on in the chambre de guides at the Auberge Sahara as to whether or not I'd make it back, with bets drawn up as to how long I'd last, as I was setting out on my 'Buy a camel and walk the Sahara scenario."

Me; oblivious to everyone's betting and speculating, I was in seventh heaven. Over and around the small collection of dunes ahead of me cutting across the piste north to south, the desert suddenly opened up with a huge expanse of sky above me and the desert of this corner of the Sahara mushroomed outwards in a 360° fast focusing sort of way, all at the same time, sky and desert simultaneously moving away from me. I suddenly felt very, very small. Nothing more than a speck of dust. It's the most wonderful feeling in the world to be so suddenly insignificant. I remember stopping breathing for a moment or two and taking a huge breath when I restarted as if breaking the surface of the sea after being wiped out and endlessly dragged along the sea bed by the force of the sea. I believe it was the first time I orgasmed without an erection . . . I love the desert . . . I love it that the Sahara doesn't give a fuck whether I live or die.

## CHAPTER TWO

# INTO THE BLUE AND
# A CULTURE SHOCK

I HAD WALKED all morning right up until midday and began searching for a spot to begin making lunch and rest up over the hottest part of the day, being 13.00-17.00 hrs and then carry on until 21.00. As I walked onwards, looking for a sizable bush in order to have both shade and feed Wahad, I saw two riders summit a large dune off to the east, less than a kilometre away. They stopped and watched my progress a while before making their way to me, at speed. Two scrawny untidy Bidan on good camels arrived, wearing identical black turbans and blue booboos. I immediately took note of their brands and their gear. They each carried a 5-litre bidon, had identical cheap purple plastic sandals strapped to their saddles, sat on their blankets inside their saddles and a sac el badiya (food bag, made from a plastic grain sack) tied behind. One man, I assumed in his thirties had a scar that traversed his face, starting underneath his right eye, moving across his mouth to finish mid-left cheek. The other man slightly older and relatively blemish free but equally dirty. The first man grinned a broken and rotted tooth grin that I had seen often enough during my short stay in the capital.

The Mauritanian dental hygiene is exceedingly poor, relying on scraping their teeth with a stick for most of the day. It's the high quantity of sugar they drink in their tea and the complete lack of vitamins in their diet that does it, believing that the sugar gives them strength. Three container ships arrive at Nouadibou from Brazil every month loaded to the gunnels with sugar, that's an awful lot of dental caries, not mention an awful lot of sugar.

They walked their camels around me, surveying my baggage and no doubt Wahad too. He was a magnificent beast. The entire conversation with me is in French. After the formal greeting of Salaam aleykum (Peace be unto you.) with which you reply Aleykum salaam. (And peace be unto you.) It can become complicated, long and involved and doesn't allow for the modernity of the mobile phone or the fact that you don't have the credit to enter into a ten minute of how's your father/first cousins/ brother of your aunt twice removed? With ca va? thrown in every other two minutes! We did not shake hands because they did not dismount or I walk towards them. I simply lowered my turban from my face to show that I was who I was as is the custom. He immediately asks me for some of my rope, which is quality and therefore expensive.

"No." I reply.

"Do you have a present for me?" He asks.

"No." I reply.

He suddenly saw my kukri, attached near at hand on my baggage. On seeing that he had seen it, I took it out.

"C'est bon, n'est pas?" I said, brandishing it in the sun.

I showed him where I'd cut a throat with it and where I cut to hack a head off. I indicated that it would only take one blow.

"It's the knife of a soldier?" He asks.

"Yes." I reply.

He quickly speaks to his friend in Hassaniya. I interrupt them by asking.

"What's your name?"

"Mohamad." He replies.

Smiling a wide macabre smile accentuated by his scar but I see from his eyes and the fidgeting with his cord and baton that he is very nervous.

"And your friend?" I quickly ask.

"Mohamad." He replies.

Mohamad 2 smiles nervously too. I run my finger across my face to draw the line of his scar, in perfect mirror image (for a very good reason) and ask, "Accident?"

He grins nervously, "Yes." He replies.

Very quickly I add, "Pleased to meet you both. And where are you going, the camel market at Teinweich Two?"

They both nod and not giving them a second to speak, I add.

"Good, because I'm going this way, good luck."

I resheath my kukri and move off, leaving the two to quickly say good-bye as they turn their camels and ride off. Over my shoulder and looking past the inside and underneath my water sack I watch them ride off in the apparent direction of the market. Even at the distance they kept away from me their body odour was terrible. I'd also not forget either of their faces, especially Mohamad 1. He really didn't like my kukri. Perhaps the memory of his 'accident' was too soon for comfort or the fact that I was all too ready to display it and point out its, finer qualities. If necessary, I was fully prepared to give him and his associate a scar each, and in the case of Mohamad 1, mimicking the Saltire on his ugly scrawny face, which why I was sending him a subconscious message. I believe he got it.

Several months later, I'd be back at the market, with stock. On arrival at the central arena, Ol Loli had Mohamad take the 17 animals from me and instructions were given to have Wahad eat and drink. Wheat, not the poor quality animal feed normally given to stock.

"Trying to steal my camel Ol Loli?" I asked.

He merely smiled and waved his forefinger, the equivalent of 'Not me old boy, wouldn't dream of it!' 'He likes him, a lot.' I thought. He said that there were two people he needed me to meet. I liked that he didn't make a fuss of me, although on this particular morning, I was on a high. It was like having a birthday and nobody knew or cared even if they did know. This was the first time I had brought stock into the market. Unspoken recognition is worth far more than public adulation and later on in the morning when it began to be mentioned by Ol Loli's hangers-on and others in the market, I immediately waved them off. On passing his limbur (a 5x3m concrete base with a small retaining wall and four metal posts holding up a fabric or tin roof, resting on a wooden frame) he ordered zreig, tea and tagine with vegetables.

"Beaucoup des vitamines!" He said as he looked aside at me smiling.

I had given him the health lecture on vitamins a while back. His cook's daughter, Alia, scurried off scrunching up the money Ol Loli had given her in her little hand, to buy all sorts of 'exotic foods'.

We traversed the market; way out back, in silence and his mood much different now. His eyes set in a long distance stare. There in the distance, beyond the last stock pens, were two figures huddled around a charcoal grill making tea. Their camels hobbled and resting nearby. They were dressed exactly as I had seen them on our first meeting and no doubt still unwashed. I spoke quietly as we approached.

"I met these two on my first day out in the desert. Mohamad and Mohamad."

Making the scar on my face. He merely grunts. He stopped as close as it was possible to stand without being sick. 'Practise makes perfect.' I thought. Though if I were blind I'd know these two were nearby, even if I were in a sandstorm with a major attack of the flu. He spoke directly to them without greeting, in Hassaniya, in a measured voice. Different camels I noticed with different brands that I didn't recognise. I later identified them as coming from Nema. The two did not smile and their eyes did not leave Ol Loli for one second, except for a quick glance at me, at the end of the monologue. I said nothing; I was merely the stooge to the main act.

"SMAATINI?" He said directly and with force.

The two Mohamads nodded like the little dog you see in the backs of UK cars, trying ever so hard to please. 'Ain't gonna work.' I thought. 'He really really doesn't like them.'

'That's good.' I mused further, 'I'd hate to have to kill his friends, should it go bad between us.' This was the only time he had raised his voice and roughly translates as, "YOU HAVE HEARD EVERYTHING I HAVE SAID?" said everything I really needed to know. Sometimes Hassaniya can be so very simple, other times it's a quagmire of complication, like a chattering machine gun. He turned away, controlled but clearly angry, despite his voice being measured throughout the brief lecture. As we walked back to his limbur he tells me, "If you should happen to need any reason to kill them, any reason what-so-ever . . . no-one will miss them . . . and I'll make sure you get a medal."

He further added what he had briefly summarised for them, that if they were responsible for the theft of a grain of rice from me, he'd flay their skins and hand them over to me, to finish them off. Toe by toe, finger-by-finger, limb-by-limb. We never spoke about them again. And although I see them here and there, they always stay well clear of me, for obvious reasons.

The owner of the stock, was a very surprised man. He thought that when I had phoned, it was to say that I hadn't found them as he had first expected. How could I? I wasn't Mauritanian. He arrived within the hour at Ol Loli's limbur, talking with Ol Loli before me. He then asked me where his stock was and after inspecting them, therefore had to hand over the money, of which he had only 15 000 UM because I didn't have the experience, he said. I said, "No. 20 000UM was what we had agreed, whether or not you now think I have or have not enough experience. I'll hold one of your camels until you pay me."

Ol Loli spoke out at length and the owner suddenly rushed off. Ol Loli winks, he eventually returns to give me my money, in full. I thank him and pocket it. He then goes and hangs out with his buddies. Over the next two years I'd see him and some of them come out to my camp and even work for a few. There was never a problem getting paid. At least, not by this shower of bandits.

As you will find out, Mohammad, Mohamad, Mohamed and Mohammed is a very popular name here in Mauritania. As is Maryam, Meriam, Mariem and Merriam. In fact a great many Mauritanians have so many different names that they use and even if they produce an ID card they still insist that it's completely different from the official version. It's bloody confusing to say the least. When I converted in February 2006 I decided to take Mohammad Ibrahim as my name, as the second was close to my christian name and the former because there are as many Brahims as there are Mohammads. Therefore the two together, fairly uncommon would mean that I'd know what Mohammad or Brahim they would be referring to. Everyone on-line, good. My mobile is therefore full of Mohamads + abbreviations, also Sidis + abbreviations, Brahims + abbreviations. I have long forgotten who the majority are and have to ask, "Quel Mohamad ?/Quel Sidi ?/Quel Brahim?"

It always raises a laugh on the other end, as they believe I am joking.

"No, I'm just senile you imbecile!" I tell them.

It's a little different from your normal greeting I suppose.

It's only on the second night after my meeting with the two Mohamads that I feel comfortable about rolling a joint. I have 50 grammes in my baggage and at one euro a gramme I'm well chuffed! It will be my first joint in the Sahara proper and not at an auberge in the Sahara, with a full night sky of stars and howling African wild dogs as my television and not a bunch of half-assed mentally unstable howling drunk and stoned rallyists who have only by good fortune managed to exit the desert in their clapped out bangers, en-route for Dakar. As if Africa needs any more of either! Not for a moment does the vista stop. With the glow from my charcoal fire heating water for more tea and wrapped up in my sleeping bag I see at least five meteorites coming down, three with large tails and two just short pyrotechnic displays in the sky. The Sahara is littered with strikes, as it is with archaeology. (I once traversed a field some 500m² with Ethnayne (Two) my riding camel, crunching his way over pottery I felt every breakage in my ass.) There are satellites above me, slowly traversing the sky seeming to move in and out of the near stationary constellations; and using my GPS to identify them is unnecessary but fun. It stops me talking to myself fro two minutes. This first night's television is accompanied by Pink Floyd's, Wish You Were Here, blasting around in my head, fantastic!

In the morning, I would wake up as I had gone to sleep, resting against a giant Acacia tree and Gong's Shamal playing away. Oops! Luckily I can get 60 hours playing time on my little Sony. Getting out of my bag and walking to look for Wahad, I came across the prints of a Dama gazelle that has passed by my camp by ten metres or so. It would be the first and last sign of the gazelle that I'd see in my territory. The Mauritanian has hunted them to extinction, first the Nemadi with their dogs (more on them later) and secondly, the Bidan and his car, huge spot lamp and ancient shotgun. I would later talk with many Bidan acquaintances about this subject and be sickened at the response of one hunter; and I use the term hunter very loosely, to shooting a pregnant female. The idiot who had performed this feat of stupidity simply said that it was two meats! Would you kill your pregnant camel/goat/sheep? No you wouldn't, so why kill a pregnant gazelle? Because it's two meats comes back the reply! If she gave birth then there'd be two gazelles, perhaps another female who would give birth to, perhaps yet another female? He simply grinned like the idiot he is. Like Air France, the concept of conservation is way way over the Bidan head. He thinks with his pocket first and second, because the gazelle is free meat and last of all his stomach and so very very far behind, arrives his head but only by proxy because it's attached to his shoulders. The tracks were moving ESE towards Mali. Not that it was going to be any safer there either as the Nemadi are between them and hungry Tamashek who want to kill its ass too!

Despite the huge number of rabbits in the desert the nomad doesn't eat them. Or more importantly, they are seen as the food of the Bidan. The Patron comes out to feast like a medieval lord; perhaps with or without friends, to have his meal cooked by his berger's wife. He has simply put the barrels of his shotgun down the rabbit hole and blasts away to then have his berger's son dig them up or, stunning them in his headlights, he leans out of the window and does the deed. I've stayed with a great number of nomad families on the occasional day or two here and there and perhaps all they have to eat is rice, goat's milk and sugar, everyday for lunch and dinner. In Scotland we call it rice pudding and it's eaten after dinner as a dessert. Or couscous, just that and nothing else. I make it a habit to arrive with or go for rabbit when I stay at an encampment. But the response is always the same. They treat me like a Bidan, and that stems from not just my colour but because this food is strictly for me as a boss no matter if I'm working for a Bidan and arrive with his camels! I refuse to eat unless everyone else does and it takes some doing to persuade them.

The well and encampment was where Ol Loli had said it would be, on line from the spot where Mohamad had me stand and point. It would be a trademark of the nomad that I would very quickly pick up and as time passed I would use my compass less and simply rely on the sun, wind and time of the day and stars as my aids to navigation. Necessity when distances are great and landmarks as such are few and far between, until that is you form a map in your head. In the case of my 4000 km² territory, not of dunes which move, but of pistes, wind-swept trees, bushes, a blue Nike training shoe, bricks and a collection of rusty old cans that have become as familiar as the landmarks in your home town. There were five khaima (tents) and no sign of life. No camp dogs either, for if there were it wouldn't have been a surprise to the Maryam, (all Bidan) the grandmother, her younger sister and three younger women, two teenage girls around 14/15 (who chased my ass the entire time I was there) ten children and Moctar, the grandfather, and his younger brother sleeping in their tents in the late afternoon, as to my arrival with a snorting camel and its creaking baggage.

The other three husbands arrived at 18.00 hrs with the camels, and three boys, 10, 8 and 7 with the huge herd of goats around the same time. Both herds and humans have covered 30km, as they do every day.

"Salaam aleykum." I shouted out.

At first nothing, again "Salaam aleykum."

Then a very quiet "Aleykum salaam."

The camp then woke up to see me unfurl my turban . . . the older children went completely mental and took off in all directions screaming, "It's the devil!"

The babies and toddlers crying hard, with the mother's and older sister's trying to hand them over to me making them scream even more!

The adult's merely laughed and expected me to go after the children who were now hopping barefoot on the hot sand. No chance. I ain't television for nobody. After everyone had calmed down and I had drunk my zreig and tea; under the ever present and adoring gaze of Aminetou and Maryam, constantly adjusting their mehlafahs for me to see their hair, necks and tops of the breasts. Strictly forbidden of course, to look at their hair. After I had finished, I was accompanied by the girls, a scrum of kids and two mothers who came to watch me unpack Wahad. Aminetou had taken Wahad's cord and was proudly leading him away to hobble him for me to set-up my camp. The game continued as it had started and Aminetou is a very persistent young woman. So that my baggage would be safe from most of the prying eyes in the crowd, I put it immediately under a tarp I carried as a shelter and therefore demands for cadeau much lessened, though this is the game here. I simply told the assembled group that all I have I need. If I don't have it, I can't cook, cut meat or stay warm at night or make and drink my zreig. Aminetou's mother mentioned that for the gift of my knife I could have her as a wife to keep me warm at night, to the shrill of the rest of the girls! She is the oldest of the two, though if she were the same age as Maryam, it would make no difference here. First baby, one year later!

Zreig is a mixture of water, soured camel or goat's milk and sugar, the Coca Cola of the Sahara. When moving herds I drink straight from the camel, up to six litres a day which helps save my water and will sustain you physically. 'Aman Iman Ahk Issouder' is a Tamashek proverb, 'Water is life, Milk is food.' My saddle is old and therefore of little or no interest, so that only leaves my rope, which I was careful to bag before I arrived at the encampment. I realised from the wanton gaze of Mohamad 1and 2 that I'd have the same trouble everywhere. As to my other possessions they never saw the light of day when the nomads were in the vicinity. To those future persistent demands I encountered, the nomad was left in no doubt as to the lack of cadeau, as my kukri kept any objections they had to a bare minimum. I would display the various uses of the knife's cutting edges as I did with the Mohamad and these future persistent agitators of my peace and tranquillity are immediately ensured that it will remain so, with a direct refusal and no negotiation possible or necessary on my part due to the presence of the knife. I am also, an unknown quantity.

So on my first night with the nomad I was persuaded to sleep in the khaima of Moctar, the eldest man of the camp and therefore the only logical choice. Everyone bedded down and Maryam, his wife then proceeded to hack and spit. Fuck me! The door of the khaima was closed, as it was bloody cold! Where the fuck was she spitting? After a half hour or so I had to leave, as it didn't seem she was going to let up any time soon. I took myself and my sleeping bag out into the cold night air. It's perhaps 12-15° C during the cold season at night and 22-26° C during the day but having a bag rated for −17°C with a Gore-Tex bivvy bag I've no problem, so I slept beside my saddle and baggage, Wahad having long since pissed off in search of food. A camel eats approximately 20 kg of fodder each and every day. I awoke at 06.00 to find the camp covered in mist. I stayed put. No way was I going back inside to endure the torture of Maryam hacking and spitting first thing in the morning, wondering where the hell it was going to fall next. I was to find over the next four days that the personal hygiene of some of the nomads and therefore the Mauritanian leave a lot to be desired.

The children use the space in-between the floor covering and the wall of the khaima as a toilet, as well as a general area for bones, spat out pieces of food, date stone, with Maryam continually spitting at the walls as well as emptying her nose into her hand and throwing it at the wall . . . and cleaning her hand on her mehlafah. I kid you not! I needed to share that as I carry it around in my mind's eye, so now you do too. Happy birthday! The area facing the front of the khaima (always south facing) is a veritable minefield, where broken glasses, cheap Chinese plastic toys (the likes that you'd never see in the UK) with metal spikes protruding from them lie pointing upwards waiting for someone's eye, batteries and debris are simply launched out from where their former owners sit or where ever it breaks. Never walk there or around their campsite without good sturdy sandals. Never. The nomad are like a plague of locusts in reverse. When they strike camp, rubbish will be strewn around for hundreds of metres after departure. Stainless steel bowls with the remains of God knows what inside, old suitcases, handbags, shoes, plastic bags filled with, I have no idea what's in there and even if there was a lab, they'd more than likely incinerate it. I once found the black bishop of a nomad who had left with his family to feed his goats elsewhere and gave it back to him months later. There are old mehlafahs, perfectly good clothes, broken glass bottles, lots. Batteries by the lorry full, plastic bottles and boxes, broken bidons. The list of course is inexhaustible as is the nomad's fervour in littering his little part of the Sahara. I of course can recycle some objects and it's always worth a look see even if you know what's there as sand travels and can reveal hidden treasures.

And now it's back to khaima hygiene. Babies and toddlers don't have the benefit of nappies and simply do the toilet where they sit or if they manage to reach the outer perimeter or where they are perhaps tied to the main post of the tent to stop them wandering into the afternoon heat when the mothers are sleeping, where they lie and wait until someone eventually pours water over them. The women's mehlafahs are used to wipe noses, bowls and asses not in any set order or priority but on an ad hoc basis. As a water filter, excellent but only when clean of course. They are also torn to make rope to tie up children, make a camel nose ring or to hang something from the tent or cloths to clean pots. I stitched two together to make a towli, a portable khaima. It acts as a sunshade and when the Irivi (Harmattan) is blowing it keeps you cool and when the cold wind from the north is blowing, it keeps you warm. An intelligent piece of equipment for two bits of cloth. Where there is spillage of any kind it is simply washed through the mat with water and hand and of course, their hands are dried on, their mehlafahs. Now you're in the zone! It's a filthy world, the world of the nomad khaima.

Where there is an older female child around she instantly takes responsibility for the younger children. A six year old will have seniority over a four year old that has seniority over a two year old. So Aminetou is positively ancient in comparison. Boys don't enter into this equation at all, the biggest slaps everyone, who passes it down the line as a matter of course, in order of seniority and the boys of every age slap all the girls of every age, and parents, aunts and visitors are all slapping all of the children. Parents have used me to chastise their children, saying that if they don't behave the nasrani (whiteman) berger will roast and eat you.

"Give him/her/them a severe slapping and use your baton/or my belt if necessary!" is the cry I've heard so many times. I have only done so very very rarely and only when pushed by the male child when all vestiges of tolerance has totally evaporated. Generally I tie them to the khaima post and grab my baton to restore order and to deter them from untying themselves. It's a very violent society.

For a people who are life dependent on water and especially here because they live next to a well, they waste an awful lot. Even when the nomad has to travel a six hour round trip hauling plastic bidons on donkeys to collect it, it's astounding to watch. The other choice is for the patron to come out twice/three times a week with supplies of water. He will also bring other supplies to them that will be bought on credit. Rice, medicines and tobacco, whatever it is, it will be entered into the book and when the berger eventually leaves his employ he will be paid what's due. If indeed he pays in full. Perhaps it will be with animals instead of money or both or not.

I know of one berger, Brahim, a Black Moor, (20% are freeman and 40% are Haratin—slaves) who after serving the same lord and master for ten years was discarded much like the rubbish the nomad throw away when striking camp. He was given only half the money owed in goats and one old camel, a bag of bones. He became depressed, was violent towards all of his family and refused to speak to me or allow me near their roadside camp on La Route L'Espoir when there, 10 km or so from Ouad Naga, the equivalent of Dodge City. I eventually met up with his boss, through chance one night in Nouakchott many months later and confronted him, to try and speak on the family's behalf. The answer was short and sweet.

"Allez! Degagez-vous!"

I told him exactly what I thought of him in Zreag, a mixture of Hassaniya and French, in front of his friends, who asked me to forgive him.

"Never!" I said, adding, "It is for Allah to pardon him, me I'm only a little fish but the boss, he's a huge shit bag and everyone knows it!"

I vented some more abuse on him before taking my leave. I thought that this would affect my employment chances. Far from it, it actually increased the number of bosses seeking to have a toubab berger.

I did what I could to help Brahim and Maryam at the beginning, I even found Brahim work but his depression was too advanced for him to want to work. His hatred of the Bidan is all encompassing and fills his every waking moment, unlike me it's every second minute! My employer gave them four goats and said he could do no more. He too of course is a Bidan and these people are well below his dignity to give more than a second's thought to. He only did so because of me and I repaid him for two of the goats by working for him for an extra month for nothing, though he did feed me. My assistance is much too little and my visits are too sporadic to make any difference other than give them moral support. I take them necessaries and a few luxuries when I can. Maryam always tries to give them back as my role of patron to show her family her respect of me. I pass them back to the kids and a banter and competition revolves around it. I am television for them. I don't mind.

Mauritanian nomad/townie food (and I use the term food loosely) I briefly touched upon but will endeavour here to give you a small guide and perhaps as a dare, when you're pissed or are thinking of having a nomad theme night or want to invite friends round to do something a little different at the weekend or as a themed birthday party for your little dears perhaps. For complete authenticity it should be served between midnight and 02.00, wakening up your children, who have only just been sleeping for an hour or two. It's really quite simple and can be cooked with the one large pot, a knife and a spoon.

For six to eight people you need a huge pile of pasta at least two kilogram's, of macaroni or spaghetti broken up into small pieces and boiled. Half a kilo of low quality diced but fatty meat, a quarter kilo of broken bones with marrow and fried in cheap vegetable oil until just cooked, adding two onions along the way, a little water to make the sauce along with two or three quartered tomatoes which will disappear leaving only small flecks of skin, flavoured with salt and pepper. The cooked pasta is spread over a large flat serving dish large enough to feed your assembled guests and the meat and sauce evenly arranged around on top of the pasta.

Instead of pasta, you could boil three potatoes, three onions, cut into small pieces in the same pot after you've cooked the meat in oil, with some water, salt and pepper. When cooked, arrange on the same dish with the meat and bones distributed evenly around and serve with two or three day old baguettes. Please allow sufficient sauce for the food to swim but not drown. For true authenticity scale down on the bread. If you decide to use boiled rice as your base then it will only be served with the meat, bone and a lot of freshly ground pepper, again distributed evenly around the serving dish.

Then there's diner el badiya (dinner of the desert). This is so simple. Make a huge pile of rice pudding and serve as above, substituting with spoons because you're toubab (White man). Add more milk if necessary or pour into individual bowls, eat and drink.

The diners are seated on the floor, with a large plastic sheet underneath the communal dish, and everyone sits around the dish, right hand washed and you only eat from in front of you. No shoes please! The women can be seated at one dish and the men at another. If you so choose, the women can wait until the men have finished before eating what's left. This then saves them washing up two dishes!

You grab a handful of rice/pasta and form a ball to throw into your mouth. With the meat, bone, potato and onion combo, you break up the baguettes, giving every their fair share to then tear off a piece of bread to use as a spoon. Here you can use both hands but only the right hand to put the food into your mouth please. The last person eating at the serving dish has to finish everything left and so obtain the strength and companionship of the assembled group. The nomad calls this barakalaam.

And you students out there could do the budget form. A pile of pasta and a tin of sardines. Cook the pasta and stir in the sardines until obliterated from sight. Use plenty of freshly ground pepper though to disguise the flavour of those bloody sardines. Believe me, I've tried all manner of complicated sauces to no avail. And with up to 150 tins of the little bastards out at my camp, I've had the practise! You'll just have to grin and bear it as well as the heat on your fingers! For those students's whose budget has completely evaporated with debauched drinking and whoring sessions, there is the tin of sardines and packet of small dried biscuits recipe made and eaten cold on a small serving dish. Soak the biscuits with a little water to add bulk and to assist in breaking them up, adding the contents of the sardine can, mixing well, using the lid to cut them up and mix so no equipment necessary. This is really scraping the bottom of the barrel and should only be done as a dare or when life is so bad that you have no option. Sadly for many nomad families it is just so and considered a treat.

There is a language to eating nomad . . . before you start eating, Bismillah (In the Name of Allah) and throughout when burning your fingers on hot food, Hammi . . . hatte . . . HATTE! (Hot . . . very . . . VERY). When commenting upon your hosts culinary skills, no laughing at the back there . . . Zeine hatte . . . HATTE (Beautiful . . . very . . . VERY) When you're finished and can't be persuaded to return to the culinary masterpiece, please, no giggling there at the back . . . Hamdoullah (thanks to Allah).

My first pasta and dried goats meat dinner with Moctar sent me reeling in laughter when he described the three flecks of tomato skin as, tomatoes! He put them in front of me; a great honour, and I ate two, only just. I barely managed to put the other back in the centre of the dish; because hysterics were beginning to take over, saying I was full up and could only manage two. Whereupon, I totally lost it and had to leave the khaima in tears. The assembled diners in their male/female groups, believed I was sun-stroked, dehydrated or simply mad or a combination of all three. By the time I returned to the male group they had eaten everything and I was as hungry as hell until I decamped for the night and made a late dinner!

As your guests arrive you will of course have prepared zreig. This again will be served sitting on the floor. You can do the quickie version and a litre per person isn't unheard of. For the aesthetics amongst you, there is the prepared version but both require mixing in front of your guests as a mark of respect to their arrival at your khaima. Here you can play a little with their sensibilities and bear in mind Maryam's personal habits when doing this. You'll love this. Okay, the pre-prepared version is three tablespoons of powdered milk, okay Mr Smartass at the back, it does say 50g on the packet but I like a little substance to mine. As I assume you haven't got fresh goats or camels' milk to sour in a goats skin, make up to one litre and put into a glass bottle with 5 mls of vinegar. Wait until it sours and please for fucks sake, don't put into the fridge or panic and throw it out when it separates thinking you have made a chemical weapon! In fact, leave out in the sun if you like. With a litre bowl you mix some of the shaken concentrate, cool water and sugar to make a refreshing drink, which of course you must taste adding what ever it is you believe; sugar, water or concentrate, it is you need to make your guests happy with their zreig. If your thumb happens to go into the bowl, all the better. Or you can sneeze into or around it, wiping your face with your hand and then onto your clothing—this part is only for illustration of the actual events I have experienced and not recommended if you want to keep your friends. In the desert, the nomads will use the action of the hot wind passing over a large, say 5-litre stainless steel bowl filled to the brim to cool the water. Oh, during the summer, I wouldn't expend too much energy wafting those pesky flies away, they'll only come back!

Then quickie version is the same as making the concentrate and whisked until all the lumps have disappeared. Here you should begin with very little water and add more water only after you have a creamy consistency. Whisk as you add the water until you've covered the tip of your thumb and give to your guests. Tasting is of course also necessary. Then there's another version, one litre carton of UHT milk and two cans of Fanta. Perhaps the Scots could use Irn-Bru instead. Mix the two in a large jug and serve in glasses.

Now for Mauritanian Atay. This is a national obsession, and a way of life for all of the Saharans. The tea ceremony takes one hour to make and drink three small glasses. It is a little complicated and lengthy to prepare and the tea maker isn't allowed to move during the process so all cigarettes, joints and the passing of the tea tray will be ably assisted by those drinking the tea. Though in your khaima you can simply throw the glass back across the floor at the tea maker. It might not be a good idea for those of you with wooden tiled floors or other than soft surfaces. I know it may seem a bit obvious folks, but it is rather easy to get carried away in the spirit of the moment. Common sense should prevail as to whether or not you elect to throw. The tea maker is the master of ceremonies so due respect please. This will come after dinner and is a requirement. It cannot be missed out. All of the equipment needs to be assembled before you start.

Right; for those of you still awake, you will need: a portable gas stove; camping gaz would do, two small teapots, four small glasses, cheap unscented Chinese green tea, fresh mint and sugar, a mountain of. This is the cheat bit, a small plastic bottle to make the froth. You also need a small tray to serve the tea on and a basin to pour out old tea, water, cigarette butts, roaches and old mint into, a supply of water and of course a lighter, because the gas will be switched on and off a lot. You will of course be sitting down on the floor, as will everyone else will have been doing since zreig and dinnertime! A look on the Internet will satisfy you as to the size of teapot and glasses. Here it is a standard.

Okay, here goes and it would do no harm to practise for at least ten years before inviting your friends around for the perfect tea but as you probably don't have the time and dedication, once or twice around the block will suffice. Heat two glasses of water in the pot and measure out one half glass of tea, when the water is boiling chuck it in. Re-boil for a few minutes at a high heat and then pour out and reserve the first glass and throw the second; with the impurities in it, into the basin. I forgot to mention that you'll also need asbestos fingers or have suffered from frost-bite! Re-fill the teapot with one glass of water, the reserved tea and re-boil, vigorously for a few minutes or five. Pour in half a glass of sugar and using the glass and teapot, pouring from one into the other to dissolve the sugar. Again pour out one glass and retain, adding another glass and bring to the boil. Here's the cheat, put the tea in the bottle with another glass of water and shake like crazy, to make the foam. This keeps the sand from getting into the tea, honest! This saves the endless pouring from glass to glass and the subsequent humiliation from the massive loss of tea. If you feel that you'd like to, as it is an art from after all, practise beaucoup but NOT when making tea for your friends for the first time, you'll only make a cunt of it. This piece of advice comes from personal experience, obviously. When it has boiled taste, before adding more sugar, re-mix and re-heat with a sprig of mint. Pour out the froth into the glasses to perhaps a third of the glass; you will have to shake lots to make up the foam for all three glasses. All those guys without girlfriends should have no problem making industrial amounts! Please, pour out any excess tea remaining in the glass at this point. Wash the outside of the glasses under running water and pour in one third of the tea into each of the three glasses and serve piping hot on the tray, everything meticulously clean. The tea should be drunk as quickly as possible because other people will be waiting for their tea. Pour the tea from the foam making process back into the pot for round two, top up and start again. The trick is to keep two pots on the go should you have lots of guests.

The protocol for serving is, the first round and glass is served to the male owner of the khaima you are currently in and should it be you, then someone else needs to be making the tea, stupid. Next glass will be served to his or your wife/concubine, then the next oldest male, the next oldest male and so on. The wife/concubine can elect to give her next glass to the next woman in line. You can refuse after the first glass if you so choose but it is considered bad form. Three glasses are all you serve, using the patron as the marker. I make a light version, which includes a fourth glass just to play with the Maure's head a little. It's great to watch their disbelief as they stutter and feign heart attacks or are they real? Either way I don't give a fuck, I like my tea, drunk with a sprig of fresh mint in a Moroccan glass, a big tea. If you like, I can import well-trained tea boys from Mauritania to the UK. They will perform this task endlessly should you so desire and should you have guests that come to your house unexpectedly on a regular basis, then you really should have one. You won't have to pay him, just food and a corner of the floor to sleep on, an old sheet or blanket will do as bedding. He'll do everything around the house for you when not making tea, run to the shops for cigarettes, bread, phonecard etc.

"If the above exercise goes belly-up, then it's you that fucked up and not me pal! Best of luck. I mean that most sincerely folks!"

Along with an introductory course in basic Hassaniya and rope making skills, I learned much from their way of life in a very short time that I could never agree to. They in fact gave my own camel to drink milk from, as they believed that I would dry up their herd. Given that my female gave me 10 litres each day, didn't seem to register with them. I also drank goats' milk, which never ran out either. I knew immediately that I didn't want to recreate their lifestyle for myself. It clearly stamped my determination to stay who I was and face the Sahara on my own terms. With my former experience and knowledge, there naturally would be many aspects that the nomad could never embrace or even begin to understand about me on some levels. I am not denigrating them. They are a very simple people who seemed to have missed out on an important evolutionary step or two along the way, as far as manners are concerned. I could never, ever totally embrace their way of life and live with myself, knowing it wasn't me. When I set up my own camp I was quick to raise the Saltire above my khaima and establish that inside my khaima it was Scotland and that there were standards of a different persuasion here. I had no want or desire to live in a petrie dish and to this day I maintain that stance at all costs. My Bidan acquaintances continue to tell me that I am Mauritanian to impress the tourists and in the early days I used to play along for the sake of their egos. Now, no. I clearly define myself as to who and what I am. I no longer care that it upsets them. We are the product of our upbringing and that can never change. They only want to become 'British' because they believe they can make a fortune out of it and live happily ever after. If anything, I believe I am a Saharan, a toubab nomad, whose heart and soul are truly in the place they desire to be.

So with my short induction into nomad life in Mauritania over, I decided to move on before: I was smitten down by any number of dormant notifiable diseases I imagined lurking underneath the khaima or at best from food poisoning attributed to Maryam's less than hygienic practices, as well as Aminetou's desire to make babies with me. Beautiful as she is, she's too young, I'm no paedophile. It is to my complete and utter astonishment that I didn't succumb to something during my stay there. I walked out with Moctar and his sons towards the next water hole and they left me after two hours to take the camels to feed on new grasses in the dunes. Again, I was given a precise direction in which to travel. As would be my practice for a little while longer, I whipped out my compass and took my bearings, scanning the horizon for landmarks.

It would be three weeks before I met up with anyone else and to my great surprise and pleasure it would be to meet up with the true nomad of the Sahara, the Tuareg or as they prefer Tamashek, which is their language too. A truly calm and gentle race. The Tamashek calm and gentle I hear you shriek in denial! Get a grip, there are bandits everywhere and the majority aren't Tamashek. If the governments of the Sahara stopped persecuting them then there'd be less of a problem. It was to my great surprise the other week when talking to a friend here in Nouakchott, that he said I was one in spirit. I was exhausted. Totally pissed off with Nouakchott, the Bidan and life in general. I said that, "I'd love to buy myself a camel and piss off into the desert. A bag of food, a bidon of water and my mp3 and I don't give a fuck if I die in the process. At least I'd die in the place I truly wanted to die in."

"That's all?" He asked.

"Do I need anything else?" I asked.

"No. You are truly are a Tamashek."

I have been on a high ever since. It is what I work towards today and every day to achieve. Not to die but to live, as long as I possibly can, in my chosen home.

## CHAPTER THREE

# SCHOOL BEGINS . . .

I CONTINUED TO wander around seeing free range camels in ones and twos or in big and small herds. The wild dogs weren't a problem and at no time did I feel threatened. Though later on I was to spar with a family whose area I had moved into permanently. My bitch with them was, that they treated my encampment as a MacDonald's drive thru as far as my goats were concerned. Lesley would later help me with information on breeding cycles, number of families in their tribe, range of territory etc., that she gleaned from the internet and relayed to me by sms. It didn't concern me in the slightest that there was no one around. This is part of why I had come to live in the Sahara. In the future, it could well be two to four months in-between talking to people. Both waterholes are GPS'd and I was en-route to another, given to me by the two old men with their huge herd of goats. I have experienced solitude before, when out hunting mink in the Highlands for two/three weeks on end during the winters and in more remote regions of the planet. Though in the Highlands, it was easy to end the solitude if I wanted to and easily seek out locals to talk with and it was only three weeks! Having an OS map of my locality made the option of hitting a hotel for a day or two so easy as not to be taken up. In fact only once, when I had succumbed to frostbite in my hands and toes after four days of blizzards and temperatures of −25°C, did I sensibly walk out and seek mankind. In only a few months mobility after recovery, it would be at the other extreme end of the Celsius scale that I'd soon be living with. I knew that I was at the mercy of the desert, that my life would follow its own course and it was what I had come for. A cleansing of the soul.

In the Sahara there is one unspoken rule. If you see someone, you walk or ride towards him as he will you. It matters little that it is only to say hello. Perhaps it is to ask for water, make tea, pass on a message or to ask about the location of herds. It's a necessary part of your work as a berger to use all means possible to find the herd and necessary to your survival, to know if there's an encampment or a well en route perhaps which now is no longer a viable option. You won't know if you don't go and it will weigh heavy on your conscience if you don't go. I went into the desert without Hassaniya. It is always possible to communicate. I began learning what I needed to know for all the important things in my life there. Direction, food, water, illness, camels, simple stock phrases that became life dependant. With the Mohamads it was completely different. As close as I was to civilization and the direction I was heading, they'd have guessed easily enough where I had come from and perhaps going to. They were out fishing and I wasn't as small a fish in a big pond of sharks as they first thought!

Wahad and I continued to tussle over as to who was the actual boss and I soon learned by keeping him close hobbled that I could keep better control of his anger and stubbornness. Hobbling means tying a rope around the fetlocks about the normal width of his stance. Close hobbling reduces his ability to shuffle and therefore cover more distance. It would be still be possible for him to travel 5 km over the course of the night in this manner. He could still leap in huge bounds if he wanted to and chase my ass, but only over short distances. That's a moot point really, he could cover 50 metres hobbled as such in the blink of an eye, with me having to negotiate stalks of grass, bushes or trees! He simply believed he was the boss and I knew I was. You have to have the instincts of a mousetrap when around camels. If you are in any way distracted it could cost you your life or at the very least a broken limb. I have been kicked in the chest once and on the back of the head, once. Both times I thought I had breathed my last.

It then suddenly occurred to me; after sampling some Moroccan produce mid-morning . . . "What's the big deal here!" that I could use the desert to re-educate Wahad. It simply arrived to beat his ass up an incline and exhaust his rebel spirit. We did a day or so of this as well as the up—down—up—down—up—down routine. That is, having him kneel (shshshshshshsh) then rise,(tutt, tutt, tutt, tutt, tutt—similar to the clicking sound you make with your tongue when chastising a child) then quickly make him kneel and just as he settles, rise and so on. If he doesn't get up, you kick his shoulder or beat his ass–

'Oh, I can see all the horrifed faces here,' and if he won't kneel gently tap the back of his occipital bone or whack the back of his neck! He moans and bitches of course and you do this until he's out of breath or your mouth's dry from all the repeated shushing and tutting.

'Ain't life a bitch?'

Think how frustrated you get when your car won't start in the morning and you've only given yourself the thirty minutes to get to work before you're due to start! I may have walked 7km to find him and 4km to return to camp, saddle up and go. When he decided to be difficult when I wanted to mount, the answer was to pull his head around to the right-hand side of his body, facing backwards and get into the saddle and keep him there briefly to show that I could do it all day if I wanted to. Of course, when you give him his head he didn't always want to get up. So here you kick behind his scapula with your heel. Or whack him on the left shoulder. Hard.

"What? Phone the animal rights groups for fuck's sake and have them come and see me!"

"And for you there in the tweed twin suit and pearls, the RSPC's in the Yellow Pages. It ain't your ass on the line here and they don't hold sway in the real world anyway."

As I've already said, watch Michael Palin's Saharan journey on DVD if it's too painful. Of course, he's giving you the sanitized version and he didn't do camels as far as I'm aware. Which is a bit of a folly really, seeing as how it's the fuckin' Sahara!

My remedy for dealing with his obstinacy didn't come from nomads or bergers but from having to find a solution to a major problem, Wahad and my need for him. He doesn't need me. No camel needs its owner. Also, without your one metre baton; cut from the root of an Acacia tree, you're fucked!

"You must never let this go!"

Perhaps using your new beautiful girlfriend's inexhaustible supply of cord, you can have a wrist strap to ensure it goes nowhere. This is your badge of office and is handy not just for whacking errant camels and smally boys but searching for snakes and scorpions before sitting under the shade of a bush or tree. Imagine if you will, you're in your car speeding along the motorway and the steering wheel comes off in your hand. Same thing atop a camel. Only, I can clear the saddle like a kamikaze parachutist. You on the other hand, would have to rely on your air bags and seat belt. The same applies to the cord attached to the nose ring. The reins are from anything between 3-5 m long, and I've seen longer. The high dismount impressed my European guests of which, only two French girls have ever done so. Then just slightly older than my new beautiful girlfriend, they weren't too concerned about their personal safety or what might actually lie under the surface of the sand, until that is when they landed. I did say of course, there might be the possibility of hidden treasures!

"Ah, the folly of youth!"

Wahad soon got tired of the process but during those momentary lapses in concentration, I now had three options I could use on an ad hoc basis to pacify his rebel spirit. I'm sure the RSPCA would have a word or two to say in my ear for the above revelations.

"Well sir, with all due respect, you can kiss my toubab nomad ass! The Sahara is a savage place and you and your sensibilities can go and take a flying fuck!"

'Just wait until I tell you all about how I trained my dog!'

That's not to say that I'm a cruel berger, not by the standards set here in R.I.M. by some bergers and owners, who can be despotic by comparison.

"I'm just protecting my ass sir, that's all. I'm hard not cruel. There's a difference and I'm alive to tell this tale."

I had decided to replace Wahad's metal nose ring at Moctar's camp. I had seen the effects on his stock where they had opened up and sliced through the nose like a knife. The nasal tissue in a lot of camels is virtually destroyed by the use of nose rings in something akin to a habitual user of cocaine. This is either cause by the frustrated or uncaring berger pulling heavily on the nose ring or the animal itself refusing to walk and yanking its head backwards. They are unnecessary. I elected to tie the cord around his lower jaw when he was carrying baggage. Uncomfortable, but given that he was a powerful male and he's not eating when walking so it didn't matter.

"Calm down there at the back, he's only a fuckin' camel!"

I use the nose ring for riding only.

The process of inserting a nose ring in virgin territory is as follows. Take a small stick, about 15 cm long and the width of a pencil from one of the many bushes around you. This is the same stick you can use to clean your teeth.

"Obviously not the same stick, the laughing imbecile in the third row!"

Sharpen one end to an ouch point when you stick in your finger. Have your new beautiful girlfriend rip off a strip from her jolie mehlafah and fashion into a small cord. Tie a rope around your camel's lower jaw behind the canines, the knot tight under his chin. You can use a small stick to hold it in place as opposed to a knot. All the better if you get some hair caught in there.

"Oh settle down there at the back or phone the RSPCA! But it'll be another lifetime before the door bell goes . . . oh I forgot, I don't have one on my fuckin' tent!"

Close hobble him and have him kneel as instructed above. Take one smally boy and have him grab and pull the lower lip downwards; which is very sensitive, holding on for dear life with both hands. Put the end of the rope attached to your camel's mouth under your foot, pulling downwards on it to exert pressure on his mouth. Not around your foot. This is merely psychological reassurance for all three parties involved. Take out and open your knife, place the stick in your mouth, making sure that your new beautiful girlfriend has the new nose ring finished, that she will then model in the typically nomadic feminine fashion, by holding it against her nose.

'She's a bad, bad girl your new beautiful girlfriend.'

Now, insert the fingers of one hand into the camel's snot filled nose and make a one cm cut at the back of his nose, using your finger underneath for pressure. Swap the knife for the stick in your mouth. You have to keep the knife handy in case there's any gristle to negotiate. You then drive the sharpened end of the stick through the slit until you can feel it with your fingers inside his nose. Rotate as you wiggle it back and forward until there's a decent hole. As you can guess, this he really doesn't like and you'll be surprised at the amount of control an eight year old smally boy has over an animal 180 kg heavier than himself, just because of where he's holding onto to. The same could be said of grabbing and squeezing the balls of a much larger man and flooring him thus. Same difference. If that were the means by which you had to perform this task, Wahad could just bugger off for all I care, baggage and all. I ain't goin' there, no way, no how!

By this time, there's a small crowd gathered, which your new beautiful girlfriend chases away to quickly come back and carry on adoring you. Out with the stick, to take the nose ring from your ever attentive new beautiful girlfriend who has sashayed over, modeling it next to her own nose feigning sadness at having to hand it over. She then quickly skips away, telling the crowd who've tried to sneak back to "Imshi khaima!" ("Go back to the tent!") slaps one or two around the head and proceeds to make a nose ring for herself. Shaking your head at the circumstances in which you find yourself, thinking that being an underpaid and overworked intensive care nurse was so much simpler, at least from a legal standpoint given the age of your new beautiful girlfriend and yourself.

Concentrating on the task in hand, you insert the sharp end of your stick into the tight loop. The other end is knotted and the nose ring is perhaps 12-14 cm long. You then stick your fingers back up his nose, nodding reassurance to the smally boy who's chest is puffed out with a look of self importance all over his face, and drive it through the bloody hole. Which again must be quite sore; given the amount of objections he's voicing. Grab the nose ring, pull out the stick and casually throw it away. It's at this point as it sails through the air, that you hope that you won't look like a prat in front of your new beautiful girlfriend should the nose ring slip out and you have to go looking for it.

'Smile as if you're in control berger of one.' Take the knotted end and pass through the tight loop at the other end and hey presto, finished. Holding onto the nose ring, your new beautiful girlfriend duly arrives on cue with water to pour over the camel's bloody nose, and steps back after congratulating you with those big beautiful eyes and her new nose ring, which she places in your top pocket with a gentle caress! Again, she chases the crowd of swarming imbeciles, slapping harder this time! It's surprisingly and disturbingly horny to watch.

Holiday over as you exit an Austin Powers moment and it's back to the task in hand. Given the nod, the smally boy then does a runner with your camel rearing up onto his feet, giving you a mouthful of camel abuse . . . remembering of course as he does so, to let go of the rope with your foot as he shakes blood and snot all over you. At this point, he is instantly prepared to do battle with you, the smally boy and your new beautiful girlfriend. The small crowd that has reappeared scatters off in all directions adding further mayhem to the proceedings. Your new beautiful girlfriend then runs after one errant imbecile who's passed within a hairbreadths of the camel's rear legs and proceeds to contribute to his future mental instability by beating him around the head and face, in a severe and dangerous fashion.

'Ah! She's beautiful in full flight,' until you remember the age of your new beautiful girlfriend and the fact that this treatment could come your way too, quickly evaporates all carnal thoughts! The imbecile departs smiling like the village idiot he is, no doubt due to past beatings from the same new beautiful girlfriend, who instantly reverts to adoring mode!

Your ever adoring new beautiful girlfriend and accompanying choir, shrills out as the camel continues to do his 'I ain't fuckin' impressed,' dance but soon calms down when he's over the discomfort or when the anger over the discomfort subsides or when the crowd of imbeciles calms down and stops baiting him. Mostly, he probably didn't like the water being poured over his head. Mwoiny would freak out too when thrown into the Atlantic Ocean. She wouldn't walk over the smallest trickle of water. You then run after him, to take his mouth cord. You untie his close hobbles (remembering to stay alert) and re-tie normal hobbles and lower his head to grab the nose ring, which he knows you're going for and doesn't help.

The other place to grab a camel when he doesn't have a cord to control him is the skin and hair of his cheek, to then grab his lower lip. This has to be done very quickly for it to be effective, also bearing in mind that the animal's not hobbled either and it can go either way, good or bad, for you that is.

'He is very big and you are only very little.'

Eventually, you get a hold of the nose ring by twisting the rope under his chin, "Oh fuckin' behave everyone," and test it by pulling on it to get him to kneel, and of course it hurts! Reassurance in English lends a comic value to the proceedings. He doesn't like you one little bit, in neither French, English or very basic Hassaniya. Untie the mouth cord, holding onto the nose ring, which is where the stick version comes in handy as it's less complicated to do one handed. You then chase him away to find solace through his stomach, even though he is pissing off! This exercise definitely reasserts who the boss is, or so I thought!

I had seen this done at the market the day I bought Wahad and it looked and was simple enough. No-one at the encampment needed to know it was my first time, least of all the smally boy holding Wahad's mouth, so kindly donated by, my new beautiful girlfriend.

'Isn't she wonderful?'

The nurse's motto is: See one do one. Your smally boy is then given the first wash as he's in too much of a hurry to go and tell everyone who's prepared to listen on how today, he became a man, all day if need be. He's now an important person in the encampment, second berger to Wahad and up for the second glass of tea. The wash I have is with soap, which my new beautiful girlfriend has been keeping for a special occasion such as this. French soap from Marseilles. Tres joile. My blood, snot and spit covered clothes are simply left to look after themselves until the next day, which of course are lovingly washed, by my new beautiful girlfriend.

It is now some one/two weeks after this event and it seems like a millions years ago. Wahad and I are resting up during one afternoon under a huge bush, when a passing berger stops to ask about camels. It was Wahad who knew about our visitors first, naturally and I think he was a little too snotty for his own good on this occasion. The berger dismounts and joins me for tea, which he makes. He draws the brand in the sand, gives me their colour, the numbers of females and babies, which funnily enough, I'd seen four/five days previously, moving north. In return, he gives me the location of an encampment five days away. Tea over he takes off. There is no lingering, no long goodbyes, it's up and off after the third glass is finished. A little too strong and sugary for me but the company was good and thank God he spoke French, otherwise it would have been a long hour. I elect to go to the well with the small encampment, to further my schooling.

Three days later, I wake up late at 08.00 to a splendid sight. Perhaps, two to three hundred camels, four riders, over three hundred goats and sheep herded by four boys, with two other men walking back and forward, one of them very tall, and traversing the huge piste in front of me. This piste is about 4km across and 10km long and the herd looked tiny, until you get close. I'm up and off walking directly towards them. One rider on seeing me comes towards me.

"Salaam Aleykum." He calls out.

"Aleykum salaam." I reply.

Straight off I remember thinking, 'He's not Mauritanian,' as his saddle and clothes are fundamentally different, though his clothes are not so very different from the Senegalese and Malian men I'd seen wearing them in Nouakchott.' I reach up and shake his hand.

"What country?" He asks.

"Scotland." I reply.

He's searching, then a smile of recognition.

"Laing." He says.

I smile a wide smile.

"Tuareg?" I ask and nod in his direction. He simply raises his head, very proudly.

"What are you doing here?" He asks.

"Travelling, going nowhere in particular." I reply.

He then starts to ride off, "Come with us then." He says.

I watch him go back to the herd and saunter back to my camp. He's either given me an invitation or an order to join him. Or I could simply carry on my own path. No choice really. I believe I've just graduated into high school. Perhaps the same will happen to me happened to Laing. I won't know until I join them. Anyhoo, that wasn't the case, his guide was a member of the 1800's version of the Salafist, akin to the Algerian militia GSPC who live in the modern day territory that encompasses a tiny part of Mali, Mauritania and Algeria.

I eventually catch up, as the dunes that arrived between us made passage a little difficult and we traveled on a parallel path for about an hour. I then fall in behind and walk with the goats. The boys and two men walking back and forward are Sudanese slaves. Moussa, the man who came to meet me is the head berger, and of the other three, Ibrahim and Mano are brothers and Abdallah the youngest, is a cousin. Moulay, the oldest goatherd would become my aide de camp, assigned to me by Moussa. Although we didn't speak a common language, I spoke English and he Tamashek, we knew what the other was saying. We take an afternoon break, with the two Sudanese men and the youngest boy making lunch, whilst the others continue to monitor the herds. The animals don't stop just because the bergers apparently do. For the animals it's a continual process of eating and searching for something to eat. The goats it seems never stop. They have to be continually watched, shouted at and sticks thrown at all day. I wander in and out with no specific role other than as an observer and the berger of one. But I'm watching everything everyone is doing and very soon without knowing it, I have been roped in to do this or that and the movement and rhythm of a large number of animals soon becomes second nature. I couldn't have paid enough for this experience. It's a natural process that over the next two weeks or so becomes both my daily life and an obsession. The life of a Saharan pastoralist.

The owner of the herds is Hamada, a Black Mauritanian/Malian Tuareg who drives an ancient white Land Rover, and keeps his bergers supplied with food, water, tobacco and news from home. He's over the moon that I've decided to come to Mauritania to discover the world of camels and knows Scotland's history intimately, through the Maj. Alexander Gordon Laing connection, the first European to reach Timbuktu. My rope making skills become second to none; for me that is, but always in last place with the youngest boy whipping my ass as we race to finish our hobbles. I'm really trying hard to beat their ass and it's a great source of amusement for everyone. It's for the first time also that I hear toubab. White man. Not a derogatory name, it's just what I am. Moussa is the first person to call me toubab nomad. I have used it ever since.

Although the routine is the same day in day out, it's not boring, not the same, the same work but different. Here you are, surrounded by animals and men and boys but perhaps not talking to anyone despite being in their vicinity. It's too hot, there's too many imbeciles to be shouted at or sticks thrown at and you're turbaned up. Wahad had calmed down somewhat, I think due to the numbers of available girlies around. Always showing off, the dog. It was as the guest of Moussa, that he first displayed his ability for theft. Or perhaps he'd not had the opportunity for a while! A 10L bucket of camel's milk, gone in seconds. A mere mouthful for an animal that can drink one hundred and twenty litres in a minute! Moulay went crazy and then everyone was chasing Wahad's ass, whacks from baton's raining down on his body as he leaps off. I joined in too giving him a mouthful of Glaswegian. Then Moussa whacked the boys because they weren't paying enough attention. I didn't dare interfere here. Then everyone was laughing their heads off as Wahad looked back, milk dripping off of his face, giving comic value to the moment.

'Son of a bitch,' I was so embarrassed.

My punishment was to go and get more milk with Abdallah.

"And no salary for three days!" He adds as we move off.

He was right, it's a lot of money to have your camel to hoover up. I then reminded him I wasn't getting a salary.

"Then you'll have to pay for it then!" He said.

I was stunned, then he burst out laughing and translated for the others. My face was red hot.

"Putain! Sac a merde! Fous le camp!"

I then let rip with some Glaswegian phrases. The boys were dancing and singing. At this exact moment in time and for ever more in the desert good or bad, I love my life! All morning, singing and chanting the likes I'd never heard before. They had sung often during the day and at night, using plastic bidons as drums but this was so different. Even the goats didn't need to be shouted at as much, though the sheep, the sheep are so fuckin' stupid! Talking of stupidity, It would be the first time I saw a camel walk into a huge bush and fall out the other side. I thought, 'She can see it, she's not . . .'

Wham! She fell into and out of, down onto her knees, sand flying everywhere, to quickly regain her posture, looking around to see if anyone had seen her. Ibrahim was in hysterics and rode up to her to give her a whack. She must have sensed what was about to befall her and she took off, Ibrahim whooping and calling after her.

My job as it transpired was nursery patrol, as had been the case almost from the morning of day three, and it was huge. They would group up and go back to their mothers throughout the day at certain times, but a hardcore group would stay put, causing all sorts of mayhem. I was supposedly stationed to stop them from causing too much trouble or when they began to wander off in bands it was yours truly, given the nod and helped by the others or not, to round them up. You do not simply walk in a straight line with stock. You cut back an forth, retrace steps already taken, circling around to sneak up on . . . Wahad had little or no time for them, the grumpy bastard. Day seven, middle of the afternoon, five disappeared without as much as a by your leave. Moussa called over and asked me as to when I had last seen the two piebalds.

"I honestly didn't know." I said.

I immediately felt about two cm tall.

"It's okay." Moussa said, when he saw the look of shock and horror on my face. He rode off and returned half an hour later with Moulay. He and I were sent off to look for them, Moussa taking us to their last point of contact with the herd. Two days, two days the little bastards took us on a song and dance tour of the Trarza. Again, because they don't simply go in a straight line and they're children.

This song and dance tour would be repeated at various times throughout my time in the desert with different herds. It won't ever change as baby camels are just like children. In fact, if you have five people sitting at a table there are five different personalities. It's the same with camels.

Like children, they can wander off and get lost. They don't worry about being lost and continue to play. It does mean that you cannot take milk from the mother though. Herein lies the problem. With as many lactating mothers as we had it wasn't a problem if milk was the only issue. But if they are all you have, you can see the seriousness of the problem of lost children. Not to mention that they are worth money. Three of them are females. A female becomes sexually active at four years old and gives birth twelve to thirteen months after mating. She will normally calve every two years which maintains good health in the mother and future babies. It is possible to have the female calve every year but not recommended. She will continue to calve until she is between twenty and thirty years old. Say, twelve babies. If half the babies are female, you can see the projected available revenue in terms of meat, milk and more babies. The males will be good for meat and therefore not as valuable, still money lost though.

The piebalds have different mothers but the same evil spawn of the father, who was sold to the abattoir as he had gone mad. Dangerously mad. We long hobbled them, that is, hobbling from rear to front breaking up the full stride to discourage running off. They didn't like that either and Wahad wasn't impressed with the noise from them either All the way back to the herd! For once we were on the same side and it was a major shock to my system. Moulay didn't let up on the babies for a moment. He also liked my cooking and we dined on rabbit stew and potato scones with raisins. He didn't go a bundle on my tea but as it was my food he let me have my moment. We talked endlessly in our respective languages it seemed, without end and the subjects varied. He played a game, called maru maru. This is a mime to explain how the tribe works and it's very entertaining. When we arrived back at camp he had the other boys mime too, bloody hilarious! We shared the guard duty of our AWOL babies but the last shift before dawn, I let him sleep on. You should have heard the language when he woke up. For someone so young he has a filthy mouth! We arrived back at he herd to no more than a hello. It's a truly leveling experience and totally at one with the nature of the Sahara. What if we hadn't come back? Inshallah. If God wills it. Moussa would have continued to move the herd onwards to Mali and our bones left to bleach in the sun. It's what you have to expect. No-one says Bon voyage here. C'est, "Bon chance m'sieur."

After two weeks of non stop movement, we had a weekend off to rest. Though I couldn't have told you what day it was. There were times when

I got back into Nouakchott after say four months, I didn't even know what month it was. I sms'd Lesley once to ask her what the 16th was of what month? I say weekend off, the herds stayed relatively stationary and we had a regular camp for two days, but they still have to be watched. In the early morning I got my ass kicked during Tammazzaga, camel racing accompanied by the drumming of bidons by the boys. Wahad and I gave it 100% and it was never going to be a gold medal but brass good enough, fourth equal. Ibrahim and I comrades in despair at being beaten, badly.

After lunch had settled in our stomachs, they had asked if I would wrestle with them. I'm not built for wrestling and anyway I have different skills, in which I ultimately redeemed myself for the poor showing at the races. I persuaded the six men to fight with me, all at the same time. Three with and three without batons and asked them to do their worst. There was complete and utter disbelief accompanied by much laughter at first until I gave Moussa an order to line themselves up and I bowed. The others did a half hearted version, totally confused as to what was about to happen. I gave Moussa a direct no nonsense look signaling everyone to circle me. I said that if anyone could KO me then they could take Wahad. Moussa translated and everyone flashed big white teeth and each and everyone was determined that he would have my camel, arguing amongst themselves. I love over-confidence.

"As there are so many who think that they'll be the one, then you'll just have to eat him for dinner!" I shouted out. Moussa translated and everyone began talking all at once.

'Then I'd really show Wahad who's the boss, if I got my ass kicked!' I thought and I laughed out loud at this. The chattering continued as everyone set themselves up for the attack. I like over-confidence; it makes a man make errors of judgment. There was much baiting about me being smaller or older, except for one person, Moussa was there but not 100%, I could see it in his face. Then it began. Abdallah was first down, and then to his complete surprise the biggest Sudanese, gasping like a fish out of water as I slammed the heel of my hand upwards and through his solar plexus. Ibrahim got smacked on the head with his baton as did Abdallah when he got back up. Mano throws his away, very far away. I was in and out, here there and everywhere. I dropped man after man. One got up to go down almost immediately. Strikes to the solar plexus and groin and sweeps to their feet and strikes to the backs of their knees kept my work to a minimum. The occasional throw for Hollywood effect for the boys, who screamed and drummed in delight. Not so the recipients, Mano and Abdallah. Of the throws I was as gentle with them as I could be. This after all wasn't war. The surprise in the fallen six was deafening by their silence and it was deemed finished when no man stirred or wanted to stir and the boys began drumming. Everyone soaked in sweat of course. The boys went so mental that it seemed they were calling to their tribe in Mali to war. The boy's cries giving me shivers down the back of my neck. I walked back from the scene of chaos, knelt down in the sand and gave them the traditional Japanese bow for thanking them for allowing me to use them for practice. My stature immediately elevated to that from a virgin berger to that of a warrior. Everyone was a little unwary to shake my hand afterwards, as during the sparring I had done so to devastating effect. It's a natural reaction to grab the wrist when offered. In retrospect very silly as they were now only too aware of. I demanded their camels as my prize. For a moment they weren't certain but when I laughed everyone went hysterical as the thought of losing their mounts would be akin to losing heir lives. In fact, a Tuareg won't leave his dying mount and will die along with him.

"I'll have your saddles instead then!" I said, after everyone had calmed down to again make everyone uncertain, until I burst into hysterics followed by everyone else in sheer and utter relief.

After everyone had settled down and had rested, I gave a master class in basic aikido in the hot afternoon sun to Abdallah and Mano. I allowed them to throw me a few times. Well, helping them to throw me would be more exact. I was then given as my prize, a display in traditional wrestling called Tallibant and then in Solagh, which involves running as you wrestle. Not for me, too bloody energetic, all that grabbing and grunting and so undignified. The night was spent singing, all night long. Takket I think it's called, I can't be certain as to my shame, the little Tamashek I picked up I've lost. Then again, I've English, French, a moderate amount of Hassaniya, a little Arabic and a little Wolof all running around my head, the dictionaries opening and closing or not opening when they need to be. The next day we patrolled the herds, slept in shifts, ate, played games and talked. The big Sudanese declined to help me practice again, even when I made the sound of a chicken laying an egg. He just nodded, walking away holding or protecting his groin rather, to the derisory laughter of everyone. To help him out I then scanned everyone who soon shut up, and sniggering took over. The boys played a game, melga. One boy remains next to the well, and the others run away and hide. This boy has then to go and search for them and catch them before they can return to the well and drink, only in this case it would be the bidon. The weekend over and we moved on, the daily routine of chastising the babies and not letting them escape, my goal and obsession for the day.

I knew that when I next saw Hamada, my time with the herd would be up. We were moving ever closer towards the Tagant and in conversation with him, I had said that this would be the time that I turned back. Not that I had an agenda, it just felt right. I had asked Hamada to buy me supplies and he had taken my list and subsequently wouldn't take the money for them, as he said I was due a salary. He was too kind but he is a wealthy man. Like the arrival of the crescent moon and the star that heralds the end of Ramadan, Hamada's ancient white Land Rover heralded my return six days after our weekend break. That night on his return, dinner was a feast of a slaughtered sheep, vegetables, fruit and Coke. The singing went on into the early hours. In the morning as breakfast was being made I packed up Wahad, took a full supply of water, ate and drank my three cups of tea, with fresh sprigs of mint. I then shook hands with everyone. Moussa gave me a silver pendant. The Tamashek believe gold harbours bad spirits. I think they may be right given the numbers of people who have died for it. No long goodbyes.

A gentle, "Bismillah." from Abdallah.

I turned to walk back, the way we had come back, through our tracks we had made, with the men and boys singing. Tears streamed down my face inside my turban until I could hear them no more. I walked in our tracks for two days before moving off taking a new direction. It would have been too easy to carry on. I had my own path to find and follow.

## CHAPTER FOUR

# LOOKIN' FOR SOMEWHERE TO HANG MY TURBAN

I WONDERED BACK and a little sideways, now and again, towards Nouakchott. I stayed with a nomad family here and there, which was little more than an extension of what I'd experienced at Moctar's encampment. At every stop it seemed I had a new beautiful Bidan, Black Moor or Haratin girlfriend, just as beautiful and as young as Aminetou in most cases. Very beautiful Haratin girls the like of which I'd never dreamed possible. All vying for my hand.

'Et m'sieur, je ne suis pas jolie!'

I was, over the next two years to receive some 32 offers of marriage. On one occasion, I was asked to accept the Muslim standard at the one sitting. The Bidan girls ages ranged from 14 to 22. The middle two, 15 and 17 were very beautiful and their sisters, ordinary by comparison, but still pretty enough. Can you imagine having to sleep with each in succession night after night? And after Ramadan!

"Oh my GOD! Donnez-moi!" I can hear you say, but wait! Four wives and four different sets of problems and clothes and children and . . . . I mentioned to the father that I had only one camel, one 5L bidon of water and a sack of food and my dog and that I was out looking for a herd

"They can walk and they don't need any baggage!" He told me.

Or any nourishment or blankets it seemed. Then again I'd have the equivalent of another four camels, trailing behind me if I did indeed have a mountain of baggage. I left at 05.00 the next morning, at the gallop! My sister liked to rub this in by sending me postcards from Spain, the one's that have four naked girls on the beach.

"Thank you baby sis!"

The last one I sold for four quid at Café Tunis, auctioning it off to a Bidan.

"Keep them coming Lesley!"

I continued to meet and travel with bergers and their herds. Though the herds were as Big as Hamada's it was still experience, the Mauritanian way. I would hear that repeated hundred's, nay thousand's of times throughout my time in the desert, "It's not the Mauritanian way!"

At times I would have to swallow my frustration and anger and accept that these so-called bergers and some owners would indulge in mindless violence towards the animals in their care or possession. Thankfully, it was rare but happened enough to be recognised a national trait. The Qu'ran forbids it. The Prophet Mohammad, May the peace and blessings of Allah be upon him, was a berger. Who better a teacher is there in relation towards the animals in your care in a Muslim country? The mindless violence seems to be for no other reason than they could indulge in it and that it is mindless, like the perpetrators. I would later learn about the violence dished out to Haratin. I could imagine what would have happened if I had done the same to Hamada's animals. My guide would have done the same to me as Laing's had, I expect, when on the night of the 26th September 1826, 30km north of Timbuktu, a normal day's journey by camel, Laing lost his head, literally.

On the second morning, at the encampment of one Ahmedou El Mamy, the Bidan owner who had arrived the evening before with three friends for a two-day stay in the desert. This meeting would have future implications and would bring ill-will and misfortune into my life. I unexpectedly woke up on day three to preparations being made to brand 5 females and their babies and 3 males from the total of 22 females, 13 babies and 7 males. The youngest of three sons, 9 years old, took the scrum of goats and sheep off for the day on their 20km foray. Ahmedou had a sheep slaughtered on arrival and one after the branding fiasco as a celebration, no doubt to celebrate the fact that no-one was killed! Sidi Mohamad took the responsibility of showing me how to butcher a sheep on both occasions. Boring! Seen that, done that, got the bloody T-shirt, but I gave him his moment, as only you must because even if he knew you done this before, it wouldn't have been done properly in his opinion. A full day's work ahead of us, we'd go it alone as the other two boys would accompany their father, a Black Moor called Hajj and the youngest of these two, around 10, would bring back the males. The hobbled females (on one leg, fetlock to foreleg) and their off-spring remain, without hobbles, at the encampment. This is normal practice and assists in the milking of the females, at 06.00 and 18.30. The males; like their deer counterparts in Scotland, live apart from the nursery.

You would have thought that Ahmedou would have said something the night before, as he and the others tucked into the sheep's head on a bed of couscous at one o'clock in the morning. No thank you on both counts. My dog Mwoiny, can devour a sheep's head in less than fifteen minutes! This lack of free flowing information is a trademark of the Mauritanian. I should start a list! You are last to know even if you should be the first to know, not that I was. You and I would have simply considered it good manners to ask for my help not just simply expect it. Manners unfortunately are in very short supply here.

Also; 'we'll start the fuckin' list,' the Mauritanian will ask you a question then ten seconds afterwards, completely ignore you as you reply. Their attention span at best is less than that of a gnat's. They will often tune into a nearby conversation and completely ignore your presence for your spoken word to tail off in an embarrassing manner. Except that no-one gives a fuck and you are embarrassed only by yourself, with yourself. As Ahmedou and his cohorts discuss the day's work over bowls of fresh camel's milk and glasses of tea; endlessly supplied by Hajj's wife Moilemein, who is wrestling with her toddler brat. The Harmattan Kid is single mindlessly intent on toppling every bowl, the tea tray and playing with the gas cylinder. She is eventually carried off by her left ankle and securely fastened to the tent post. When she cried Moilemein returned to her and slapped her across the face. On crying more, she was again slapped and when Moilemein raised her hand for a third, she stopped, suddenly, no tears. The flow of tea then continued unhindered. Everyone except me of course, ignored this tussle of wills between the mother and the wild force of nature, momentarily becalmed, silently plotting more connerie.

It was the babies that Ahmedou had elected should be branded first, as being the easier option and therefore the job would be done much quicker!! I must point out that the conversation throughout the two days was conducted in Zreag. This is akin to Franglais. Only it's French and Hassaniya. Ahmedou and the others mostly spoke French for my benefit but when tempers and frustrations arrive, then it's full on Hassaniya. It's only now that I can see Hajj getting himself ready for the day's work with a look of calmed reassurance. Like he carried a secret that could change the course of history but wouldn't tell anyone. I kept my mouth shut, as my sarcasm arrived like a juggernaut without a driver, slipping its brakes. As far as I was concerned, there is never an easy option as far as camels are concerned when having to manhandle them. Moving a herd is so simple as to be, so simple that a child can do it. But actually handling adults or babies, the options for disaster are the exact same. As my limited experience had shown, it was the baby's inherent unpredictable nature that was to prove my suspicions correct and therefore my mounting sarcasm justified. This is the national trait of Scotland, I expect we all have them. A line from a Camel song duly arrives in my head.

"Time on your hands, doodle all the day, shuffle your feet and turn on the news to hear what they might say . . . they've made a machine, a new fangled device, they're lighting the fuse, there's no need to worry, your world will be alright . . . Time for a smoke a pipe and a joke . . ."

'Just might be a fuckin' good idea, anesthetised for when the end of my life should arrive any time soon.' The first thing that occurred to me was that they perhaps weren't as experienced as they professed to be. That list again, if a Mauritanian thinks he can do it he will because in his h-bar sized brain in his Tardis type skull he can, even if he can't. He won't ever admit to not knowing he can't or hasn't. At least my philosophy of, see one do one means I therefore have had some experience!

"Well, see it as you like I don't give a fuck!"

Ahmedou surprisingly enough didn't have Hajj present. He had nodded at me as him and his sons took the rest of the herd away; long before the proceedings started. Ahmedou, the others and myself were to handle the females and babies. 'If it were me,' I mused as I tied a female to a tree, then hobbled her, that 'I'd have had the boys take the herd and use Hajj, as being the one constant element in the day to day existence of the stock. 'Still, what the fuck did I know, eh?' Secondly, why weren't the babies being secured beside their mothers? Ahmedou had waved me off when I suggested that I do so. It's only now that the smiling face of Hajj registers in my mind's eye . . . 'Bon chance?' Surely, it was asking for trouble to have the imbeciles running around, and I don't just mean the babies! My reference for seeking internal stability was Moussa. Natural enough when you need a solid point of reference to hang onto like a rock in the middle of the raging ocean, after your ship has gone down. I would endevour to keep myself safe from the impending storm as much as I could. I tied the baby to the same tree.

Despite the lecture Ahmedou had given me that morning at milking about being quiet around the stock, they were all chattering like excited schoolboys. Primary two. It was at this point, purely on a point of self-survival that I went to tie up another baby beside her mother. Sidi Mohamad nodded in agreement as he led a female past to a nearby tree. As Ahmedou came back from the Hilux with his iron he shouted at me to let her be but Sidi Mohamad intervened and common sense prevailed. There would be many differences of opinion between Ahmedou and Sidi Mohamad throughout the day's proceedings. The others reacted to this Grand Canyon in the otherwise perfect planning and soon all mothers and babies were safely secured. Though Hamadou had made two fundamental errors. Sidna one, which less so, was still an error of judgment.

"Patience dear reader, later. It's not as if there's not an endless supply of connerie coming your way in this book."

Then came the townie/nomad fire ritual. This consists of arguing for a very long time about choosing the best wood to burn and throwing away wood deemed unsuitable going back for it for it to be thrown away, again. I could have had two joints and listened to Topographic Oceans waiting for the jump off. It would all be used up eventually! See what I mean! Hardly a sentence goes by without some reference to stupidity. They just looked even more stupid having to walk after it after throwing it as far away as they did on what, three occasions! Finally, standing around the blazing fire warming their hands, happy with their choice of logs, Ahmedou selected the first baby. I stayed on fire duty as the Fantastic Four ganged up on him, Sid Mohamad and Sidna discarding their boubous in the process of dragging him over, throwing him down and trussing him up. Hamadou was the only person to start out minus his and Ahmedou kept his on through the entire process. He continually scoffed at my choice of clothing and every two minutes; as they do, readjusted the huge expanse of material, pulling it back up onto his shoulders or wrapping it around his huge stomach to stand with his hands behind his back like a puffed up peacock. I've worn one once and don't like it. A Western style shirt, white patterned material with fancy stitching on short baggy trousers and the boubou, a voluminous tent with the same stitching with a black turban and sandals made me look and feel like a clown. It mattered little that this boubou and trousers were expensive. I didn't want them. I later gave them to a berger to sell and help feed his family, the equivalent of three weeks salary.

Hardly what one would call professional start. I was given the head to sit on and held onto his lower lip and an ear.

"Go and phone them for fucks sake!" Sidi Mohamad on his flank pulling on his tail and the other two on leg duty, Ahmedou took the red-hot iron from the fire to place it on the neck just in front of the left scapula. You've seen enough cowboy movies to know the scene so replicate it with a camel in your mind's eye. Smoke rose from the skin as the iron marked him as owned. As the fumes wafted up my nose he was naturally enough, howling his head off and I could hear and see his mother trying to pull the tree down telling us what she'd like to do to us. Thank God sense had prevailed and they'd tied up the babies too as they were trying to bolt despite being beside their mothers! The others now knew that we weren't having a barbeque or that we were perhaps trying to barbeque their step brother! It also made the others that followed a different proposition and this is where the fun started. The men, so very pleased with themselves relaxed just a little too much. Sidi Mohamad threw a handful of sand onto the wound; I would later use Sudocrem on my camel and it worked a treat, and went off to collect the next baby as the first bolted and sought refuge and solace from his mother, suckling. Only there wasn't any milk to be had as the females had been milked at dawn. I fastened him to the tree again. The mother gave me a mouthful but not as in the case of Sidna, who got a stomachful from the mother he dealt with. He stank. Oh he really stank! Been there, done that, had the smelly matching African combo; exactly like theatre blues, for what seemed an eternity. I later burned them as washing did nothing to alleviate my olfactory discomfort.

Let me first tell you about branding, that I've since discovered wasn't the process going on here, well at least by the book as it were.

"Should that surprise you, man in the third row? Didn't think so."

The iron should be glowing red-hot. Like you see in the cowboy movies, or the Burger King advert, where you think the wrangler is trying to cook his steak live! It should be pressed onto the skin for between twenty and sixty seconds until the skin turns white. Ahmedou held it in place when it wasn't red-hot for the minimum time allowed. Then perhaps reapplied for another five seconds or so. When red-hot, it was in place for perhaps fifteen seconds, occasionally for twenty seconds. If done properly the brand will heal within a few days leaving a smooth black scar. I had no idea as to the length of time of the healing process so of these animals, therefore I cannot make a qualified statement. I will say that it didn't look good for half to two-thirds of the stock on the morning of my departure given that the process was a complete bordel. I believe that their wounds would have been harbouring inflammation and infection. Not rocket science eh? It was hard to see from the number of flies swarming and resting on the wounds. Then again what the fuck did I know? Hajj simply shook his head and tapped his right temple with his right forefinger. Says it all really.

Vets in Europe apparently used to use branding to treat muscle and joint problems in horses, which I didn't know about. How would I as I've had no contact with the equine world. It is now considered barbaric but for some diseases, its continued use is supported by professionals. The rationale is, that branding using a red-hot iron turns a chronic condition into an acute condition and the body's defence kicks in and healing then takes place. It remains controversial and should only be used when there really isn't another option. This also supposes that the herder is using a red-hot iron as he is supposed to! As well as those conditions affecting horses, it's supported for use in contagious skin necrosis (caused by bacterial and fungal infections), abscesses and swollen lymph nodes.

"Get a fuckin' medical dictionary or you'll be here stuck here, whilst everyone else carries on without you!"

The list for the Sahara then goes on with: diarrhoea, kidney problems, cough and infections of the udder and womb, vomiting in calves and intestinal obstructions. The branding iron is a bar about fifteen centimeters long and the width of a thumb. As I have said, it use remains controversial. My thoughts are firmly in the natural medicine and modern vetinary medicine, school of thought. When it comes to the selection of stock you can identify what diseases the herder/owner believes the camel has had and therefore is a clear indication that you should stay clear of buying these animals. Given that you are an intelligent man, the animals you choose to buy, should only have the previous owner's brands on their ass, sorry flank, neck or shoulder and not a grid pattern of branding in the aforementioned places or anywhere else the owner deems necessary. What I will do and keep it in general terms; and perhaps keep the contents of your stomach in place, that there are many camel diseases where branding is still used by many nomad peoples across the Sahara, who simply have no other choice available or are firmly established in their use of it. You also have to remember that this practice goes back over centuries of being handed down from healer to healer, father to son. To us in the West it may seem barbaric. As a cauterisation tool it's second to none. It's used on nomads too.

Finally, we return to the episode in hand, where you may remember me saying that there had been two errors made. 'Mmm, so unusual.' The next baby is dragged over again duly hobbled and manhandled down onto the sand. Everyone's about to get into their allotted place when the mother, not wanting her off-spring to suffer any more, rips her nose ring out and proceeds to race towards us. Sidi Mohamad and I are the first to react, racing to intercept her. Ahmedou has scarpered leaving the other saps to hold onto baby. Let me say that this baby is perhaps three/four years old.

"Not so fuckin' little! It's maybe because I used the word baby, eh?"

En route Sidi Mohamad picks up a length of tourja, a brittle stalk which produces a high heat charcoal the thickness of tissue paper, and breaks it a cross the left hand side of her face to stop her forward momentum. I reach up, blood and snot flying around and grab her right cheek with my left hand and with Sidi Mohamad and I both grabbing her lip and then her left cheek, we wrestle this one hundred and thirty kilo maniacal mother to the ground. Sand showering us both, legs flailing as Sidna arrives with hobbles. He stands back, grinning like the idiot he is, until the baby arrives with Hamadou and she's then hobbled fetlock to foreleg. Ahmedou struts up giving everyone a mouthful, me included! I tell him in Glaswegian that, he can go and take a flying fuck to himself and if he opens his mouth again in my direction, then he'll need a fuckin' dentist! Sidi Mohamad translates this as, "He isn't happy and he doesn't like you very much!" adding 'Dishwadi?' "Where did you scarper off to?"

I then asked who'd tied the camel to the tree. Hamadou owns up.

"You're a prick and a waste of space." I tell him.

Sidi Mohamad understands a little English but not full-on Glaswegian. I scan the other mothers and see another female attached to the tree with her nose ring. I point at her and look directly at Sidna.

"You as well!" I tell him.

I'm angry because these Bidan jokers are playing with my life and aren't even aware or bothered that they are. Left in the hands of God, mainly an excuse for laziness and stupidity. Ahmedou then does his peacock thang for ten minutes, pacing up and down lecturing at the two imbeciles. Sidi Mohamad grabs Sidna to deal with the hobbled mommy as Ahmedou continues with his monotonous monologue. It's at this point that Sidi Mohamad takes over, with Ahmedou giving his twenty ougiya's worth now and again. But by and large and not before time, things have gotten more serious now and the larger animals don't necessarily take up more time, just more energy to restrain. I'm on head duty throughout as Sidi Mohamad seems to favour the flank end the most dangerous place to be. I later learn that he is a retired Gendarmerie officer with extensive experience up in the Zemmour, The Wild West of Mauritania. He's okay, for an officer. We keep on going until all are done then eat. The boys are so tired out that they immediately go to sleep. That's another national trait, sleeping in the afternoon heat. I thank Moilemein for lunch, beg a bowl of milk, grab my turban, wacky backy, mp3 and head off into the dunes nearby. I'm followed by the 10 year old but chase his ass, in a kindly manner.

"Yimshi khaima!" Less direct than Aminetou's version and also without the head slap.

I arrive back after milking and the day's events are replayed for the benefit of all. There is as you will remember no TV here, we're it, everything we do, is TV. I have listened to a great many nomads singing and as my Hassaniya grew I could make out the line of the song but essentially I remained lost as to the deeper meaning. There isn't folks. A typical song would go thus:

'Mohamad, he looks after the camels, everyday he looks after the camels . . . today, he fell asleep and the camels went away! Maryam . . . she's been beating the children on a frequent basis today because the children have been exceptionally naughty, all day, and she's tired! But all's well, because everyone came home, we've eaten couscous and had camel milk because Mohamad, he found the camels again! Mohamad, he's fantastic! Three cheers for Mohamad!' Sung without a melody and perhaps accompanied by the occasional paradiddle on a bidon.

"C'est pas jolie eh jolie!" My song for this day's events would be far longer, far bluer and ten times more sarcastic!

The Fantastic Four left for the capital soon after breakfast. There, they'd relive their experiences for all and sundry who'd listen and that would be a considerable amount of people who'd then take it back to their families and friends. Soon all of Mauritania would know there's a mad Scot walking the Trarza. And perhaps an opportunity to make some money from his association or marry a sister off to him or get an invitation to live with his family and a visa for Europe! But most of all, I'd be TV for the masses, who have little or no life to excite their daily drab lives, which they are more than content to live. Eat, talk, drink tea, talk, sleep, drink tea, talk, rest after eating, drinking tea and talking, to continue to eat, drink tea, talk and drink tea and obsess about finding enough money to marry their first cousin, buy a car and house . . . to be able to eat, talk, drink tea, talk, sleep, eat, talk, drink tea, rest and talk.

I stayed with Hajj, Moilemein and the kids for two days more before continuing my walk back to the capital. I took away a gift of a goat sack in order to be able to sour my milk like a nomad. I would have it filled at various camps, or from passing herds en route to the Auberge Sahara. I had decided that I would turn up at the door and stop for four/five days, to be able to be able to organize my future life in the Trarza. I'd find somewhere to set up my tent, which I'd need to buy of course as well as everything else to sustain me. The list grew and grew as I walked on. For one person it would be substantial. Eventually in my campsite for one I would have: one Mauritanian khaima for paying guests measuring 6x6m, one Saharawi khaima for me measuring 5x3m, and one Mauritanian khaima for food and baggage measuring 2x2m . . . five saddles and a huge quantity of rope, five sleeping mats, five Spanish blankets, one very large mosquito net to ward off flies for my tent, tapis for the 6x6 and 5x3 khaima, two one thousand litre water sacks, six cushions. Food: 50kg of sugar, 50 kg of flour, 35kg of lentils, 50kg of pasta, 25kg of rice, 50kg of dried milk, one hundred tins plus of bloody sardines, one hundred tins of tuna fish, paprika, turmeric, all spice, 80 L of olive oil, glass jars with clamps in which I'd store tomatoes and peppers, 10kg of honey, 2 kg of dried chillies, 2 kg of pepper, 10kg slab of salt, 10 kg potato powder and 35 kg of potatoes, 35kg of onions, 15kg of Tunisian dates, 25kg of hard biscuits, slow cooker, two wooden spoons, a ladle and a sieve, toilet paper a mountain of, matches, twenty boxes . . . a small library of Chekhov, Arabic language course, Hassaniya language course, a translation of the Qu'ran, two translations of Hadith, petanque and a hunting rifle with an infra-red telescopic sight . . . but for the moment I was unhindered by baggage or responsibility.

Nothing stays the same for ever. I had a plan, of sorts and with no-one to talk to other than Wahad; and to be honest he didn't care either way, my head was filled with possibility. Within three years I was to lose everything. Mwoiny and I would leave the desert, her with what she had and me, my African combo, my turban, 10 000 UM (30 euros) and my passport which had been stowed under the sand. I had 1L of water when we arrived at the site of my former camp that morning around 08.00 and 34°C. At 13.00 around 42°C and at its height, 50°C. We slept all day, moving around in the shade of the bush every half hour and as soon as the sun went down, we left. Hours in which I plotted revenge, hours in which I would have killed for a glass of dirty hot water, 11 hours can seem like a lifetime. 'March or die. No fuckin' way I thought, NO FUCKIN' WAY!' We Scots are a stubborn shower of bastards!

On the subject of not having water or only a short supply of, listen very carefully. It is your life! Without water you will last two days at 50° C, if you simply rest in shade that is. With no water walking at night having rested during the day at the same temperatures, you can walk perhaps 30-40 km and during the day, perhaps 10km. With 2L of water you might be able to walk 50-60 km. It is necessary to drink 1.5L of water for every 2L lost in sweat. Less water does not mean less sweat. If you drink too much water you will simply lose it and it will be of no benefit. He knew or would surmise that I would have little water. He had tried to kill me once and was hoping for his conscience that the desert might do the same. As I've just said, we Scots are a stubborn shower of the off-spring of non-married parentage!

This period was also the first time I experienced rain in the Trarza. I remembered from school the story of the Scottish physicist James Clerk Maxwell who spurred the chaotic thoughts of a teenage Einstein with his theories of electromagnetic theory of light. The memory of the Van De Graaf Generator came to the fore as the force of the coming storm took over my body. I could taste it, like joining the terminals of a small 9 volt battery to your tongue. My hair on end, my eyes very gritty, the air very heavy and Wahad touchy. We made for a huge bush which I could get into but would make no difference as it would funnel water down on top of me but keep the force of the storm off my body. Wahad simply got down and ass towards the storm continued to eat the bush. Priorities in hand he was abundantly happy. The storm raged for four hours, relentlessly. My head at least had stopped pounding. The rain was no release from the heat and it stopped, just as someone had turned off a tap. The birds began to sing and the full force of the desert hit me like a high definition picture.

The colours were so vivid. The sand seven different colours whereas before only two/three. The trees transformed, grass so green, as to be almost painted. The smell of the sand so pronounced and Wahad, smelt like an old damp rug but not unpleasant which was just as well as my chosen life would include freshly showered camels!

Later at my camp, I would again be at the mercy of the storms. The ridge opposite was 2 km away across the piste below me. The sky when it went black on the horizon would give me five minutes to prepare for it. Everything would be stored in preparation for this time, in heavy duty plastic bags, even wood for cooking as I would have no idea how long it would last. Everything piled up into the centre of the khaima and the tapis used to shelter me and the baggage from the rain. The sides are up as I had no wish for my khaima to take off like a balloon. And the air heavy with static electricity, again my head pounding. First, there's the cold wind that hits making you shiver, followed by a sandstorm. At first a few crops of rain then WHAM! The fire hose is turned on and for five hours easy, it keeps going. From the four drip points in the khaima you can collect rainwater. I would store 120L in six 20L bidons treated with a little iodine, from the storm. Superb for making tea and soup, quality soup. The bounty of the desert that Saharans have collected for centuries. The bidons would then be stored dug down into the sand for two thirds of their height and covered with a piece of tarpaulin in the shelter of the bush behind my khaima.

At night, the sky would be a wonderful display of lightening strikes and thunderclaps, all around me. A huge Van de Graaf generator switched on for my pleasure. I love these storms. I love that I have no control. I can see the huge arcs of electricity come down and I have no way of knowing where they'll strike next. Camels are pretty nonchalant when it comes to storms. They simply get down ass to the coming rain and ruminate. "Well, what else can they do? Unlike you, they don't sleep either, girlie in the third row."

I remember one storm being so heavy with static that I had prepared a joint and debated whether it would be safe to strike a match or go up in a huge ball of flame! 'Imbecile!' I did and smoked a double strength joint to wait out four hours of high winds and torrential rain. I had to simply hunker down and hope that I wouldn't have to walk lots of kilometres to retrieve my khaima, as I would do in the future. It's great having trees around you, the only problem is the majority are Acacia and twice suffered the same horrendous wounds extracting it as I would my second camel Ethnayne on two occasions. It's also at night that the pounding headache that alerts you to a coming storm as it doesn't necessarily mean there will be a cavalcade of thunder and lightening to forewarn you. The same storms in the capital are horrendous by comparison, dirty, with pools of stagnating water everywhere as there are no sewers. On the terrace it's fine, but on ground level where the Haratin live in small bidonvilles (town encampments) it's squalour magnified by ten thousand.

## CHAPTER FIVE

# "NOW, YOU ARE A BERGER..."

T WO DAYS OUT from the capital and on track for the Auberge Sahara; I had GPS'd the auberge, I came across a small camp of two tents and a huge herd of goats. I move on as the approach of night arrives and pitch camp about thirty minutes away. I'm lost in the moment of setting up camp and a man appears, quite suddenly. A Tamashek. In fact, it is "Salaam aleykum." I hear first before I see the man, in the light of a full moon. Mwoiny and the wild dogs would and do go absolutely mental when the full moon arrives. From the valley on the ridge where we lived, there's another ridge just over two kilometres away. The full moon creeps up from this horizon and it is a full twenty minutes before it's high in the sky. Like a huge searchlight it arrives, its craters very distinct. One day I'll know which ones. And she and they go mental! Running around, howling, barking, hiding behind bushes and coming out to go, well go completely mental, for a full twenty minutes until it's up in the sky.

"Aleykum salaam." I reply.

He motions for me to come. I repack what I had taken out to cook with, secure everything and giving a last look at Wahad's departing profile. I grab my sac el badiya; a present from a new beautiful girlfriend, which contains all my worldly possessions. My kukri, money, passport, blow, compass, map, mp3 etc and I follow on. I look up at the stars above my camp. He introduces himself as . . . you've guessed it, Mohamed. He is married to a Haratin girl and is a goatherd for a Bidan. We arrive to the smell of dinner, rice pudding with fresh goat's milk, it's delicious. But when it's all you have to eat, then it's boring.

Try eating it for lunch and dinner for one week, I challenge you. The equivalent of three/four tins of Ambrosia creamed rice per person per meal. With tea and milk to drink for breakfast, you can drink as much water as you like throughout the day. Tea mid-morning, mid-afternoon, early evening and after dinner. One week. Seven days. (Appropriate chicken sounds.) You'll never ever complain about food ever again! His brother-in-law had seen me when he returned with the goats that I had somehow missed!

He has two very well behaved daughters about four/five years old and a Black Moor brother-in-law in the other tent, again with two well-behaved girls, a little older, another Haratin wife, his wife's sister. This camp is clean, exceptionally clean. The pride in their Spartan surroundings is outstanding. A place for everything and everything in its place, even though they have virtually nothing. Their clothes, bedding, tapis and utensils almost perfect. With dinner just over, a 4x4 arrives, it's the boss. Mohamed's up and off to meet him as is his brother-in-law. I follow on and am duly introduced. There's a brief discussion and the brothers take off. The Bidan then tells me that I've to use the camp as if it's my home, that they will look after me, cook for me, wash my clothes etc. I smile and nod in agreement but have no intention of using Mohamed's family as my short-term Haratin. Mohamed arrives with twenty litres of milk and stows it in the back of the 4x4 and the Bidan takes off.

We go back to the tent and Mohamed's wife hands him a small sack, as the others arrive to drink tea. I elect to keep to the goats milk which I drink in huge quantities. He then takes out a small pipe, fills it and smokes. It wafts over and is strangely familiar. I motion for him to give me some. It's very harsh, dry but hits like hashish. He nods his head and hands me the sack. His wife, brother-in-law and sister-in-law all smoke too. The two pipes doing overtime. I pull out a small boule of hashish and make up a pipe, first Mohamed, then his brother-in-law, wife and sister-in-law all smoke in turn. There's much giggling and laughing and they blab on, with Mohamed remembering every now and again to translate but the moment in the conversation is long past and I'm laughing two minutes after everyone else that starts everyone else off again. A second round and then a third, as everyone has three pipes of wild and cultivated mix. Just like the tea ceremony! The girls are soon KO'd.

"C'est fini!" His brother-in-law says as puts his wife over his shoulder, and with the girls following behind, staggers back to his tent. He drops her so hard that I thought that her breathing would have stopped as did Mohamed. I ask Mohamed to ask if she was alright. He shouts over and what seems like a lifetime, the reply comes back.

"She breathes!"

We're in hysterics. With the girls tucked up beside their mother, I eventually decide to go and Mohamed tells me that he needs to walk me back. I tell him that the stars there are my guide. He persuades me otherwise. 'He's a Tamashek who knows the desert blah blah blah.'

We wander back and eventually arrive at camp. I ask if he would like a joint, Ecossais style. Long roach, cool smoke. He accepts and we smoke and talk. After we're finished he tells me its time to go. He gets up and walks off. I watch him sniggering. I let him keep on going and when he is just out of sight I shout out, "Tuareg lost in the Sahara!"

There's a stream of abuse; I believe, as he staggers back to sit down and duly rolls up and goes to sleep. The next morning after breakfast, I go to give him a small gift. He shakes his head, "Never again!"

The wild hashish we smoked the night before, he showed me that morning. A small bush, 10cm high and about the same across, sometimes smaller, that arrives after the rains and grows in the driest of places, on hard piste. The fragrance in the morning as it wafted through my tent is as heady as patchouli oil. It has many, very small oily leaves impregnated with pollen that is better dried out of the sun and makes wonderful tea rather than smoke which is very harsh. The camels love it and devour dozens of bush at a time; though it never did anything to calm Wahad. The goats and sheep love it, Mwoiny loves it too, eating and rolling in it, the bergers and their families smoke it, so it must be okay? And it's free!

"We Scots love free!"

I moved off after striking camp and made directly for the Sahara. I skirted around the verges of Nouakchott, something akin to a Mad Max landscape, very surreal. The feral dogs here are more dangerous as they are in-between two worlds and have no fear of either. I carried a small bag of lumps of concrete and throw to hit hard, not to scare. I'm quite good at this. In any confrontation I've had with these dog's, I throw to kill. I'd later shoot them instead. Every year there is a cull as the numbers are huge and a problem as far as children are concerned. Indeed, a year or so later, around the back streets one evening, I saw a young boy running past being pursued by four dogs, big bastards. Along with four other men I took off after them. Three dogs stood us off while the top dog was determined to have the boy. He had grabbed a stick and was waving as hard as he could, screaming at the dog. I threw a piece of concrete and downed one. As it yelped and fell to the ground, it caused the top dog to turn on the fallen dog and the others then joined in. Membership of the club, terminated. One man grabbed the boy and they took off. Bloody savage and this is the capital!

I spent the next day filling three sacks of wild foodstuffs for Wahad, including 15kg of wild hashish. Hoping to pacify him whilst in the auberge. I'd buy fodder in the market and mix in the wild food for the little dear, spoilt bastard. I then slept as near as I could to my point of contact for the half hour walk from the desert to the auberge. Though now, you'd need to do the same journey by 4x4 with your camel, as Nouakchott has swallowed up this route and would take you hours to negotiate.

"Yes I know, PHONE THEM!"

Using a small dune at the side of the road, you place your camel in the back of the 4x4, hobbled, and then a cord is passed under one foreleg over the neck, pulling his head down, under the other foreleg back over the neck and secured in place. "Sorry, what I forgot to say, was that first of all, you put down a nice thick soft blanket and cushions, on the bed of the 4x4 and . . . NOT!" It's commonplace and they generally don't mind, too much. Wahad used to complain more when I took his saddle off! Which just goes to show how stupid they can be.

We arrived at the main doors to parking at 17.30; where else would he go he's a bloody huge animal, and Khalifa let us in to an empty parking area. Parking for camel's is free of charge and is the ultimate 4x4. No diesel, spare parts, tax or insurance required. Can you imagine what I'd need in the UK for Wahad? Stables, veterinary certificate, proof of purchase, family tree, seat belt for my saddle, helmet, chest and back protectors and a man walking in front carrying a fuckin' huge red flag when I wanted to go out riding!

"Oh and if I beat his ass! SSPCA, eh baby sis?"

I took Wahad up to the back and set up a small camp. It would be better for me to sleep beside my 4x4 given that at any moment it could fill up with vehicles. I strung a mosquito net up and roped my camp off to discourage people from approaching Wahad, unless by invitation. As I finished I met with Hermann and Sidi Mohamad, who at first were in complete disbelief at Khalifa's story. Both had been out when I arrived. Sidi Mohamad got on his phone and ordered up take away for Wahad. I was taken away for zreig and tea, the traditional Saharan welcome. The next day the guides were in and out, wanting to buy Wahad and asking me about my experiences. It was over tea that I discovered about the lottery on my life and that Sidi Noir (there are a few Sidi's here) had scooped the prize as he alone had said I'd return. Though not with a camel! He didn't give me the 10% I asked for either.

One Bidan guide Brahim, who hails from Atar, stopped me one morning "Yager, ente rais! El badiya, zeina?"

The second phrase I recognised, "The desert is beautiful?"

To which you reply, "El badiya zeina hatte!"

"The desert is very beautiful!"

The first phrase he repeated over and over, certain I would know what he was saying. I just had a stupid look on my face and finally gave up, shaking my head.

"Now you are a berger." He said and shook my hand.

"Berger of one." I reply.

"It's a beginning." He says.

Then he was off, back out into the desert. Over the next four days I had lunch/dinner with three French girls who were so impressed with Wahad; 'Good man I knew he'd come in handy for something,' that they just had to have every scrap of information on him, the desert and all. Not though, about my new beautiful girlfriends.

"Shhhh."

I was invited on the last evening to the wedding of a Belgian chef Alex; friend of Hermann and one time boyfriend of Kanya, (she was to have three in-between splitting up with Hermann and marrying Sidi Mohamad) who had a restaurant, Café Brussels, ten minutes walk from the auberge. It served the best cheese burger in West Africa. A slice of steak, Gruyere and salad, with mayonnaise and mustard. French fries and ketchup. Delicious! Herein lies another tale of woe, attributed solely to the greed and the single-minded viciousness of that greed, of a Bidan who forced Alex to sell up after a year of intimidation! I danced the night away with the cook of the auberge, Maryam, a radiantly beautiful Pulaar girl until 05.00 and then took Wahad, and my fully stocked food and water bags back into the desert. On reaching the first sizable bush for shade and food at around 06.30. I slept all day. The sounds of the wedding party in my head.

I walked back in the direction of the piste opposite the camel market, and began my journey exploring campsites eight hours walk from there. I spent two weeks, cutting back and forth the piste surveying sites, watching the entry and exit of herds to and from the market. It occurred to me when I was about four hours away from the market, that here was a carrefour, a crossroads. The herds arrived here and departed north, south and carried on eastwards. It would be good for tourists, bosses who wanted TV and the chance to meet bergers and herds. I walked around, across and up and down the ridge and found a small valley, like a bowl. Here then a place arrived, behind a large bush that would protect me from the north wind. Surrounded by trees and huge bushes, a good supply of grass. Two kilometres away on the piste below was a small stand of, what I thought were, dead trees and tiny dunes. Ideal for a tourist camp. Nearby but far enough away to give me peace and quiet. The piste below me would also supply a goodly amount of wild hashish tea, sorted! I would later build a Robinson Crusoe brush wall in an arc to protect me from the Harmattan. Also one right around the supplies tent to keep the goats and camels out. They wouldn't remain a problem for long as the bloody African wild dogs would have their asses for dinner.

For the moment I would stay here and establish that I now lived here. The equipment would arrive later, there was no rush. I explored my new neighbourhood. From the top of Wahad I had seen a great deal of archeology on my travels and it was no exception here either. I decided that I would pursue my amateur interest in that field as a hobby. It was to become a little more than that during the next three years and is now an obsession, in a long term association with The National Museum. In a little over two weeks; with Wahad under close arrest at the market, I was back at the auberge. I spent the week negotiating prices for all I needed. Here there is no fixed price and you have to deal with bandits on a daily basis, until you get to know the prices and they get to know you. I bought tents from the Marche de Tentes behind Marche Marocaine. There in Marche Marocaine, I bought my 2 x1000L watersacks, and all the equipment I needed: posts, rope, tapis, huge iron tent pegs, sleeping mats, new kitchen equipment for my khaima and crammed full the small khaima with food, all the vendors within spitting distance of each other. I had done this on the first three days and waited three days for a 4x4 and left at 09.00 on the last morning to go and collect all I needed at one sitting. Sidi Noir then drove me out and by lunchtime we were under the shelter of my tent. We had lunch and I was then driven to the market to collect Wahad. In the following year I would have the 6x6m khaima, fully stocked for my European guests. I arrived in darkness to feel instantly at home despite never having slept in it. I had found a little niche of the Sahara to continue my education.

From my new home, I walked and rode around getting to know every quartier, choosing areas to take tourists for different daily excursions. I'd be in and out of the market for water and took two extra 20L bidons with me on my first visit. The African wild dogs, ah the dogs. The daily ritual of contact arrived from the first night. We competed for the same rabbits, along with the eagle owl who patrolled the piste during the morning. At night as I slept, they would pass close, some twenty metres or so, left and right as they traversed the ridge en-route for take-away Bugs Bunny. And on those occasions when I went out hunting at night, two of the young would go into to my tent. It then became a major concern, so I began sleeping with my baton and kukri beside me. My tent was little more than a canopy as it was hot at night and more especially during the day, but even at that, they could burrow underneath. Again the children. Always a problem. More and more as I became familiar with my area I began to notice the wildlife. Huge tortoise I had seen living near encampments and small villages. The nomads at one encampment had said that the huge tortoise over a metre in length was three generations old! Desert foxes, jerboa, sparrows, swallows, swifts, hawks, vultures, feral donkeys (dangerous fuckers) and wabbits of course. The swifts would leave the piste and fly right through my tent without a sound. One day I was making zreig and two flew past on either side of my head, like Red Arrows, perfectly synchronised. Birds of every description would come into the tent to drink from my bowl of water, left out in the hot wind to cool.

When I went out and about for my daily constitutional I would be accompanied by two crows, a couple. When they weren't around I'd occasionally mimic the crows and drive Mwoiny mental. They would stay with us for the next two years, until one day, the male arrived, alone. He was noticeably sad. He, or rather they, had taken to baiting Mwoiny on a daily basis when we were in and around the camp. Dive bombing her or hovering just above her to float downwind, sitting ten metres away, waiting for her to chase them. We would walk the point to point of 15km, perhaps twice a day, accompanied by the happy couple, mostly in the morning as I expect they had a pressing engagement elsewhere. He took no interest in Mwoiny and in less than a week, in which he wouldn't take any food from me, he had left the piste. I never saw him again. Though there were others of course, but didn't interact with us in any way.

Some two months after my arrival, and a little while after my conversion to Islam, a tent pitched up some two kilometres away and I went over to see my new neighbours. Bidan grandfather and grandmother, two sisters and their off-spring, first cousins in their early twenties, Maryam and Mohamad. Also husband and wife. And a Haratin goatherd. The family quickly ascertained my former life and I was approached by Mohamad to examine his wife. The mother had agreed also, everyone except for Maryam, who nonetheless agreed. I said that I would the following day and left. Mohamad and his grandfather were off to water the camels but as the mothers would be there it would be fine for me to carry out an examination of her back, which she said she had problems with. Early morning, Maryam arrived to speak with me. In the first instance it was to remind me to come for lunch and then she blurted it all out in a torrent. She had never wanted to marry her cousin but her mother had handed her over. She would not sleep with him because she knew it wasn't right and had seen the product of other first cousin marriages, handicapped babies. She was terrified. She would if necessary, feign illness for the rest of her life, rather than let Mohamad touch her. Or if he did, she would kill the baby and herself. Would I help her? I said yes. I said yes. It wasn't her beautiful big eyes set in her pretty face, attached to her lovely slender body but the real look of fear. The same look of fear I'd seen as a nurse, when the patient is told that they are, 'going to die, lose a limb, become a vegetable slowly, oh so very slowly. I'm sorry but' . . . I told her that I would arrive this evening for dinner and afterwards carry out an examination of her spine. I then told her how we'd play it. I'd start at her neck and move downwards. When I reached her lower back and increased the pressure, pushing hard she was to wince and move directly away from me, blowing out gently, two/ three times. KISS. Keep it simple stupid. She'd then be made to lie on her back and I'd ask her to raise her leg. Not very high and not very long, wince and drop it suddenly. Arch your back slightly again to relieve pressure. The same with the other. Two/three short breaths each time. The last test would be to stand up and bend over, slowly to touch her toes and then get back up, but to use her hands on the tops of her thighs to push herself back up, slowly to stand up straight, going backwards ever so slightly to relieve the ache, again blowing out, two/ three times as if to relieve pressure. When performing lifting tasks to bend at the knees, not at her waist. She was to slow down and occasionally here and there after tasks, to rest up.

If I had suggested this to someone in the UK, I would have been prosecuted for teaching someone to defraud Social Services. Here there is no system to defraud. If you are injured/handicapped/ill you either have the money to pay for treatment or don't. I knew they hadn't the money to treat this 'illness'. 'No doubt about it Mohammad Ibrahim, go directly to jail and DO NOT collect two hundred pounds!' I said yes, because her fear was palpable. I said yes, because I had seen those babies too, and in one case, three from the one pairing of first cousins who were intent on trying again for a, normal baby. I managed to diplomatically dissuade the kissing cousins from doing so. She then took off for her camp. I spent the rest of the day in agitated anticipation of the theatre we were about to perform that night. It didn't rest easy as I waited to go and my conscience has suffered ever since. My fear was for Mohamad also. What if he became really frustrated and indulged in the violent rape of his wife? She I believed, would then take herself off and end her life. The family would have been totally mystified as to her reasons for suicide. The Qu'ran forbids it. It would and is the act of a truly desperate person, who sees no other choice. If I didn't intervene, I truly believed it might certainly happen. It is for my God to judge me.

My intervention for the family was that they were having free medical advice, for Mohamad, hope to be able to consummate his marriage, for Maryam, a get out clause. For me, it would simply be more baggage. My head's a bloody mess at times. I carry a lot of other people's secrets around in my head. Things I wish I'd never have known, done or things that I'd rather other people had kept to themselves or told someone else or that I was asked to keep as a matter of my work. A nurse's baggage is carrying other people's problems. It helps mask your own, until you have to face them. 'Once a nurse always a nurse, no matter how far away you run, eh!'

I duly arrived saying that I was sorry I couldn't come for lunch as invited by Maryam but that I had been studying and had lost all track of time. It would be better if everyone, Mohamad that is, was here. Which was agreed upon. We ate, talked and the moment finally arrived. The others left. Mohammad and Maryam's mother sat opposite. I asked permission to touch her naked back, which of course was given. Inside her top, I gave her spine a general examination and then increased the pressure at the pre-arranged the spot and Maryam, coached reacted perfectly. I of course had my professional face on but my heart and mind in complete turmoil. Next, I laid her down and asked her to raise her right leg, again perfection. Then the left leg and a little imperfect but good enough for the audience. More uncomfortable this time and I mentioned that the slipped disc must be affecting the left side more. The sciatic nerve I said in this leg, was more of a problem, winging it a little here, going off script. She looked at me, surprised but caught on straight away. Good to show a little shock. I then coached her on how to get up from the floor and had her stand up, holding her hands as she stood. 'A little too much pressure and lingering touch Maryam, but thank you I'm alright.' The final test she breezed.

If she had lived in the UK, she'd have had the full disability pension. Little Britain flashed into my mind, with the swimming pool sketch. Little Mauritania. Art imitating life, life imitating art. I gave her mother and Mohamad my opinion and verified their worst fears. Mohamad was angry and claimed she was acting. Maryam was distraught, playing it to the final curtain. I gave her advice on how to alleviate the pain, especially at night. The reasons for her headaches and tiredness at the end of a long day. That it would be expensive for surgery that might not work considering how long ago she had injured herself. Yes, you think it's all so simple but your back is a dangerous place to injure blah blah blah. Some people who start off with simple injuries, go down hill rapidly. I felt like shit. Still do as I write this. Maryam and her mother would come to visit now and again over the next week, until plans were made by the boss to move to new pastures for the goats and camels. Mohamad had chilled out after his mother had spoken to him. He apologized for being angry with me. Now I really felt like shit. 'Professional face, no matter what.' The day before they left Maryam came over to see me alone. She asked if I would like a wife. Her. I thanked her but said no. I was happy to been able to have helped her. She kissed my cheek, thanked me for my part in her deception and left.

This is a major problem that the Bidan faces, consanguineous marriages. If a girl is very beautiful, she'll be married off at 14, perhaps to a paternal uncle many years her senior. If not, then first cousin marriage normal. Why do you think I've been chased after by so many girls and their families for? New blood and money. The Bidan society believes it's keeping control of what it holds dear, its lifestyle, its slaves and its dominance of all things great about Mauritanian society, by breaking the laws of nature and justice. When exactly will the message get through? Perhaps when their society's near extinction.

So for the next month or so, I was alone with my thoughts, plans and daily life. I patrolled my 400 km², mapped out the archeology I found on a daily basis, got to know the animals, hunted rabbit, studied but mainly basked in a smug, egotistical sort of way, and traveled in and out of the market for water, fresh fruit and veg. Then one day, a 4x4 arrived. A Bidan summons me over, "Where's the berger?" He asks. "I don't know. I'm alone here, have been for a while." I reply. He tutts humphs and haws.

"Can I help you?" I ask.

He shakes his head.

"My camels have gone." He says.

"What's your mark?" I ask.

He draws it on a piece of paper. He then starts to laugh.

"What do you know about camels?" I go over to my covered saddle and expose it for him. I point to the tent where my baton is hanging. I tutt and shush, I show him where to strike to gallop, rise and turn whilst the camel is on his knees, which I mime. His face is a picture.

"Besides I saw the ten females and seven babies with this mark five days ago." I say.

"Where?" He asks.

I shake my head and waggle my finger, and rub the thumb and fore-finger of my right hand together to indicate that he'll need to pay me. He writes down his number and holds it out.

"Give me a call if you find them!" He says.

"How much will you pay me?" I ask.

He looks at me.

"How much do you want your camels?" I ask.

"15 000UM." He replies.

"For 20 000UM I'll do it." I say.

I don't care if he does or doesn't hire me. He's looking directly in my face and he can see it's the truth, he thinks.

"Go for them." He orders.

As he starts up his 4x4 he leans out of the window as I walk away to my tent, "Oh, by the way, you're the berger here!" He shouts.

He drives off. I have my first job. I have a new position, that of the job of berger of the area I live in. It's unpaid, as are most bergers, until someone sends you off to get their stock. Or you have a village pay your salary of 30 000UM a month. Never ever volunteer information to the Bidan that you will need to bargain with in the future. Nothing's free in the khaima of the Scottish berger, except: dinner, tea and a corner to sleep in, oh, and cut badly if you noise me up or piss me off. Generally that's the case for both a Mauritanian khaima and a Scottish household, except the cuttin' bit.

## CHAPTER SIX

# MY WORKLOAD INCREASES AND THERE'S A GIFT FROM THE SAHARA

THE NUMBER OF visits from the Bidan steadily increased as my whereabouts becomes known. Mostly for TV, for them to come and see the European berger but there are serious jobs too. And I'm off here and there to search for herds or camels in two's and three's or holding herds to feed them up before taking them into market. I can manage about 24 camels alone, given the nature of the Trarza. And I very soon, have my favorite places to feed and hold. Having a mount helps too. You cannot search for camels as the Bidan is want to do in his 4x4. He takes the day off to search with friends. The two up front are watching the sand choosing the best path, with the other two in the back, talking smoking, making tea and generally having a good time. Occasionally the men up front will ask if there's anything to be seen.

"No nothing!"

Comes back the answer for perhaps the herd to pass behind them! This I have done only once and would never repeat the exercise. It's a complete waste of time and simply an excuse for the men to have a day out. Your camel is set on course. He is constantly looking for other camels and will generally see them first. He turns his head, stares out at them but stays on the line you have set him on, until you change his direction. You therefore have four good eyes which are focused on nothing else. As opposed to four watching the sand in front and the other four half-way up their own asses. You simply guide your trusty mount towards them, look for the brand and move on. Next herd. Go directly there. Move on. You cannot take a 4x4 into the dunes, where camels love to go for the young fresh grasses or simply because they love to go there, as I do and hang out. You cannot hear or smell camels on the wind, from a 4x4. You are also traveling too fast in a 4x4. A camel walks at an average of 5km/hr. You need a camel to find camels. I would have thought that an abundantly simple and straightforward concept to understand. It's not the camels, as I've said that the boys go into the desert for, it's simply to play truant or do something different before lunch, their afternoon nap and have something to talk about when they get home at the end of a very tiring day doing fuck all. I, on the other hand, am still good to go.

It's in the early days here, that I make 'friends' with a local family, who it seemed had lived not far from me and regarded this area as their own. It would be the same Ahmedou El Mamy I had met out in the desert and had the branding fiasco with. He came out to remake my acquaintance and to seemingly give me permission to stay there. Pompous git. Not that I needed anyone's permission to do anything out in the desert. Open range. You go where you want to do what you will. He also seemed to visit every two weeks or so and I was slowly introduced to his wide circle of friends, being taken into town for the odd afternoon or morning here and there. The El Mamy's, second or third rung in the same tribe as Col Ely Med Ould Vall, the 'President' that took over in 2005, and the man attributed to having introduced 'democracy' to Mauritania. He was also the puppet master of the next President, Sidi Mohamad Cheihk Abdallahi, who was placed in office after a rigged election by Vall and best chum, General Abdel Aziz. Therefore it is the military who was the Head of State, who then deposed Le Poupee in the coup of August 2008, the tenth coup d'etat since independence in 1960. Birds of a feather. Maaouiya, the deposed President in 2005 was out of the country at the time and by all reports a very bad egg who was in place for twenty years. The General was the Head of the Presidential bodyguard for both Maaouiya and Sidi, who now promises free and fair elections once more. Give me a fuckin' break pal! Same singer, same song! Aziz retired from the military in 2009 and duly became President. His banner headlines were: 'President for the Poor.' 'I'll build roads and supply you with electricity and water.' The tents at the roadside displaying his poster were paid the equivalent of a month's wages ($77) each week. I personally know of one family who had four tents, who do not like the man in any shape or form! The posters by the way were printed in China, despite the fact that there are media companies in the capital, capable of producing them. He is also reported to be the boyfriend of Khatou, Sidi's wife and herself under request by parliament for investigation into financial irregularities of her Khatou Foundation. She is protected by the General, obviously. Details of their lives can be gleaned from the Internet from a wide variety of reliable sources. I know what everyone else knows here in Mauritania, because it is a very small place and everyone knows everyone, among the Bidan that is. Nothing's secret for very long here. The Haratin, Soninke, Pulaar, Wolof and Black Moor of course know everything too but his lord and master doesn't think he does. We'll cover the minefield that is Mauritanian politics later on.

Ahmedou is of course of the same insidious spawn, only at the time he was very carefully hiding his true intentions, masked by apparent good manners and an apparently intelligent and enquiring mind. Like they all try to do, their feigning manners is an art, a black art. Here's the list again. Their concept of manners differs greatly from the generally accepted Scottish or European manners we use everyday and take for granted. As my grandmother used to say, 'Manners costs you nothing.' No excuse me's, please or thank you, except in the field of finances, your finances as they whimper and moan about needing your money because they "Don't have enough to blah blah blah . . . and you are The Bank of Africa blah blah blah . . . I need it and I want it now, you must give it to me!" 'BIG FUCKIN' YAWN!' They will interrupt you when you are talking or as you are being served in a shop. There's no concept of queuing.

Ah, except for Agence Mattel, one of three phone companies here in Mauritania, that is. I was there on the second or third morning in operation, the security man handing out numbered pieces of paper. Men would look at them and still walk to the counter to be told to sit down. More than a few objected, "I'm a boss you can't speak to me like this!" One Bidan said. "Not my boss, sir please sit down." He left muttering all sorts of obscenities. Also the BNP Parisbas, very clean, a jolie mehlafah to welcome you and indicate that you should sit on the very comfortable couch to wait and she will call you when an opening is free. Everyone in order of arrival and no favouritism. Generally speaking, it matters little that you may be talking to a doctor or having a tooth pulled. At Western Union, it's disaster lurching from disaster to disaster. I am very forceful in chasing people away who think they have a right to look in my transaction.

In other words, chaos reigns supreme here. There's no concept of decency. You can piss and shit in the street like a dog but woe betide if Mwoiny does the same and war breaks out!

Except that is, amongst the Bidan I consider friends, who by and large have lived outside of Mauritania or have European wives and essentially want nothing more than friendship. It is also interesting to note that they all apologized on behalf of their fellow countrymen, soon after we made our acquaintance.

I was also introduced to family from the same tribe who lived at Teinweich One. One Mohammad Leomine Ould Sba and the reason for my departure from the desert to take up teaching English in Nouakchott in August 2007. I have taught in a primary school, two private language schools and have private students. All of my clients are Bidan and African professionals and their rush to learn English seemed to arrive; like the plague of grasshoppers in 2005, after the attack on the French tourists in December 2006. I believe, as a way of severing the existing old time French colonial link, that has since resurfaced with Sarkozy's recent olive branch giving public French support to the General, so soon after it had been taken away. It's all to do with money of course. The other reason for the rush to learn English is that it is seen as the language of business, and the professional classes want to get some and get out of Mauritania.

Leomine is lower down in the order of feeding at the tribal trough and therefore has a bigger chip on his shoulder. My demise at his hands, is much further on in the story. I am his arch-nemesis. I wait for my time to exact my revenge. I have the dead centre of his homestead GPS'd. I can arrive in the middle of a sandstorm, or in the blackest of nights. Two months after my departure from the desert, I lay up in the palmeraie 30m from his house arriving at 03.00, watched him and his family all day and took off at 03.00 the next morning. I didn't see any of my baggage there. It's probably in K'sar (pronounced Luksar). He thinks he is so safe. "Ah Leomine, your time will come!" Ahmedou sent potential and actual employers out my way and was instrumental in giving me, or dictating to me rather, his version of desert life, as if I were a complete virgin. Mauritania as you will find out has fucked me in every way possible, that I calculated at the daily price of 2500 UM, half the price of the cheapest whore.

The list again, superiority complex. The Bidan's is as big as the Sahara. His opinion was that, "The nomad, sic Mauritanian, could not be trusted and would steal everything I had. I needed people to look after me. You must only trust the Bidan, we are your friends." El Mamy wanted to give me a family to tend to my needs. They were to be my bodyguards. He knew of a family of Haratin, that I would only have to feed to look after me, who could be brought out for my inspection the very next day should I say yes. I refused point blank. I said that," Scots never have been, never have had or would have slaves." That Scots had in the 1800's, been the first Europeans to come to West Africa with the intention of ending slavery as well as securing commerce and opening up Africa. In competition with the French, Germans, Dutch, Portuguese and Belgians, who would embrace widespread abuse of Africans. And in the modern world, it is the Islamic countries that have persisted with slavery. He became very angry when I repeatedly used the word. I asked him what he meant by Haratin. I asked him what he meant by only giving food for work done and no salary. I knew straight away even if I did give them a salary, he would take it. He would not tell me what Haratin meant. I said that it meant the 'Captured Ones or slaves.' He said that I was wrong and he refused to speak on the subject again, thank fuck.

It later transpired in conversation with his wife, Boya; and to be honest she looked like an obese boy . . . moustache and all . . . that my family would have been a 15 year old girl and her two younger brothers, aged 9 and 7. It was implied that I could sleep with the girl but not marry her. She didn't have the right nose, her mouth was too big, she wasn't fat enough blah blah blah. In fact, she was quite pretty and had a gentle soul, despite, despite, the slapping and shouting she experienced every day of her life at the hands of her so-called betters. Her brothers of course, suffered the same fate but with more violence. Any off-spring from my use of her, would be her responsibility alone. These children would simply have been taken from their mother and handed over to me. I smiled the smile of an imbecile and anger raged inside my head like Hurricane Ike. My respect for these people can fall no further than it has, zero. You couldn't pay me enough to cross the road and piss on them if they were on fire. I'd keep walking and that makes me a very bad Muslim. For the first time in my life, I am a racist. For the first time in my life, I really really don't like myself.

Over the next year the brother-in-law of Leomine, Mohamad Baba and Sidi Mohamad; the retired Gendarmerie officer, would be regular visitors and drop by for tea and a chat, or on occasion to ask me to go hunting. It's not my thing to career all over the desert in a 205, armed with a searchlight and ancient shotgun chasing wabbits! I watched them for five hours one night driving all over the place, the searchlight shining in all directions. I never knew wabbits could fly! I watched whilst my wabbit cooked and Mwoiny had the carcass and entrails, me scraping the stretched skin with my Neolithic tool. The two like Elmer Fudd gone berserk chasing the wabbit with a passion second to none. Forty-two shells blasted into the desert that night and when I met Baba weeks later and asked how many he had gotten, "None!" He replied with a wide smile.

I thought, 'You are a fat, stupid, specky bastard!'

I told him that they could have eaten with me and Mwoiny.

"How did you catch them?" He asked.

"Snare." I said.

"Ah," he says, "It's not the Mauritanian way!"

I reply, "No, but I did eat dinner though!" I then thought, 'No, you're a double fat, stupid, specky bastard!' I have to thank Max, a school friend, for that line of abuse. I knew I'd get to use it one day. Sidi Mohamad would eventually go off to live in Paris with his fourth wife, an 18 year-old girl, leaving his other three wives, 40, 32 and 26 and their children, his children I might add, to fend for themselves. Though the idea of having four wives may sound endearing, it's a huge responsibility if you have a conscience. Many men simply don't have that and therefore there are many one-parent families who have to go it alone.

Leomine and Med Baba were constantly asking me to find tourists for them, through my contacts at the auberges. I knew exactly what this meant. I would do all the work and they would pocket the money. Essentially they were looking for a White Haratin. I didn't like either of them, from the minute I met them, I knew they were trouble and I told them no way. I added that I would work with another berger, as he had a family to feed and had been cast aside like yesterday's newspaper, like so many other berger's and their families had been of late. You on the other hand sirs, had many camels, a large family and a fat belly. I could tell that he didn't like to be told no. His hate I believe began to fester in his rabid mind at this point. His future attitude towards me was haughty and detached, like a puffed up peacock, strutting around a big garden with no-one looking. A Mauritanian national trait. When I had guests staying and the minute I saw their 4x4 arrive, I told them that these two men were 'gentlemen bandits', that on shaking their hands they were to count their fingers and see if their wristwatch was still in place. Everyone got the message straight away. I knew they were having the piste watched at the Teinweich end, so when guests would arrive so would they. It's what I would have done in their position. I soon got tired of their visits and never made tea or gave them zreig. Water only, warm water at that.

A typical five day stay in the desert with me is as follows, though I did have three day trips too. Loose fitting clothes, no underwear, as it make riding uncomfortable, sandals, a jacket, a turban for women too, and your personal items in a small backpack. It will cost you 20 euros per person per day for everything and you buy the goat for the final night's dinner and pay for the taxi to and from the auberge, driven by my friend Thioub. He will of course be available should you need the services of a driver in the capital. He has been certificated by an Australian company to drive their employees so is au fait with seat belts and has passed a road test and therefore a much safer option. The price you will of course negotiate, for yourself. The party will be up to a maximum of four people, of reasonable health and of a sporting physique. "No Tellytubbies on my watch!" Your party of four people will arrive at the backend of Teinweich Two at 04.30. Carrying your small Karrimore, and accompanied by the ever attentive and professional bergere, (I'm carrying my badge of office, therefore she knows its work time) we will walk two km and rv with the four adult camels and one baby with the second berger, Brahim a Black Moor, who will give everyone a glass of tea. If only one or two persons, then no Brahim and no tea. Just two camels and the goat which has traveled in the boot of Thioub's taxi. "Please, calm down there at the back." We then walk for four km, where we leave the dunes bisecting the piste behind us and it opens out. It will still be cold so keeping your jackets on, everyone can mount if they want to. Most do for about an hour and walk for an hour then mount and so on. We're called in by the African wild dogs to our left. "Hello."

We then arrive at the large khaima around 09.00, set up on the piste below my ridge and as Brahim takes the camels away, his wife Fatiea, makes breakfast. Mamadou 5, is a gentle soul like his mother. They have a small khaima about 40m away. As he is the goatherd, his responsibility is to look after dinner; sorry the goat, which he takes very seriously and you mustn't interrupt him as he works! Although he is none too comfortable with the new arrivals, Fatiea persuades him to shake hands. The first day is simply getting to know your immediate area and to acclimatise to the ever increasing heat of the sun. I give your party the safety lecture. Always check your bedding for scorpions. If you see one, kill it immediately. If you don't, Mamadou will because he will be protecting you. He doesn't know that he is a child of course.

Before you sit down in the sand under the shade of a bush or tree, check the sand with your baton for snakes and scorpions. (I have four batons standing by). Fateia will keep you supplied with zreig and tea. Lunch at 14.30 and dinner because it's my habit, at 20.00. Though on the last night you will experience the true nomadic dinner at midnight, and listen to Mwoiny crunch her way through the head afterwards. If I have stock, Brahim will take them off for the day. If I'm alone, then I'll keep them on piste, with one day out free range and cover 15km or so, instead of the normal 30, to show the daily life of a berger with his bergere. It does mean that you will get lots of milk to drink! If not then everyone hangs out together. At night, I will sleep in my khaima and you therefore will be reliant on Brahim and Fateia should you have a problem. It is necessary to put your trust in them and they will diplomatically chase away any passing 4x4's for you. If in the case of the two rouges; and you will have been briefed earlier, Brahim will arrive at the run and we will return at the run to welcome and send away the two aforementioned scumbags, I mean visitors back to their hole in the ground.

The next day after breakfast we will spend the morning walking around the piste, in the small dunes and here Mwoiny will show just how easy it is to traverse a dune by running along the firm path, where the wind breathes over the uppermost curve of the dune. You will of course, be up to your knees before she shows you! I will demonstrate why Wahad does not like to career down slopes and will always take the off-ramp when stepping off dunes, even f I try to make him. He's also handy for carrying the water. How he always then goes back on line, the compass in his head firmly set on the path I have chosen for him. We return to camp by late morning as it begins to get hot and you will be flagging badly and this is the cold season!

In the late afternoon, I set up snares with those who want to come and all day you will have the opportunity to see birds and animals at your leisure. Although cameras are naturally permitted, I don't like being photographed but I will do the group hug thing at tour beginning and at tour's end, with one or two in-between, if you insist. Mamadou would prefer you didn't at any time, much to the amusement of Fatiea and Brahim, who are only too happy to oblige every time.

Our next day is spent out riding. You will, after having had breakfast come with me at 07.00 and perhaps Brahim, to find our mounts. Here you will learn how to track them, and who may be at least five km away. No sunglasses, turbans only. You will not be able to see the graduations of sand and tracks if you keep them on. You will in effect be blinded. I of course haven't implied at any time, that we might not find them. Slowly and surely you wind this way and that, walking directly in their tracks like a train to suddenly lose all trace as they've crossed another piste. Panic sets in. You will be asked to get down low and scan the surface from where they last were. Brahim of course knows immediately, I some two/three minutes behind him and you, may never know. Until that is someone say's "There!" We're off. Brahim and you wink at each other, 'He's a swine 'cause I said not to help!' There's huge sighs of relief when we see them feeding off in the distance. Nose cords attached by myself and Brahim, you are then each given a camel in turn and we go back to the camp to saddle and pack up. Fateia has everything ready for us, everyone downs at least a litre of zreig and we move out. Of course Brahim and I are walking, two camels each under our guidance, until as such time as you feel confident to steer your own. We make for the big dunes, discovering archeology all over the place and there on a patch of hard ground in between two dunes, is a meteor strike, spreading out for 150m. Everyone is given a momento, handed up by myself and Brahim.

We eventually find large bushes for the camels to eat from and for them and us to shelter from the sun and we unpack for you. Towli's are strung up (two mehlafahs stitched together to form a makeshift khaima) as Brahim makes tea as I serve peanuts and biscuits, the standard Saharan snack. Mwoiny of course takes the opportunity to go and sleep. You will have noticed that she runs from shade to shade, waiting on our arrival before running off again. This is because the sand is hot. Our conversation is interrupted when two camels have a set-to over who's section of the bush is who's. They are dealt with quickly and efficiently, the instigator is whacked, to break it up. It's not Wahad this time. He gives me the look. He too gets a mouthful and this sets off tittering within the group. Someone mentions Laurel and Hardy. Another mentions Tom and Jerry and I mention that it is a big big place and that you can easily disappear, with no witnesses. My smiling face belies the fact this is indeed true and can be easily arranged. Everyone smiles back in a cheery, friendly apologetic sort of fashion. After tea, Brahim and I put on a race. He lets me win, he knows that I know. We play to the gallery. It simply won't do for the boss to have his ass kicked in front of the clients. The exchange of cigarettes between the guests takes place and no-one wants to race me. We pack up and move on, winding in and out of big and then bigger dunes. Lots of photographs and lots of oohs and aahs. The camels and therefore us, suddenly look so very small and insignificant.

Dismounted and sat upon the summit of a dune here and there, everyone is lost in their own train of thought. The huge dune field stretches far out into the horizon. I leave you to come out of your meditative state, voluntarily. There's silence on the way back. Dunes do that. They make you travel in the mind, they have a way of redefining who you are, what you are. Out here, you are nothing. A fuckin' huge mortar and pestle is photographed from atop your mounts. The wife probably told her husband to leave it as she never liked her mother-in-law's present. It is fuckin' huge!

The next day perhaps two of you will elect to ride with me and two elect to stay in camp and do chores and annoy Mamadou. We arrive after a short gallop on the piste, in high spirits. Your love affair with camels has begun for real now. You have tamed your fear with a huge animal and you didn't fall off. You will though, I promise you. Eat and rest before we leave an hour or so before dusk.

We are then off to cross the ridge going past my khaima on foot and onto the next piste for three/four kilometres, to then lay up in a set of small dunes, overlooking a very large tree standing on its own island, some one kilometre away on the same piste. We are here to stalk my neighbours, the family of African wild dogs. We cover up with huge military turbans the colour of sand. We use my 6.5-15 x 40 infra-red scope without the rifle and the 8 x 21 birders binoculars to survey the entrance to the den, and wait for dusk. There's a lot of fidgeting, too much. The family exits the den just as dusk approaches and the three younger dogs play and run around, the parents are wary. Of course they know we're there, it's only you who thinks we're hidden! Mwoiny of course isn't with us as she'd just lay in and spoil everyone's fun. The family depart their den and fan out, two young go west and then south, the father east then north, the mother and the smallest dog stay put.

According to research, five is too few for this family to survive. I had seen the carcass of one pup only the week before some two kilometers away. As the dogs disappear, the mother gives everyone their orders. They howl back and soon all is quiet. The youngest dog plays around its mother, with her looking over our way and soon persuades her off-spring to leave with her. She knows we're there. There's too much fidgeting and whispering. My party is on a high as we make our way back to the khaima. After dinner there's an impromptu soiree with Fatiea providing the drumming and musical accompaniment.

The next day everyone helps gather wood, fill and carry bidons from my camp, there's petanque after breakfast, everyone's happy to remain in camp and chill out because we will strike camp at 04.00 the next day. Braham's khaima will be loaded up onto two camels and everyone will walk out. I will have Wahad with me for the return journey. Mwoiny elects to sleep as she has been on guard duty all night. At 09.00 Thioub will be waiting at Teinweich for you. It is both elation and depression that drives the day. You will reminisce over the past few days and laugh or die from embarrassment. It is the late afternoon that the goat is slaughtered. The girls help Fatiea prepare vegetables and the camp is buzzing with the excitement of the coming feast. A member of your party thinks he can make the tea. Mamadou spits it out as do I . . . "No way!" He ain't drinking that but the rest of you think it's okay. Fateia takes a glass and drinks it and diplomatically refuses a second. The goat is slaughtered with the men in tow and they form a procession of butcher's assistants, to and from Fatiea as Brahim performs the job of head butcher. Mamadou and I chill out. The two berger's have had a busy day and deserve a rest. The feast is upon us and everyone is stuffed, sleepy, sad and excited. There's talk of having showers and ice cold Cokes, until one by one everyone's asleep.

Brahim, Fateia, Mamadou and I are almost packed by the time you rouse from the beep beep beep of a Nokia alarm going off. Tea and milk is handed around and everyone's ready to go. I'll dismantle the khaima when I get back later. Mamadou rides on Wahad. It's cold and he's a mere bundle in the saddle. Mwoiny is at her usual place and half way along the piste we're called upon by the dogs again. It's their way of saying "Goodbye." The walk out begins in high spirits but as the sun gets up and the deep sand takes over from the hard piste, it suddenly becomes a little quiet, sadness too of course. The sun burns at our backs as we approach

Teinweich. I tie up Wahad at the place you first met Brahim at what seems like a lifetime ago. I transfer Mamadou to my shoulders and on we walk. As we approach the outskirts of the village, Brahim takes Mamadou and we shake hands. Fateia shakes hands with the girls and thanks you all for coming out to see her in the desert. She gives you a guerba, a water sack made from a goatskin, she will make another with the skin of the goat we had last night. After photographs are taken and thank you's and bon chance, they move off left to take the camel piste to the market. It's where they live. We carry on into the village, where Thioub is waiting with his Merc. "Bismillah." You shake hands and get in. I wave you off and turn back for Wahad.

It is hoped that you learned something from your time with me. Navigation using the sun and wind, that water is really precious and shouldn't be wasted. That the Sahara is full of life and that it needs nomads to look after it. That you might not need all those gadgets and stuff you chase after, working hard like a beaver for the next DVD or car or CD player. That there are always other options in life. Mostly, I hope that you have found something inside you that gives you a buzz when sitting in your office on Monday morning, swamped by an enormous amount of paperwork, with the boss asking you to bend over and kiss your ass. I have had wonderful emails from past guests which keep me going. I had no idea that I had such an influence on people and the decisions they have taken since. It humbles and pleases me to know that they've moved on to not just make a difference in their lives but make a difference in other peoples lives less fortunate than themselves. Water projects in Mali and Niger . . . teaching in Burkina Faso, Asia and South America. All because of what I have said in the course of our conversations. I thank them for their trust in the first place to come out into the desert with me.

My advice for what it is worth is, work until you are 40. Sell up everything, give everything to charity you can't and piss off. There are millions of people who need your skills and experience. We all live on the same planet and need to look after one another. It doesn't necessarily need to be that to which has taken you to this moment. You're thinking, 'What can I possibly do?' Make a list of your experiences, hobbies and dreams and see how others could benefit from them. It's just a cerebral exercise after all! Nothing may come of it . . . then again!

I would continue to leave to look for herds or transfer them to other areas, and be gone for perhaps a month or so at a time. It was always a surprise on my return, that my campsite was always there. It was about six or seven months into my stay in my 3000km² territory, that 60km out from Boutilimit into the desert; the eastern extent of my known working territory and about 150 km from Teinweich, that I came across a 6 month old dog, a female. I dismounted, tied Wahad to a nearby bush and waited patiently with a bowl of biscuits and sardines for three hours, sitting under another bush. A length of rope behind my back. She'd run from bush to tree come in and go away, sniffing the air continuously until she couldn't resist it anymore and the moment she came to eat, I had her. She fought as I lifted her by the scruff of her neck and had the cord quickly fastened around her. I then let her tuck in. As she did I checked her over. For someone so young she had a lot of scars and not caused by fighting other dogs! Very quickly she was to become my very newest and bestest girlfriend and woe betide anyone who later would have a go at me. This would later include Leomine in his 4x4! Mwoiny was as adoring and vicious as Aminetou, but with bigger teeth and an unflagging spirit. Come to think of it, much like Aminetou really and as with all Mauritanian females, she's a bandit. A thief of the highest order, who would cost me a small fortune by consuming an entire fish dinner for six people, when she slipped her cord at the Menata. She simply trashed the vegetables. Cow! We moved towards the road, found a small shop and I bought eight tins of sardines, four packets of biscuits and other assorted tins and foods. We moved back into the desert to resume looking for the camels, which we found a week later. This isn't always the case. Sometimes you just can't see them for looking at them. Or they're simply not where you were told they were or just fucked off in another direction.

She was attached to me by her cord for the whole of that week, walking on my left hand side in my shadow or attached to Wahad, who did not like her one bit. She on the other hand liked Wahad and would later chase his ass when he got a bit terse with her. He would give up trying to stomp on her after a few minutes, then usually have to put up with a mouthful from the lippy bergere. Mwoiny I later learned was a Malian breed that has a penchant for children. "Hold on there she's not a fuckin' savage!" I simply meant to say that if children began to wander from the encampment this particular breed would chase them back, similar in fact to the North American Song dog of the Sioux. Only they like to catch fish and love water, whereas Mwoiny loves to eat them and will only drink in the morning and at night." Children like baby camels can soon get disorientated and unlike baby camels children rapidly collapse due to heat stroke. Mwoiny is very submissive towards me and very intelligent. She learned very quickly my non-verbal commands and calls for the camels to move left and right. HAA! HAA! and whistle. HeyHAY! HeyHAY! HEYHAY! (for stubborn females who choose not to hear you!) for stop which obviously wasn't meant for her because, she isn't a camel I reasoned. I had my own call which carries for a kilometre or so . . . AaaaaOUUU! It has to be heard to be fully appreciated and would bring her instantly to my side as well as alert the herd that I had arrived and for everyone to get their act together.

Let me stress from the outset that she wasn't a pet. If need be I would cut her throat if her injuries were severe enough or leave her behind should she wander off. This happened once and we hooked up four days later. Lesley never doubted for a moment that we would. We had walked into the face of the Harmattan for almost four days. One minute she was there and the next, not. I hadn't enough water or energy to go and look for her. I AaaaaOUUU'd but nothing and I kept on going, eventually reciting prayers for her. It would take me fully a week to recover from this and nearly a week after this before she was match fit. Imagine a hairdryer blowing in your face, on full and on high heat. See how long you can stand it for, even at a gentle blow. We have no choice here. March or die. At the end of the working day, she would have twenty minutes rough house with me. That's it out of twenty-three hours and forty minutes, where she works non-stop even if she's sleeping. She has three calls which took time to stick in my head. A low growl for people who approach the camp either by day or night, a low growl and low yelp for 4x4's and a full on barking session for the African wild dogs. She guarded my khaima and my life and she herded camels and goats and was mostly professional. I am unique, in that no other berger in the known history of Mauritania has used a dog to herd camels. There is now one other, Moctar, and of his story you'll read about later. Mwoiny is now his bergere, and he takes a great deal of pride in his association with her.

The Bidan continued to arrive and occasionally scoff at me for having a dog, though always very careful to keep an eye on her. She would unnerve them by sitting as close to the khaima demarcation line and guard me. I would be asked time and time again to tie her up. I refused. I simply said that they were free to go. Her display of her role as bergere would completely stump them and although they accepted that she could do the job, they would never readily agree to pay for her services. I simply refused because I knew that the job would need two bergers and that the boss would have to pay out. I insisted that for herds over 24 the boss pay me half to perhaps a negotiated half to one third for Mwoiny or go elsewhere. Some did and some paid. It also increased their stature when relating that their berger had used a dog to herd his stock. There was also much hatred for her, given the fact that the Qu'ran states that the dog is the only animal to carry germs. In these instances I simply said that they were free to discuss it with her. None ever did. One man at the camel market stupidly got on my bad side when he upheld Leomine's attitude towards me as being warranted and started to approach me in a violent manner. She chased his ass into a small cabine and he slammed the door. She sat outside for just over an hour until it was time to go.

I disagree with the Qu'ran in many respects, we all have germs. I once had a conversation with a Bidan. She stated the obvious and also that I shouldn't let Mwoiny drink from the same bowl, which I did. Not on a regular basis, only when really necessary as I'd normally carry a polythene bag as a water bowl. She said that her mouth was filthy and that I'd die as a result. This from a woman in her 30's with a mouth like a graveyard with broken, blackened and rotting teeth. My sarcasm so much wanted to spill out but I held my tongue. She carried on blah blah blah, then I thought, 'Fuck it!'

"Madam," I said, "Mwoiny's teeth are perfect, yours on the other hand are a bloody mess, broken and rotted and your mouth as a consequence is full of bacteria that is directly affecting the health of your heart. You, will soon be dead. My dog on the other hand, will live a full and healthy life. In fact, given the choice of kissing you or her, she'd win every time!"

In French of course and not Hassaniya.

"My teeth are perfect!" She replied.

Smiling a horrible horrible smile, completely oblivious to the fact that it was her that I was referring to! That list again:

"Smile even though all around you is in chaos caused by your own hand, denying that your ship is slowly sinking! It's always someone else's fault!"

The first night at our camp, when I had finally released her from her bonds, she took off towards the sound of the howling African wild dogs at 19.30. This family lived at their nearest point, only 4 km away. There were five families in total, who comprised this one tribe. My first thoughts were as she sped off into the darkness . . .

'C'est fini! Elle est mort!'

Twenty minutes later, not that I was counting you understand, she comes back looking very pleased with herself. I thought, 'She's either killed them, chased them off or fucked them!'

The thought that I would have African wild dog puppies gave me the shivers.

'I'll kill them!' I told her.

She was tiny in comparison to the African wild dog. She would continue to battle with them, holding her own in odds of 6 to 1. When they next traversed the ridge it would be by at least 500-1000 m from our home. My newest bestest girlfriend, isn't she wonderful? Her training was along the same lines as I had experienced in Scotland with my labrador, only with a major difference. Here, this dog wasn't a pet. She had a willful streak that included theft of anything edible. I therefore kept her out of the khaima by simply hitting her with my baton her every time she attempted to come in. I would use the baton to make her yelp.

"I'm not even going to say it this time!"

She soon got the message. I also trained her to attack/kill. With two codewords embedded in her ever active and intelligent mind, she was after several months training the most complete dog I had ever owned, as far as I was concerned. Still a thief fuckin' though. Can't have everything I suppose.

There is a funny story about her not being allowed in the khaima. Okay, it's basically a canopy, as the sides are rolled up. She therefore, will rest at the very edge, her paws and nose barely touching the invisible demarcation line between inside and out. If she dared to cross even by a millimetre I'd smack her paws or nose. If you give her a millimetre she'd then take the centimetre, then the metre. I would use a bowl to put the water I'd use to wash veg or pour out tea etc into, a slops bowl if you like, along with vegetable skins, tea leaves and the like. I'd leave this trailing the back edge by at least half of the bowl and allow her to steal, so I'm not all bad eh! She knows when the booty's fair game. Bitch! I remember one night when we due to leave the homestead of Abderachman, a man I had worked with for two months whilst his son's had gone off to earn money in Nouakchott. I was his second berger. The night before I know I'm going to use a taxi, I don't allow Mwoiny to eat as she gets car sick.

She's off the rope for less than five minutes before we take off. We travel 80km and get within 1km of the auberge and she empties her stomach over me and the car naturally enough. 6000UM (18 euros) in damages she cost me! She must have stolen the food left out for goats in the morning! Kanya didn't fully appreciate the state I arrived in either! The first of my many black marks in her book of obsessional hatred towards me.

Okay, sorry, here's the funny story now. One night, as I was eating my potato scones and wabbit, onion, potato and green pepper (stored in olive oli) and chili soup.

"Yup, it's not fuckin' Mauritanian! Remember, there's a Saltire flying above me at this point."

A tiny jerboa bounds into the bowl, grabs a piece of potato scone, bounds back out and does a runner. Mwoiny goes mental, runs around the left hand side of the khaima to dive into the bush behind us. The jerboa's gone. Next night, it's a little more guarded but actually bounds off my knee this time, into the bowl to stay there when it discovers there's nothing in it yet.

'I'm still cooking them, you little arsehole.' I let slip out.

It then looks over the rim of the bowl at Mwoiny who of course is going mental but will not come into the khaima, even though she'd love to. I couldn't have her steal from guests and I am pleased the training's paid off. The jerboa then susses the situation straight off. It waits until I'm finished cooking takes the piece I throw onto the floor and is off, with her majesty running around the right hand side this time but to no avail. The jerboa's safely tucked up inside his burrow scoffing on potato scone. So every night we are there for the next year, this nightly ritual goes on between dog and jerboa should we be alone but never with guests. I daren't tell them because they'd think their host or guide was some sort of lonely mental person. The jerboa; who was never given a name and funnily enough I never used Mwoiny's name with her either, would be my TV during dinner. At least it would be someone else to talk to! The jerboa would sit in full view and eat in front of Mwoiny who would chatter, like a fish wife. With me as well, when I rolled a joint. When I rolled up outside she would destroy the joint and take the beating afterwards, actually come back for it. Now that's love. Doubt I would have done the same with Aminetou! The full five minutes or so to smoke it, would have her give me a fuckin' mouthful! Even if I made a sedray khaima; being a makeshift khaima under a bush or tree, the same rule applied and to her credit the rules of khaima was strictly observed by Mwoiny. The jerboa would scurry around just inside the perimeter of the khaima, stopping here and there making Mwoiny run around in endless circles, or it would simply walk across the inside of the tent. Or bound backwards and forwards and have her go even more mental. Always, it disappeared into its burrow.

There was another neighbour who lived in the bush behind the tent, a sand viper. It was spotted one day, a small one as if that makes a difference. It never came into the khaima and we never went raking about in the bush after it. It was Mwoiny who alerted me to the presence of it. She didn't pursue it either. You have several minutes if bitten, just enough to leave a text message and say goodbye. I have stepped on one barefooted, as it lay just buried underneath the sand. It took off. I was also stung by a scorpion and had a hellish four days afterwards.

"Kill the bastard the moment you see it!"

Mwoiny's hunting skills, despite this loss of face with Jerry Jerboa, are second to none. She'd take wabbit easy enough, pigeons she'd wait for under bushes but it would take her longer to outwit desert foxes, as this particular quarry is very small and very fast. A very beautiful little creature. I always liked to see them get away.

"That's got to be bonus points when the RSPCA catches up with me. Right sir? You can tell he's not pleased"

The other jerboas that she caught, she was brutal with and would take twenty minutes to play with, kill and eat. They're so surprisingly crunchy for something so small and soft. She'd arrive with it in her mouth, lie down and taking her time, let it go to instantly smack it. The surprising thing I discovered was that she'd broken its legs on one side! It then runs around in circles and she waits, waits and WHAM! Slaps it hard to stun. It carries on running around in circles, WHAM! For ever and ever running around and . . . WHAM! Eventually bored or hungry she lets it go, watches watches watches and body slams it, to then roll on it and eat it, the tail trailing like a piece of spaghetti. Savage bitch. Then she cleans her back by rubbing it over the sand and runs off. Her daily ritual would be to go and hunt around 16.30-17.20 if we were in camp and not working before coming back to scrounge off of me. I could always tell if she had eaten, as she'd have a self satisfied smug look on her face. Funnily enough it was about this time suggested on the GPS for hunting in this area! Either that or 0330-04.30! If I set snares, I'd have to tie her up or lose my dinner! I fashioned myself a nice little rug at one point from the wabbit skins.

During the course of simply walking around my immediate area I had gathered lots of Neolithic archeology. Stone axes, mortars and pestles, beads, jewelry. Fishing net weights by the ton. Further out I had found intact pots large and small, had cached those as they were so far out and too fragile for me to transport. As well as small and huge fields of broken pottery that had signified the raids on encampments. I had GPS'd, photographed everything and mapped everything down on paper, also an inventory of everything. I still have three caches of stone items and the three pots out in the desert waiting safe transportation. It would take Time Team the rest of the 2000's just to work in the Trarza alone. The only possible solution would be to wait for the USS Enterprise to do the work satisfactorily and completely. With Seven-of-Nine in the team, I would be happy just to be around to make the tea! The very worst aspect of working with her is that she would that have to lose the skin tight suit, as it would be far too hot. Now, the survival suits the nomads wear in Frank Herbert's Dune, I'd love one of those! You really have too much time to think, dream and ponder on so many unnecessary things. The Sahara as an entity produces enough energy in one day to power the planet for one year. How the hell do you attach the leads to the battery? Then there are the Australian deserts, Kalahari, Negev, Black Rock Nevada, the Gobi . . . so much energy going to waste and the world in need of it. I imagine the man or woman who discovers the secret will be assassinated by the oil moguls and the nuclear power industry.

Anyhoo I digress, so what's new eh? I decide one day to take samples and my paperwork to The National Museum in Nouakchott. I arrive at the other side of the market around 08.00, and tie up Wahad under a big bush. I then tie Mwoiny up to my saddle and make off for the road.

"Will you lot at the back fuckin' calm down! She doesn't and won't drink during the heat of the day. What, take them both with me in the fuckin' taxi?" If I don't leave Mwoiny, perhaps, no its certain, someone will steal my camel and saddle and the big bull of an imbecile at the market doesn't like Mwoiny. No-one not even Ol Loli would take responsibility for her as she's unpredictable without me being there! With her on guard no-one will approach her because: 1. She's tied up, therefore the Mauritanian will think she's mental and on guard. 2. She will go mental and they then are correct in their assumption even if she only wants to talk and play with them. They won't know this of course and piss off. Job done! It does mean, "Oh dear you're not going to like this, one little bit sir . . ." that she will be there for several hours all alone, with only Wahad to talk to and he's a grumpy bastard at the best of times. I don't give a fuck!

"And all you animal right's activists who now want to cut my throat, get in the fuckin' queue! There's Leomine, El Mamy, Med Baba and Ould Bou ahead of you. Perhaps one of your new bestest boyfriends will do the job for you! If not, you can send your hate mail to the publisher Inshallah, who'll pass it on and I'll feed it to the goats." By Saharan standards I'm not cruel. You there in the civilized world have a different approach to animal care, and rightly so, because all your animals are as soft as shit and wouldn't last two minutes here. There are moments even I can't take after three years. The cruelty exacted on donkeys that pull the charettes twelve hours a day every day until they drop, pulling huge loads, is terrible and unnecessary. At 5 000UM for a donkey and 50 000UM for the charette you can see where the owner's priorities lie and it's cheap and easy to replace a sick or injured animal. The sound of a big heavy stick slamming onto their spine at twenty paces makes me sick to my stomach and as mad as hell and I'd love to do the same to the driver but then I'd be as bad as him, by beating a stupid animal senseless. Not that I consider the donkey stupid, just a prisoner of war and helpless to better his life. It does amuse me to see them take off into the chaotic traffic in Nouakchott and have their owners chase after them under the hot sun. They also spend most of the night braying and causing everyone around to lose sleep. A little payback for their daily misery.

I arrive at the Museum by 10.00 to the great surprise of Hacen, the Black Moor director. I unload my samples and can see that I've only brought more of the same that fills the cases simply laid out around the not very large hall. It's a simple place because the history of Mauritania and therefore the Sahara's contribution in this particular spot is simple but spectacular by the quantity lying around. I show him photographs of the other caches and his eyes are open wide.

"Why didn't I want to sell them?" He asks.

"Because they belong to Mauritania and the rest of the world." I tell him.

I had been asked by nomads at every camp to buy stone axes and had taken to carrying a small one to show that I had found it en-route. This then stopped any further demands for money. I used a large mortar and pestle to grind wheat, a smaller mortar and pestle to crush spices and a flint arrowhead broken in half down its length to skin my wabbits,

I found it did a far superior job than my knife. I later found a curved version which was even better. Hacen is amazed at the quantity of GPS references I have and agrees to take me on as an associate without salary, of course. They have no money to speak of and it's basically down to the small number of French and Mauritanian archeologists to do the best they can in the present circumstances.

I expect the money available for one Time Team programme could fund years work here. It would take them more than three days to acclimatize never mind get down to any actual work. I love them. It was my favorite programme in the UK but even they would see the complexity of operating out in the Sahara, as daunting enough as to make it impossible on a full time basis, unless carried out by people as mad as me! I don't claim to be an expert. I am by proxy of my life there involved and can therefore hopefully make a small contribution without the need for praise or salary. I encourage tourists to go to the Museum. I go around the many stall holders who sell artifacts to give up the more unique pieces. It is small and slow work. With a country steeped in corruption, famine and 50% of the population living on less than $1 a day, it's shwea, shwea . . . small, small. There are two posters hanging up in the museum in French and Arabic, asking people to hand in items and not to sell them. I asked where the others were so that I could put them up around the city. No-one knows or claims to know. Guides who have gotten to know me, have been contacting me since my associateship with the Museum to come and collect finds in various parts of Mauritania. I simply pass them onto Hacen and his team to go and collect them. They now know I'm for real and not out to steal, which was a concern at first because these men too have a conscience and have seen may Europeans come, hoover up and make a fortune.

I was contacted by a Black Moor I knew from Boutilimit, the centre of artisana in Mauritania who said he knew of a Malian who had a Neolithic statue. I was due to head back out into the desert and didn't have the sum he asked for but not wanting to give up the opportunity I agreed to meet him. He wouldn't let me touch it and I could only stare across the room at it, so really didn't get a proper assessment, but my amateur eye could tell it was for real as well as see the uneasiness in this man's eyes. The stone was of similar I had seen many mortars and pestles made from. I had two thirds of what he was asking for and said that I could phone a friend to drive down and hand over the rest in the morning. He refused. He was scared. He took off and I never saw him again. I expect the 30cm or so statue in a similar pose to Michelangelo's David, without the definition of course, would be in a box cached away in a vault very soon, worth how much? Millions of dollars as well as being a world treasure. He wouldn't let me photograph it either. I had the equivalent of 68 quid and he wanted 100. I later spoke to Hacen. He said that it wouldn't have been shown as it was nude, it would offend the sensibilities of the Bidan. Given that not many Bidan go there it wouldn't offend many people.

Two German's in 2005 came to Mauritania and hooverd up a half million dollars worth of archeology and sold it on the Internet. Interpol later tracked down every piece and the two men were sentenced to 10 years in prison and lost their families and homes. I've had two direct requests from two Frenchmen and two Italians. Indirectly through a Bidan who needed a guide for two Germans, on a specific route. The French team wanted to go into the desert and take off towards Egypt. I was to help them buy stock and supplies and be their berger. They were unspecific about their reasons and very guarded, when I asked about visas for passage through the Sahara. Although there aren't borders as such you still need them. I gave them a list of how many camels and equipment needed and I also gave then their chance to come clean. We were alone, passing joints back and forward and I asked them directly if it involved archeology as it would be pretty hard to keep it a secret from me out in the desert. They eventually agreed that this was their aim and I said that they were at liberty to go to the camel market and buy stock. I wouldn't be joining them and I then left. They had too by my return that evening, which was just as well as I had spoken to a friend at Brigade Mixte.

Of the Italians, they too gave me the impression that they were out to hoover up and said that I was due to leave for a job and couldn't help them. I said that I would be gone for perhaps two weeks and would be back. They had told me something of their plans and knew they'd be hanging on, doing the tourist thing before moving off south to Mali. I was out on the Route L'Espoir when I saw their car about a week and a half later. I was moving stock along the road because the dunes were too big and would mean I'd move about 2 km/hr. I followed their tracks in and watched them for the three days they stayed here, filling up their small backpacks with archeology, camping out. Small fish, but if they were going to stop off all the way down to Mali they'd make a small fortune. I was just another berger out with camels and they didn't take much notice of me but I stayed far enough away as not to be recognised by my clothing. On the third night as they camped up I hit the road and phoned a friend. His message to call him arrived a month later when I finally hit the road and my list of calls and sms arrived. I phoned back. The car had been stopped by the Gendarmerie and found to be full of hashish, cocaine and of course the archeology I'd seen them take. "Thank you." He said and I cut the call.

The Germans gave me a specific route which indicated that they too were taking the easy option as far as hovering up archeology was concerned and I flatly refused telling Cherche to dump them as they were out to hoover up. He speaks good English and understands my many colloquial phrases. He thanked me and told them he couldn't find anyone. He too has a conscience and makes him unique amongst his peers as living here all of his life. There are some good Bidan eggs here. Not many.

I am not a policeman. I have no special status other than having contacts that I deem to be worthwhile in a country steeped in corruption who make a difference. I am an unpaid associate of a poor museum of a third world country, that hardly anyone visits. I only have my conscience, which doesn't allow me to agree to the theft of national treasures. I have heard tales from guides who tell me of the wanton destruction and theft of archeology in their regions, from all over Mauritania. In one instance, a rock covered in animal drawings that these bastards have taken a sledgehammer to and smashed up, to take away the best of what's left. This particular rock, Cherchefall has known since he was a toddler. His father would take him by camel to see it. He knows every line and can faithfully recreate it on paper, to scale if he wanted to. He's in his seventies. He was sobbing his heart out as he spoke to me over the phone. He was depressed for months afterwards and will now not go anywhere near the area of its location. He can't. Just as I can never go back to Culloden. I understand his pain. These treasures cannot be replaced and although time and erosion will wear them down it's no reason to smash them up!

That's the reason I do what I do. If I see you here stealing archeology from my small patch of the Sahara, I'll track your ass and hand you in. No salary required or demanded by me. I'll kick your ass into to prison for free! You are warned, with a smiley face of course!

It's while I'm moving stock not long after my new job at the Museum, that I see or rather hear my first accident on the Route L'Espoir. Mwoiny and I had come down to the roadside and were waiting for a suitable place to cross with the stock. I could see a huge green overloaded lorry approaching and it trundled past on, eventually uphill, struggling to keep momentum. A brousse taxi zips past, full of passengers and baggage, on the roof and boot, tied down with bits of rope and material. As it accelerates the hairs stand up on the back of my neck, I keep the stock moving in the opposite direction until, there's a metallic crunch, a thump, then the sound of debris falling from the sky, as dull thuds. There was nothing I could do. This is the Mauritanian way, the African way. Overloaded cars, trucks and vans and drivers with no training, no commonsense that says it is dangerous to overtake on the brow of a hill, or on a corner or to drive at night with no lights. I saw the remains of the 190D weeks later and it reminded me of the car Odd Job brought back to Goldfinger's stud farm. There were some clothes caught up in a tree, bidons that were strapped to the boot, scattered around and three suitcases, their contents spilled out. Bismillah simply isn't enough.

## CHAPTER SEVEN

# STOCK GOES MISSING . . . .
# THE GAME'S AFOOT!

I T IS A camel's duty to escape, he is a P.O.W. It's in his job description just as it's yours to drag his or their scrawny asses back again. I had bought myself another camel to ride and would keep Wahad for baggage and tourists. Ethnayne (Arabic for two) was about six years old and a very strong animal, a little less tall than Wahad. In subsequent races against bergers we would be successful 80% of the time. I had lots of offers to sell him. Some very good offers too. He could put on that extra spurt just when needed and demoralize the opposition. It also calmed Wahad down, considerably. He just needed a mate and Ethnayne was it. The two became inseparable and Wahad didn't mind becoming Number Two. He would take the bags and his buddy, the arsehole. 'I knew what he thought about me, he had the look. Always the fuckin' look.' Ethnayne came courtesy through a contact through El Mamy. At a decent enough price, 155 000 UM, Wahad by the way was 150 000 UM. The price for most stock falls around 145-175 000 UM here in the Trarza, for male, female and baby. If you buy a pregnant female, you also buy the baby. For stock in the north around 220 000 UM, due to there not being any mosquito borne illnesses. Not there are any in the desert but there is at the market. So don't buy there, only in the desert.

There you get to see the animal in its normal surroundings and not crammed in and competing for space and food, and not made to perform in the small circus, where at times you couldn't swing a cat . . . "And believe me sis I've tried!" "Only joking, sir." Abnormalities are easily spotted and the true nature of the animal shines through. Ethnayne was responsive without the need for much baton work. Show him the baton right he would move left and vice versa. Riding a camel's so easy . . . sometimes. Sh sh sh and down he'd go, tutt tutt tutt and up he'd go. The first kick, canter and the second, the transition then the third mode and he'd fly! Give his ass a whack, sorry, touch his flank ever so gently with your baton and into orbit he'd go! So very different from Wahad who by the way sported some nine brands of varying means used to put on. From the use of the branding iron to a simple cut with a hot knife. "Sorry folks, but it's the truth of the matter." Ethnayne only had one, so probably the reason for his ease in his transition to me. Poor Wahad, having lived like Black Beauty and had been passed from owner to owner, quite rightly entered into an expected battle of wills simply because he was tired of having to re-train a new owner. Again, I had to change the nose ring and this I achieved myself, without the use of a smally boy and a new beautiful girlfriend.

Work came and went, guests too and I was in a definite rhythm. Berger, guide and associate. I had gone back to Scotland to remake my acquaintance with my family in June/July 2006 and never realised how much I had missed and loved my sister. I had left the camels in the care of Brahim and Mamadou, and Mwoiny, with a French woman called Annie. She couldn't speak English, and Mwoiny didn't understand French. They were okay together and Mwoiny got to go to Boulanoire near Nouadibou, Atar and Chinguetti. She hunted and was spoiled rotten although, I had given strict instructions for Annie not to. Mwoiny was a little too overweight when I got back. At this point I hadn't been to the last two towns, and only to the camel market at Nouadibou. These being undertaken with other bergers. They eventually took to her when they soon realised she was the professional I said she was. As a team, she and I probably covered a few kilometres under 50 000 ranging here and there looking for and moving stock. I had two further branding sessions. Much calmer and professional, being undertaken solely by bergers. The second akin more to a scene from a western. Lots of incidents but no lasting injuries and mostly a loss of face involved and a great deal of baiting afterwards. The difference was amazing and not a hint of tiredness afterwards, just a smug satisfaction of a job well done. I have had a very interesting employer at this time.

At the beginning of September 2006, a huge brand new Mitsubishi 4x4. "They're shit for the desert by the way, really shit. Great for intimidating the other mothers when you take your off-spring on the school run but for the desert, complete shit." This day it was 50° C and as the electrically operated window opened; it was like a blast from an industrial freezer, as I later experienced at the fishing port, there was a Bidan sitting in the passenger seat, a rather commanding figure. There were three other Bidan in the 4x4 too. He spoke Hassaniya, translated by the driver Ahmed, when he had completely lost me. Officers I thought. Every Bidan dressed to kill in very expensive boubous, gold watches and expensive mobile phones. You could have bought two camels with the phone Ahmed had, white camels which are about 600 euros each. I asked if they were all officers and he said yes, "Except for the boss." I introduced myself as did the boss, Achmed. "Where is the berger?" He asked. "I am." I said. Achmed was taken aback. When Ahmed asked me where I was from; I have accent that automatically determines that French isn't my first language. When I told him Scotland he then spoke perfect English. It transpired that Achemd's herd had disappeared some two weeks previously and had been seen coming this way. I asked for the brand, the numbers of females, babies and males. Achmed asked what experience I had. I gave him my time since my arrival and asked for a pen and piece of paper and put down the brand of every owner I had worked for. My C.V. I suppose and he then agreed that I could work for him. I said that two weeks could easily put them in Mali as they could easily cover up to 100 km a day. There were other possibilities too to consider as I hadn't seen them anywhere around my territory. I'd have known this brand if I'd seen it. It's a little different from the usual run of the mill brand and begins on their face, on the left shoulder and then the left flank. Distinctive. Very distinctive. "What are the other possibilities?" Achmed asks after translation, "They've been put onto a lorry and driven off to an abattoir or taken to Laayoune through the minefield." I said. "Not a possibility!" Achmed replies. I was then given his phone number and mine given in exchange. The instant the window went back up, the heat hit me like a sledgehammer.

Every week I would see the 4x4 in my territory and he'd drop by at all times of the day and night. Always with the same three officers. I would broaden my search, going first to wells and asking all and sundry, en-route and all around. Always with the same smirking smile. One day I asked two bergers I knew well, Brahim and Mohamad, if they knew who this man was. They would stay over at the khaima even if I weren't there, at my invitation. They would never take more than tea, sugar and a little rice. They both smirked that smirk. "Tell me who he is!" I asked. Again the fuckin' smirk. You don't know who your employer is?" Brahim asked. I simply looked at him, no smile. "He's President Col Ely Mohamad Ould Vall's brother." Brahim tells me. I kept a straight face. "Thank you." I said. For the next six months I kept on looking. No one had seen hide nor hair of this herd. And to this day it remains so. I reported every week by text when I could and the reply came back. 'I was to keep looking.' He didn't have to pursue them as he did and could have bought the entire camel market 30 times over and not have missed the money. He simply loved his camels and wanted them back. El Mamy has been looking for 10 females that wandered off eight years ago. He too continues to drive around on the occasional day with his 4x4 full of imbeciles, looking for his camels. The consensus of opinion amongst the bergers is that they've been stolen and taken straight to an abattoir. Achmed's brand is known by all of Mauritania. Perhaps as you read this they are wandering free range, in Mali, Niger or Algeria possibly, or, chilling out unnoticed in my former territory. With camels you can never be certain. At times they are frustrating cunts.

Two months into my employment with Achmed, a huge herd of sheep and goats, perhaps 3-400 and 100 or so camels arrived with five bergers, ahead of their boss around 13.00 and had asked my opinion about staying in the area for feeding. I said that nearby there was a family of African wild dogs and about 12 km away to the SE was another of the same tribe. They thanked me and had decided to move on as he had more than enough time to move on through, when the boss arrived in his battered old Hilux. The head berger told him what I had said and the Bidan dismissed this as being of no concern, "Anyway what did I know!" The berger said that I was the berger for this area and that . . . the Bidan cut him off and turned on me. "What do you know about being a berger! You know nothing of the desert!" He gave the berger his orders and drove off with another berger, into the heart of my neighbour's garden. The berger apologized on behalf of his boss and I said that it would be to his cost not to listen to me. I live here. I watched with dismay as the bergers; who knew what I said to be the truth moved off, and that their camp would put them squarely on the my wild neighbour's patio. As we watched them move off into the distance I went and sat underneath my tree. I watched as the bergers moved the stock, always a wonderful sight for me. A little while alter I could see the 4x4 racing back, stop and move in my direction, cutting right and left. I left the shelter of my tree, on a rise and great for looking out over the unmarked piste that herds cut down behind my camp then move off north after reaching the end of the small valley some 1-2 km, then out onto the collection of small dunes with the piste behind, I walked back to my khaima, the sound of the Hilux getting closer, Mwoiny tells me too. The Hilux slews to a halt some 10m away, as I sat making a pipe. He shouted out from the cab that I wouldn't be welcome at the camp. I looked his way, lit my pipe loaded to the gunnels with Moroccan produce and sent Mwoiny after him, she did so and he took off. My code in such circumstances is, 'Talking with Dylan.' This in reference to The Magic Roundabout. Dylan; the wabbit named after Bob, loved to smoke a joint in the garden and play his guitar in the afternoons. This explanation is for our colonial cousins the Yanks who I expect have no idea at all about TMR. And of course, he invariably fell asleep, being a wabbit of course, I never do, did, well once. I was out with 30 camels, Mwoiny running around every now and again keeping such good order this day, I did considerably less as I'm the head berger anyway. The mp3 is playing Gong, and I-spy with my little eye something beginning with wild hashish. I have a little boule and I've just had lunch and Mwoiny's doing alright and why not. I duly light up and . . . it's not Gong who are playing when I come to, it's The fuckin' Eurythmics, bloody hell! There's no sign of the camels from the shade of my bush, which is only covering the top half of my legs and my feet are lobster red! Thankfully I do use factor 50 darling. I grab everything in one full sweep and crammed them into my bag, The Eurythmics are still playing and I go to the last point where I'd seen them, for Mwoiny to join me. I look round and about 40 m away is the herd, still in close order and everyone accounted for. Never again when I had stock did I smoke in the afternoon. Thank God for Mwoiny. She saved my ass, sorry flank, once again. 'I must endeavour to clean up my mouth, then again I'm not a young person and may be set in my ways somewhat.'

As night approached I heard and saw the Hilux come back and drive to the camp to leave about two hours later. We had our twenty minutes rough house, I cooked sausages and mash for dinner, with rice pudding to follow, then tea, pipe and mp3. I finished off mapping the items I had found earlier this morning and got ready for bed. With the moon relatively high in the night sky I heard Mwoiny and then the distant sounds of dogs. She was about to leave and I called her back. She began to leave and this time I gave her no choice. "Imshi khaima!" If you remember, this means "Get back to the tent!" Only in her case it was the small khaima I had rigged up for her over a large clump of grass. She had dug down, so she could escape the heat of the day, by constantly turning over the sand and it being damp further down would therefore allow her to stay cool. The Kalahari bushmen, excavate a small trench and piss in it, to then cover themselves to escape the heat of the day, there being little cover. She did as was ordered and stayed put. To reinforce this I took my baton from the khaima and pointed to her with it. This means the line has been drawn and the next action I take will be pain. Your pain. She got down further into the khaima and watched me go back inside mine. I listened to the distant sounds of the African wild dogs having take-away. 'C'est pas jolie!' I eventually fell asleep to the sounds of war.

I awoke to the sound of goats and sheep. I must be dreaming I thought, then I remembered the previous night's battle of teeth on flesh. I looked out to see Mwoiny lying down, with about 30 goats and sheep about 15m from me, it got very loud all of a sudden. I got up and went to inspect her booty. There were many female goats full with milk and I picked up my bowl and gently stalked one of them. It tried to run but Mwoiny quick as a flash had her by the throat and pinned. I took the goat from her and from the goat, her milk. I filled Mwoiny's bowl first and then had what was left. I went after a second and caught her without help, Mwoiny went back to her milk. I filled my bowl and had breakfast. I took more and filled my sack, another and left it covered in the khaima, and whilst on a roll had another 1L just for good measure, giving Mwoiny half. I turbaned up, grabbed my baton and we took off for the camp. En route we picked another five and soon arrived to the smiling face of the head berger and his associates. They had been out all night running around like idiots trying to chase the dogs off, but there were so many that they split up the herd and caused mayhem. The bergers were exhausted. It seems that two families had ganged up and had a field day. If I were an African wild dog I would have done the same. I said it was lucky that only two had done so as there were five families of this tribe. This stunned everyone and there were many heads being shaken from side to side. As they discussed the possibilities, who should arrive in his crappy Hilux. The head berger stood up as did I start to but he said to sit and ordered one of the others to give me a bowl of milk. I was stuffed but took it anyway, as I wanted to get right up this asshole's nose. 'If that's anatomically correct and physically possible doctor.'

The Bidan gave me a scowl as the berger gave him the story of the night's events, Mwoiny didn't take her eyes off of him for one minute. When the berger had finished the boss charged directly towards me and . . . Mwoiny was up and in front of me in a second. Her eyes directly looking into his. He motioned for her to go, shouted at her, went to pick up a stick and she growled a, "I will rip your head off!" type growl, which he clearly understood because he threw the stick away, thinking that she would chase it. As I've already said, she isn't a pet and doesn't do catch, chase the ball or run after the stick. It really didn't make any difference to Mwoiny as now, she hates his guts. I kept sitting and drank his milk. Scowling, he made to move towards me, giving me a mouthful in Hassaniya. Mwoiny leans forward and starts to get low, the Bidan stops abruptly. I waved my finger at him, "I wouldn't do that if I were you. She loves me dearly, and will bite you until I tell her to stop." I finished the milk, held out the bowl and asked for some more. No one moved, Mwoiny had seen the bowl and kept on looking at the Bidan. I nodded at a nearby berger, who slowly came to take it as I said he could, "It would be fine, the problem Mwoiny has is with the arsehole in front of her." The Bidan was livid. He started to give me a mouthful but I held him off. "My dog doesn't like aggressive behaviour towards me. If you start shouting, she'll go for you because you've already threatened me, picked up a stick and that, is tantamount to war in her eyes. You and I both know, thank you," as I took the bowl from the berger. I really couldn't drink any more but forced it down. "You and I both know it's your stupidity that has brought your bergers and herd to this moment in time, not me. If you like, I will tie my dog up and you can try your luck against me. I warm you though, when you leave hospital, you will be handicapped, never again will you eat with your right hand." I finished what I could of the milk, my stomach groaning and gave Mwoiny the rest, just to get up his ass again. I shook the hands of every berger and left. He was so full of rage that he was shaking. As I walked away he gave them a bloody awful mouthful, ranting and raving like the mad bastard he is. I could hardly walk as I had consumed nearly 4L of goats milk. Later on during the afternoon, three of the bergers arrived at my camp, en route for the road and into the capital to stay with family. They had tea, peanuts and biscuits and left. One of them gave me a number and said that if I needed a berger, phone, they'd arrive by foot all the way from

Nouakchott if need be. But never again for this Bidan. Surprisingly, each of them patted Mwoiny, albeit very tentatively but that they did so was remarkable. Doesn't happen very often and when it does, it tends to be special. Very special.

Most people tend to listen to me, thankfully those that don't are in the minority and they have an indomitable spirit which magnifies their stupidity. One Bidan, contacted me three times with weapons for sale. It didn't matter that I said "No negotiation! I don't want or need them!" He came out twice to the encampment with different Bidan on both occasions. The first time, he arrived in his Mitsubishi around 16.00hrs, again with the crappy 4x4, though not as lush as Achmed's and doesn't have an industrial freezer for AC. He made his introduction and asked if I had a problem with security with the other three smiling like idiots. I looked at Mwoiny, she at me, and I said, "No." "Can we come into your khaima?" I said yes, but they insisted I tie Mwoiny up. I shook my head, "She's my security!" I said. Lots of laughter. I asked her, in English of course, if she'd like to bite his fat ass. One of them translate into Hassaniya and everyone laughs. I looked at the culprit directly and asked, "English?" He replied, "I speak small." "French is good." I said. The others stayed put as the fat man got out very slowly and went round to the back and opened up the door. He motioned for me to come and have a look. There under a blanket that he pulled back, was an AK-47, mag in place. He motioned to pick it up. I could see that its safety was on. I took out the mag as it lay there and taking it out, walked away from the 4x4 a little and pointing it at the ground and emptied the chamber, which wasn't empty. "Arsehole!" I said. Again the culprit in the 4x4 translated. "Why?" The fat man asked. I picked up the round and looked the AK over. "Never travel with a chambered weapon." I said. "Bad practice always means accidents." I added. Chinese pattern, relatively clean and in good condition. The wooden stock had seen a lot of abuse. The rounds would cost me 225UM each. I could have a bucketful if I wanted, a skip full of them if I really wanted.

I had used Abderachman's AK with him and Dombo; his beautiful 22 year old, and mad as a brush granddaughter, who can fuckin' shoot by the way! She just can't cook. She kills pasta, and was the reason I didn't ask her to marry me. I had been helping her and her grandmother to move furniture at their homestead this particular day and an AK came flying out of the dark recesses of the room, straight into my hands, delivered there by a grinning Dombo. I caught it and instantly took the mag out, empty and checked it for a chambered round, empty. I looked it over and said that it could do with a clean. She had it stripped, wiped down with her mehlafah and re-assembled in seconds. I asked if she could do it blindfolded. Mehlafah in place she repeated the same exercise. I could have ripped her clothes off and fucked her stupid on the floor there and then all afternoon, all night and all the next day! She really really can't cook though and she's mad! Handy wife though, should you need an extra gun around!

I took the clip from the 4x4, put the round back in and walked towards a small dune not far away. The men all got out and followed on. Mwoiny in between me and them at all times. She doesn't like guns but will stay put, she shakes a bit though. It soon passes. I knew she wouldn't leave because of the four men. I put the mag in and on semi-auto took off a branch here and there from the tree in front of the dune. After a half dozen I went onto full auto and proceeded to cut the tree down, walking towards it as if to finish it off, until the hammer went click click. No-one said a word as I pushed the tree over and walking back to the group, handed back the AK, shaking my head. "It's not my style." I didn't mention that I had a .22 hunting rifle with infra-red scope either. Didn't think it necessary and would only keep them here longer than I had wanted, which was two seconds after I had handed back the weapon. He scribbled down his number and the four mounted up and drove off. The number would subsequently go into the charcoal brazier. As my rifle was silenced and therefore much less noisy than an AK, Mwoiny was understandably nervous, she was for the first time in her life a pet for five minutes. I enjoyed the moment too.

The second visit, some five months later, would involve yet another display of my shooting skills. He opened up with, that I hadn't phoned him, what had I been doing? As if I was an old friend or something. The list. "If Africans meet you once, it's an introduction, the second time you are family and they firmly believe they will get an invitation to your wedding or will be given an invitation to stay with your family in the UK!" This time, it was an old 8mm Mauser and twenty rounds. Heavy wooden stock naturally enough and in remarkably good condition for its age. Three different men, but the same type of imbeciles and I would choose yet another poor Acacia to abuse, as well as two empty coke cans and one full can of Fanta and four cigarettes. I shot the filters off of them and would later use them to roll joints with, having run out of tobacco.

They were surprised also that I asked them to take the cans with them and not litter the Sahara. One of the imbeciles actually clapped with glee as the Fanta squirted out of the two holes, having been shaken by the same imbecile previously. I thought that it must have been an old school science project, something he had waited to finish. Again I refused his kind offer and they left. Mwoiny a little less shaky but needed no more than a few reassuring noises before going off to hunt. Didn't spoil her appetite did it? Nothing ever does.

My third contact would be not long after the attack by Salafists on the Israeli Embassy in February 2008. Lots of vermin began to escape from their burrows and infect the city not long after the murder of the French tourists in December 2007. Knife attacks increased, rape, unheard of before began to occur and as with all countries infected by corruption, there was no real order to regaining order, it is a piecemeal reaction only and nothing more than a show of hormones. The Bidan in their enclaves of Las Palmas, Tevragh Zeina (Beautiful Land) of big houses, big walls and guardians were shielded by police-checkpoints and the rest of us had to make do being hassled by police-checkpoints. In the African quartiers the police will allow riots to rampage and clean up at a safe distance long after it's finished of course. There is no concerted co-operation between the services and the Guarde Nationale the most dangerous. Fuckin' cowboys, who are posted outside all government buildings, TV and Radio Station. A Frenchman who worked at the Presidential Palace was given a car, pass and would be in and out of the Palace everyday. He'd arrive at the same time and leave around the same time. This day, his car broke down and he arrived a little later than normal. He waved at the guards and drove on towards the main gates, which of course are closed, the guards chasing after him. He stops, gets out when they bang on the window and they shoot him in the foot as he does so! One wonders where they were actually aiming at!

One morning, I was near the Malian Ambassador's house when a 4x4 slows down to a roll and a Moroccan leans out and tells me to fuck off out of his country! I smile, then laugh saying, that as he was Moroccan, he too was a stranger here! That it wasn't his country. He took off did a Hollywood 180 and drove straight back at me. I weaved this way and that, I'm an expert at this as you'll find out later, and he finally stopped nearby and got out intent solely on violence. He approached at speed and full of rage; never a good way to begin a fight, he went to kick me and

I simply waited as his foot went high, spun him around and slammed him down onto his back, hard and KO'd him. Seven Bidan immediately appeared from seemingly nowhere and jumped on him. A Bidan in a very expensive boubou asked me to come with him and drove me straight to the Auberge Menata. I get four phone calls within the hour, one from a journalist. Everyone knows everyone and within a breath of an event such as this happening here everyone knows. In the evening, I get a phone call from you know who, "Could we meet Mohamed?" He knows I'm at the Menata. Ohhh, bloody hell, I smile and say yes. In an hour at an rv amenable to us both, he's already there. Unusual, because timekeeping isn't important to the Bidan. He's alone thank fuck, and we take off. The usual chit-chat then my story of being attacked by hordes of Salafists wanting to cut my throat. I point out that it was hardly a full-frontal invasion by an army of gun totting Al-Qaeda and it was dealt with quickly. He drives to a deserted spot and asks me to get out. I know where this is going and merely smile. In the back of his 4x4, he has two Beretta 9mm's with four fully loaded clips. "Hak wahad!" (Take one!) He says. "No thank you, I don't need it." I reply. "It's a gift!" He says. I thank him for his concern and say that I couldn't possibly carry it around like I was a cowboy. He has a shoulder strap too. I say for him to keep me one and two clips, and should I need it I'll call, as I now have his number. This country's an asylum and the lunatics are in charge. Sometimes, I don't know if I'm a doctor or a patient!

On one of my visits to the camel market, I got to briefly meet a light-skinned man. He doesn't introduce himself but I'm told later that his name's Abydi and he turns out to be a Nemadi, 'master of dogs.' He's pleased to meet Mwoiny and isn't at all shocked to hear that she's a bergere of camels. She instantly likes him. He considers his all of his Mauritanian cousins to be barbarians with to regard to dogs. The Nemadi are generally looked down upon by the Bidan as being aboriginal and therefore not intelligent, also the dog thang, it's not good even for me but both he and I continue to be surprised at the reactions of Bidan who have positive comments to make. On three occasions I have been offered quite a lot of money for her. The Nemadi are an extremely hard working people and very proud of their heritage. He was then off, having secured a lift up on top of the baggage of a 4x4 going south to Nema where he lives. He also had blue-eyes I remember. The Nemadi apparently have a different view of Islam and alienates them from the Government, who also withdrew their right to hunt and of course in the process, denied them their traditional rights with regard to their economy and culture. In my opinion this is both a racist and colonial attitude and totally unnecessary as they don't interfere politically or demand to be looked after, they simply want to be left alone to live their lives. Don't we all! Notwithstanding the prohibition to hunt, the Dama gazelle that was their main quarry; the largest of all the gazelle species, has virtually disappeared from Mauritania and only survives in very small numbers across the Sahara, though mainly in Mali, Algeria, Niger and Chad. Hunting is the major reason for its decline as it inhabits the poorest countries in Africa, with their civil wars, desertification, loss of forests and here in Mauritania, the Bidan took to blasting it industrially with his ancient wobbly shotgun from his 4x4 and Peugot 205 with a passion, doing more to contribute to their extinction than the Nemadi could ever have achieved. I take one wabbit for my pot, whereas the Bidan has no finesse. He'll stick his barrels down the burrow and lets rip a few times. The Nemadi aren't nomadic and live in the east/south eastern part of Mauritania. They speak the dialect of Azer, another tongue closely connected to Berber. Only recently, Nemadi women have taken their hunting music and love songs out into the international music scene, I do believe Tesco sells their CD! Give it a go and contribute to their welfare please.

Life in general in the desert most of the time, is spent in isolation. It can easily be two, three or even four months before I return to Nouakchott and many weeks in between talking to other bergers, nomads or Bidan out in their 4x4's. I do not mind not talking, as if you can believe that from my acerbic nature expressed here. It wasn't even necessary to talk to Mwoiny on a regular basis, as we would go about our daily work. If not moving herds or bergering tourists, she'd sit at my back as I worked for the museum, using me for shade. For hours I'd be engrossed in the finds and she, sleeping with one ear scanning for intruders interrupting our peace and tranquility. Not that the desert is quiet. I've often heard said, "Ah, the silence of the desert!" As if it's dead, empty of life that you now know not to be true. It's full of life, full of sound, never ever is it quiet. On my whirlwind trips into town, it would be deafening, unbelievably smelly and the pollution, sickening. I'd find it hard to understand people who'd continue to live like medieval peasants, who'd not notice the heaps of rubbish piled high around the streets.

Back in the desert it would take me two days to get my desert ears back and I'd be virtually deaf, until like a heavenly chorus it would arrive and my tranquility return. It's also towards the end of the year that Wahad is under performing, he's being overly difficult and his heart isn't in it anymore. It's understandable. He doesn't want to be saddled although he continues to take baggage but it's a struggle to have him walk faster than 3 km/hr. I decide to cut his hobbles and dispense with his services. He has taken off during his tenure with me four times in the direction of Nema, his compass firmly set on his birth place and is the case with all camels. I tell him he can go home if he so desires. Because he is Ethnayne's friend he chooses to come and go. I am visited not long after, by Med Baba, who then believes in that Tardis space that his h-bar sized brain exists within, that Wahad is free to be taken by whomsoever and used accordingly. I look at him in disbelief. I tell him directly, "He carries my brand and remains my camel. Would you steal El Mamy's stock just because he doesn't use them now?" He smiles the smile of an imbecile, completely lost in a storm of stupidity. I add, "If you take him, it will be theft and I'll have your ass!" He smiles and apologises, he said that he didn't mean anything by it, just having a bit of fun. I don't like his sleazy broken toothed smile.

Why would I like to march him and Leomine into the desert, break their legs and leave them without water? These men are without compassion or honour and would leave you to die for one ougiya, with which you cannot buy anything. Also with the Bidan it's an honour thing, when confronted with their crimes. There's no reasoning or bargaining except for you to lose most if not everything they stole from you and expect to be pardoned as well. They are uncouth and uncivilized. It's the little vestige of Arab they have retained that demands their loss of face to be preserved at all costs. In the case of the US military humiliating honest Iraqi's, their culture demands that they seek to inflict damage upon those who brought dishonour and shame upon them and their household. This was the reason for thousands of half-hearted attacks on soldiers and the support for the insurgency. In the main they'd fire a couple of shots, throw away the AK, honour restored. The insurgency was the summit of their frustration and the reason for supporting foreign fighters on their soil. Here, it's not that complicated because it's a simple means to covering their criminal activities and their shame on being caught. How dare you criticize and judge them for stealing from you. You are to pardon them without further discussion and allow them to keep their ill-gotten gains!

If not, they are then entitled to use violence to keep what was obtained illegally. All this to preserve their face and of course allow them to keep the money, property or animals they have no right to in the first place. The problems of Mauritania, begin, continue and end solely with the Bidan and his rapacious capacity for criminality. I don't know of any foreign national who lives here, has passed through here or has had to work here even after the briefest of visits, who has anything other than a superficial respect for the Bidan society or the Bidan.

It is a land of opportunity in which foreign nationals exploit because the Bidan won't get up off of his fat ass and do the work. They make the Bidan pay handsomely because they target the Bidan and not the African, who in turn exploits the foreigners. I came here simply because it was a safe point of contact for the Sahara, ha bloody ha! It is amongst my teenage Bidan girlfriends, who are the most vocal with me and therefore the most guarded, who would like to leave here and never comeback. They are intelligent young women who simply want a normal life. One 16 year-old beauty Aminetou, sees her life like a 30 cm ruler. Her life laid out, measured, with a definite beginning and end to it. It depresses her that she may never be able to leave. Like so many Mauritanians it is her dream to leave. She has explored Scotland on the Internet and would dearly love to go there, with a handsome Scottish guide of course. She's a little too young for me; though here she could have been married at 14 and in any case at 2 million ougiya plus a house and a car, she's too expensive a bride for me to have to buy. But if I had it, I'd still certainly not test the waters.

Mohamad Baba and his brother-in-law, Mohamad Leomine Ould Sba are scum, who have never worked, who haven't contributed one ougiya to charity. They have simply sponged and stolen their way through life. They abuse their slaves and live life large but act like the consummate gentleman they are most definitely not. They have stolen all I had. They are shit scared of me and any encounter at the camel market sees them running to their cars and driving away at breakneck speed. Both have taken to carrying their ancient shotguns, beside them on their front seats, on a full-time basis. Mauritania is full of Mohamad Baba's and Mohamad Leomine's. As you will see, climate change will radically alter their lives in the not too distant future, perhaps then when the Atlantic Ocean's lapping at their door, they'll not be too smarmy, as although in Mauritanian terms they have money, in the scheme of things in the big world, they don't have too much of anything to offer. Without their slaves, they'd be hard pressed to look after themselves. They have little to contribute, no skills to use in a modern setting, no future as I see it.

As this problem begins to arise with the Bidan scum, Ethnayne succumbs to an infection, after having caught his nose ring in an Acacia tree and spent the night hooked up with two huge thorns in the top right-hand side of his head. It took a feat of superhuman agility to placate a frightened camel and a full fifteen minutes to get him out, as his head and therefore nose just out of my reach. My head, face and arms were covered in cuts from the thorns. Having managed to secure a cord around his mouth, I cut his nose ring and then had one very large Acacia thorn to pull out and a nose ring to replace. Problems when they arrive, never arrive singly do they?

## CHAPTER EIGHT

# 'HOME, HOME ON THE RANGE . . .'

I NEVER DID understand that song, because there aren't any antelope on the Great American Plain. Any American I've asked, doesn't know of any native species, though now there is a breeder in North America who has 200 Dama gazelle . . . "Don't bring them here sir they'll only get shot!"

As Ethnayne's infection grew worse I had to consult a vet. I knew there was one at Carrefour Madrid at the far end of Toujinine. I left the two at camp and with Mwoiny in tow we took off on the five hour journey, starting out at 03.00. It would be five hours if I could get a taxi, as with Mwoiny it wasn't always possible. In fact most of the time we travelled on top of the baggage at the back of 4x4's. This day I was spotted by a former employer who had arrived at the market to sell stock and he took me to the vets in the back of his 4x4. I bought all I needed to after talking with the vet and was driven back to the start of the piste. I got back at 13.30 and then had to go and find Ethnayne, which I did about an hour later. Getting him back; with his lordship in tow, I secured him to a tree, hobbled him and tied his head down using a cord looped over his neck and under his front legs. I had done thousands of intramuscular, subcutaneous and intravenous injections in my career as a nurse, but this would be the first time I'd give a 180kg animal an 18ml shot and I would be alone. Just to be on the safe side I tied up his lordship.

I went into the khaima and prepared the injection, no mediswab of course, and a clean wet cloth would have to suffice. I had disposable syringes and needles and all in all, it would be five times cheaper for ten times more antibiotic than it would it be for me. This country mystifies me at times. This bottle of oxytetracycline; and I would later discover from published research would be no longer effective in treating camels, was made for tropical climes and needed no fridge. Unbeknown to me, this would be a futile exercise, a waste of time, effort and money, almost cost me my life and would ultimately cost Ethnayne his. It remains the standard treatment for animal diseases here, despite the research. 'These Mauritanians are crazy!' I paraphrase Obelix all the time here, touching my right temple and making the 'toc toc' sound. I have two places to choose from to inject into, the first is near to the base of his neck and being a kindly soul I injected into his left flank. "You thought I was going to say ass! I'm going to clean my act up." He had no idea what was about to befall him and naturally enough he didn't like it one bit. Neither did his lordship and I would have to keep an eye on him just in case he became a little spiteful. This would have to be repeated five days later and now he would be forewarned.

I had to refuse work this same week as I simply couldn't leave him not knowing when I'd get back. The boss went off and it would be the last offer of work at my camp sa berger I'd get. In town, I'd get the occasional phone call asking me to take herds, still do. My last offer was the 18th June 2008 from Abderachman, whose eldest son Mohammad actually came to the school three days later to plead his father's case for him. Anyway, Dombo can't cook and she's mad! I was teaching and couldn't just get up and leave. I'm going to take a few days off from writing this journal of a mad man and spend it with the family. I will sleep out in the dunes with my secret supply of food and will eat well at night. In fact, the time I was there I went back into the capital on the fourth day to buy a supply of multivitamins for a malnourished patient her cooking was so bad. Abderachman says he will never find a husband for her!

I settled down to my usual routine of daily walks and kept an eye on Ethnayne everyday, cutting and draining the large abscess on his head when necessary. At times it was the size of my fist. My own scratches from rescuing my camel had been infected too and I treated them simply with saline washes and raw iodine. Stings a bit. The fifth day duly arrived and I brought him back to the same sturdy tree and proceeded to secure him in place. He knew what was about to come next and he wasn't as helpful this time. I caught Wahad and tied him to a tree further away this time. He had become very protective of his mate as knew he was sick and that I was about to inject him again. I prepared the injection and made my way out into the early morning sun. On seeing me Ethnayne began to try and pull away from the tree. I went to go to the other flank and he moved his left leg and I started to move backwards and WHAM! The flat of his foot hit me square in the chest and threw me 2-3 metres onto my back. I felt a pain in the side of my left leg about10 cm above my ankle but couldn't investigate the wound. I thought my chest had been caved in and I couldn't breath. Mwoiny was giving Ethnayne a mouthful. I had no feeling anywhere and I could see that I was still holding onto the syringe and let it drop behind my head. I saw it fall in slow motion as I fought for a breath, thinking this possibly is the last thing I shall see. I couldn't breathe, my lungs were bursting as if I had been wiped out and couldn't surface the ocean as it dragged me along the seabed. There was a surge and rush of noise in my ears and the pain registered at the same time in my chest and leg. I began gasping little gasps of air, though none too deeply at first. I checked my ribs fearing the worst. All were intact as the first painful surge of deep breath entered my lungs. It burned like hell and with my chest heaving I rolled over onto my side then my knees, then the pain in my leg came hit a new high. I fell back down gasping like a man with pleurisy. I looked down to see a 20cm piece sliver of tourja sticking out from my trousers pointing towards my groin. I went to pull it and thought "No fuckin' way Hosez!" as the burning pain overtook my chest as I continued to gasp for air like a drowning man. As soon as I could talk, it was "Fuck, bastard, cunt, whore . . ." all in French for some reason but not in anger at Ethnayne but at my luck to be still alive and being stupid enough to be kicked and of course to release the stress of my pains. Thank God I was traveling back at the time or I think I would have been dead.

I got back to my khaima and cut my trouser leg vertically from below the sliver of tourja. Tourja, the wood that makes such hot and fine charcoal that allows just three glasses of tea. The truth behind the tea ceremony I suppose in times long past, though modern Mauritanians deny this of course, even when they smile the stupid smile they won't admit it. Even if I went industrial I'd never be able to burn it all, it is scattered throughout the desert and Sahelien regions. Tourja the wood that cooks your bread. Fuckin' tourja that could just have hit an artery and imminently your life-force will spurt out into the desert sand. My head was spinning as I gathered my first aid kit. A combat dressing, clamps, Dettol in a bowl of water, suture material and washed my hands, the easy way given my present state was to pour from the bowl all over the tapis. At least it wasn't piss I laughed. Mwoiny had her nose pressed right up to the demarcation line, she didn't look happy either and outside Ethnayne complaining remained securely tied. I started to laugh, again at my misfortune, shivering despite the heat. Shock of course, what if it had been my ass! Sorry flank. I couldn't stop shaking and I was sweating, far too much The pain in my chest was searing and the pain in my leg hot. It wasn't even 08.30 and probably around 34-36°C and I was experiencing high temperature sweats you'd expect on exertion at 40 and above. I had an emergency pharmacy with antib's and pain killers. These I grabbed first and swallowed with as small an amount of water as was possible. 'Okay, I had dithered enough, to work.' Everything ready I slowly pulled the sliver of wood out. 5 cm now that's impressive. No fuckin' wonder I was sweating like a stuck pig. And from my leg I was not, repeat not, expecting an ooze. The relief was immense and I soon had it cleaned, stinging like crazy and as it didn't need sutures as the puncture wound presented as a cut. I simply used micropore to fashion the same. A firm dressing in place and a virgin crepe bandage to finish. My breathing had considerably improved and I slowly and purposefully cleared up. I took two paracetamol and rested for about half an hour or so and then went to finish the job, with Ethnayne kicking out again. But this time, the injection went into his neck. He and Wahad scarpered with Mwoiny chasing their flanks and I crawled off into my khaima to die in peace. Such is the life of a berger. "Think camels . . . think mousetrap. A bit like . . . clunk click, every trip. Never forget, think camels . . . think mousetrap! You have been warned even if you think they are Walt Disney and cute, sir!"

All seemed to go well and he ate and ate and regained his strength over the two months. Wahad had taken off on one of his jaunts and Ethnayne and I went here and there, off visiting friends along La Route L'Espoir, where at least 12 families had come to stay after their bosses had dispensed with their services. For the Bidan it would simply be a matter of economics. The boss would save on salaries, diesel in taking water and supplies out and a berger was a much cheaper proposition. The families would live at the roadside sending their goats out on a train in the morning to return in the evening, their nomadic life at an end. The upshot is that the grasses are very poor for 8-10 km either side of the road and therefore the milk and meat production is down. The nomad is sedentary and now wants all his cousin has in the capital, only he has no money to buy it. Where there was no want or desire, there is now envy and greed. For three weeks all was well until I noticed the infection coming back.

My holiday over, I returned to camp and began with the antibiotic again, as well as emptying the abscess when necessary. Then one day, a berger arrived with Wahad. I greeted him and he knew me but not I him. It was the brand he knew and of my reputation. Over tea he explained why he had referred to Wahad as a bandit. He lived some 30km from me at this point and has two khaimas, his mother and sister in one and his wife and child in the other. They had seen Wahad hanging around but as you do you don't really take notice of passing camels in your camp. Wahad had waited until his wife had gone to the other khaima, after taking lunch on a large serving dish, and bread made earlier into hers. He then went into the khaima and helped himself to everything including 5L of milk. When his wife arrived she began to beat his flank and he then ripped the khaima in two as he sought to escape. She grabbed and roped him, formidable woman, and tied his flank to a tree. As soon as Mohamad arrived she asked whose camel it was and to return his fat flank to him the next day. We then burst out laughing and I began looking for money to repay for the damaged khaima. Mohamad refused the money saying it wasn't necessary as his wife had repaired the khaima and I gave him one of the two watches that my brother-in-law Henry had given me as for gifts on my return to Mauritania. Mohamad sampled my Scottish cooking and stayed the night and left the next day. Wahad I set free the next morning before Mohamad left. He went in the opposite direction from Mohamad. I think he knew he had overstepped the boundary or at least didn't want to tackle wifey again. I later met his wife and I wouldn't either. Bergers are lean men and his wife much taller and shall I say, broader in the flank than Mohamad. He wouldn't stand a chance if she let rip!

I then began another few weeks of nursing Ethnayne and its now that Wahad disappears from sight and sound of my life. I perservere with the treatment and again he seems to pick up but his character had changed. He's grumpy and though not unresponsive, reminds me sharply of Wahad's behavior in the early days of our relationship. Every now and again a familiar sounding 4x4 passes on its way for a well some 40 km to supply the family staying there. I know the driver Sidna, and I run out to wave him down from the edge of the ridge. He changes direction and drives to meet me. I asked if he would buy me 100kg of wheat and gave him the money, which he said he would deliver in less than a week. I was out at the time and he dropped them off at the khaima and left the change in between the two sacks. This was to build up Ethnayne as he had lost so much weight. As he slowly put the kilos back on his change in temperament stayed noticeable different. After a month or so of not riding him and his daily bowl morning and night plus the 20kg of fodder he'd find for himself I decided to try him out with his saddle again and see how he'd handle.

There was the usual moaning and groaning as I got into the saddle. He rose and walked off in the direction I had set him on. His change of direction at first tolerated and after a half hour I dismounted and walked him for an hour, then mounted to return to camp. All seemed to be going well and I didn't gallop him, all was nice and relaxed until he bolted. Straight for a huge fuckin' Acacia. He would not respond to my baton, would not reign in and would move neither left or right and even when I smacked him hard across the face, he carried straight on, Mwoiny barking her head off. If you had done this to my animal, I would drop you and beat you within an inch of your life. But this was my life here in the balance. He kept going and I decided that I would have to dismount as is. There would no choice as to where or as to how I would land. I let go of his cord and exited stage right, Mwoiny at rear left. I hit the ground and tried to roll but hit a clump of grass that sent me off like a rag doll and I hit others and was stopped by one, as Ethnayne chargeded at the tree. A searing pain in my right thigh registered. I looked down to see a small fatherless son of a twig of six large thorns, one of which was sticking in my trousers, like a small caltrop. I look up as I pull it out to see Ethnayne thrashing my saddle up into the tree, branches, thorns and twigs raining down on him as he is determined to lose the saddle one way or another. 'He doesn't like it.' I thought, as I sat back and watched him until he tired. I threw my shattered baton at Mwoiny who's giving Ethnayne a mouthful. She scarpers. He doesn't need to be scolded, he's not malicious just ill and I can see now that perhaps there is only one remedy. There is a major problem to encounter before that part arrives though.

Ethnayne then settles down into the tree, shuffling his big fat flank in towards the underbelly of the tree and a low-lying branch, jamming my saddle and therefore himself in nice and snug tight, absolutely covered in debris. 'Another day in paradise!' was my outspoken comment at this point. His nose cord is wrapped around several branches and twigs and I can see all the water leaking out of my bidon and to make matters worse, my sandals, my very best and much loved Merrells are strapped onto the saddle but on the opposite side to me. My thigh is throbbing a little and I've an ache or two elsewhere and nothing's broken. Life's already better! These thorns are a complete BASTARD to remove. "Yes I said I would, but this is different." They have the hardness of a six inch nail and everyone remembers their first. It also gives everyone the shivers to recount it and many just say, "Yes I do." But for the sake of illustration here goes. There goes that shiver again.

Here in Africa, when you continually walk as the poor and bergers are wont to do, the sun bakes your heels and huge cracks appear and you can see a red line of raw tissue inside. It's the rule. I have many large vertical scars on both heels. It also reinforces my reply of "No car and no money!" to ardent beggars and show them my feet. There's a nod of recognition and I'm left alone. It's okay to have these large fissures, and the discomfort of hot sand washing in and out of them is just part of life. Because the atmosphere's dry they don't become infected. You simply have to put up with it because everyday you walk the desert which is covered in fuckin' sand. On the middle aspect of my right heel there was a fissure and it was here that I took my first Acacia thorn, a little shudder, size large and BLOODY sore. You bite your tongue and swear in French, "Bastard, fuck, cunt, whore, SHIT!" There's heat and a shiver like a dog shaking itself that takes over. Calm restored you kneel down and pull it out. The pain is excruciating! "BASTARD, FUCK, CUNT, WHORE, SHIIIT!!!!" This sensation brings tears to your eyes. Thankfully this happens only once or twice because you have been surprised and learn to accept the pain over and over and over again. You become immune as it were and simply swear inside your head, pull it out and keep going. "Oh, by the way, it doesn't matter if it's small, if that's what you're hoping for. It's still going to be painful!" I have taken five in one day!

The Zulu King Shaka, had his battalions of male and female warriors stamp huge clumps of thorns (I forget the name, but resembles a caltrop so that one spike is always pointing upwards) flat on his parade grounds. Anyone who called out was immediately killed. "Fuck that for a game of sodjers!" Like his warriors I didn't wear sandals during the cold season, no matter if it were dune or hard piste covered in sea-shells. The dried ancient mud is a little like walking on razors at points but is generally okay. Your feet adapt to what's underneath them and you mould your foot to the uncomfortable element that you walk over. "Don't know if I'd do the hot coals thing. I'm mad, not crazy mad!" So one in the thigh barely demands a swear word. Camels strip whole twigs of them and munch away very contentedly for hours. Mwoiny if she were unable to pull it out herself, would simply hold up her paw and wait for me to pull it out, without a whimper. 'I wonder if she swears?' Then there are the millions of caltrops that emerge with a certain type of grass that arrives after the rains. My first contact with these microscopic bastards, "well they are," was with a 500m swathe of them. These tiny balls containing dozens of spines cling onto everything and are very painful. I always go around if I can as you get more infections with these than you do with Acacia thorns. The fine spine; a strand of hair at 6/1000 of an inch thick would seem like a small nail in comparison, lodges deep and even surgically removing them is impossible if you don't get them out right away because you can't see them. You wait for the pustule to arrive and burst it to have it fall out with the pus! Very pleasant if you're eating and reading at this point, as I am wont to do when eating breakfast!

So, we're back with Ethnayne lodged under the tree and covered in debris. I need my Merrell's but that ain't gonna happen, not until I extract my mad camel but I need my sandals to do this without taking thorn which are every-fuckin-where. I also have no idea as to their current status either. I need a baton. I have an Opinel No8 in a pouch around my neck and I go off to find an Acacia with visible tap roots on the desert floor. I eventually cut myself a substantial 1m debous (baton) and strip its bark and make a hole to take the cord, which I retrieve from my last baton. This baton will crack your skull if I hit you with it. The other much finer was for control not for a forlorn hope which this is now. I'll need to dislodge and break the branches of the Acacia which are generally more brittle than the debous filled with sap. I take careful note of Ethnayne's position and see that he is firmly locked in. He has no intention of coming back out. I can see numerous cracks on the wings of the saddle, I don't use the fancy leather covering that is used here as the spars make it easy to attach equipment to. The major problem is his nose cord, wrapped as it is around thorns and twigs and branches. The other problem is that the ground underneath and near the tree is littered with thorns. I begin to clear them as best as I can but cannot in all honesty cater for what lies underneath the sand. I had left my kukri at the khaima which would have been handy. You cannot dwell on what you may have done just on what you have at that moment in time. Note to any would be travellers: carry the best knife you can afford. It may just save your life one day. Fuck what the UK authorities say, they're not there to give a helping hand when you most need them. If you don't use it fine and well. But one day you too might just have a mad camel trapped under a tree.

Mwoiny has retreated to the comfort and safety of nearby shade and has no further part to play. 'Ain't life grand for some!' My momentary smile disappears and I move in and ouch, take one out and unwind the cord as best as I can without moving, ouch, too much and ouch, a scratch here and OUCH, an intrusion there, as I finally free it, ouch, and move in, ouch to change it over to his mouth, ouch. He's not, aaahh—that's my cheek and it's gone right fuckin' through, I can feel the tip of the cunt with my tongue, helping by turning his, ouch, head away and OUCH, I leave the next thorn in my foot and that one too. I grab his nose ring, unattach and then re-attach to his mouth, with Ethnayne trying to bite me and wriggling back into the tree and I'm fearing the worst for my Merrells. I need something to fixate about as my feet, hands, arms and face are, ouch, throbbing like mad, blood is trickling out it seems, from everywhere. I no longer know if it's sweat or blood until I see the red smear on the back of my hand or am I wiping blood from my arm onto my face. I'm giggling of course like a manic character from a fairy tale, as you do. Holding onto the cord I negotiate my way from the Acacia and sit down to remove my new best friends, blowing hard. I look at Ethnayne as I give time for the pain to subside. He has the look of an animal who is at complete odds with his surroundings, completely lost in time and place.

This is the medical definition that determines that a person is confused. Normal for Norfolk is another less kindly English NHS term and describes the lack of intelligence in a person and in a coma. This isn't the case here. This is more. Much more. For Ethnayne it's catastrophic. He's looking straight through me and I have Mousa's lecture on the subject in my head. "OH REALLY!" I shout out, my frustration reaching 75% capacity. My clan motto is GARG'N UAIR DHUISGEAR! (Fierce when roused! And so true.) I had just gotten up and, OUCH, that bastard went right into the underside of my left heel! I'm not at the point of hoisting the battle standard but getting pretty damned close. Note to self as I blow hard pulling the six incher out: In future, attach Merrells to my body with a shoulder strap. I have two rules, never put my hand into dark places and always wear sandals in the vicinity of Acacias . . . what do you really think? This once, you can safely say dickhead. No, neither do I wear my sandals around my body when I mount up. I didn't ever claim I was the perfect berger.

It's bloody hot and I'm exposed to the sun. I cannot wear my turban for obvious reasons or I'd end up being trapped alongside Ethnayne. The sun is beating down on my back and neck. I have no water either, and thankfully only half an hour away from home but the problem is here. As I touch the back of my neck I'm reminded, as I always am, that when a Tuareg realises his time is up and has no chance of survival, he will expose the back of his neck to the full force of the sun and slip away. 'Not today, dearie, too much to do.' Ethnayne is angry, really angry and he has the look that says, "Come near me and I'll fuckin' kill you!" He backs further in until he can move no more, he senses what's about to happen as I grab my debous. I cannot in all honesty break the low branch but if I can take out the smaller one's I believe it will improve the forward momentum of Ethnayne. So in-between ouch, OUCH and FUCKIN'OUCH, I clear what I can, to basically stop him from entangling the cord and saddle back into the tree. He's really mad now and therefore devious. I try to OUCH and ouch coax him out. No way. Brute force is all I have left. I do not want to cut the belly strap, or the restraining cord because I don't want to get kicked or tangled up in the straps and saddle if he takes off. In this situation I don't imagine that I'd survive close quarter combat with a mad 180 kg animal. So I beat his left shoulder; the command to rise, and pull on his cord. It occurs to me that, ouch, he doesn't know his commands any more, and, ouch I beat and drag and ouch until finally he exits the safety of his thorny prison.

With his freedom from the Acacia, he tries to bolt and I stand firm dragging his head down and smack him on the back of his neck until he goes down, through sheer brutality. I grimace as I take another thorn, in my left heel again. 'Is it in the same hole?' I'm sweating like a pig, and I can feel cramp rising in my left calf, and I'm close to burning the tree down in reprisal. I can see that my Merrells are indeed intact and instantly retrieve them. Ethnayne has several thorny problems himself to remove. I use my debous to dislodge those near his rear end, paying very close attention to his legs for any sign of movement. Mwoiny has joined me and I have to drag Ethnayne's flank all the way back up to camp. It's a fight all the way back and it's now I make my decision on his future and the welfare of my life. It's nearly an hour before we get back and I tie him to a tree. I tend my many wounds. I don't get my mirror out but make an iodine solution and wash my body where it hurts. Imagine if you will ladies, that your dearest five year old daughter has gotten into your make-up bag and has applied what she will where she will despite the presence of a mirror. That's how ridiculous I looked. My two-piece African combo in tatters to add to the comic touch. My feet are left to look after themselves for the moment. I drink 1L of zreig and retrieve my kukri. I reapply sun cream, turban up and grab my debous. I have another riding crop I could choose to use but now it's my life we're talking about here. With the saddle still in place I take him 5 km to the north. The wild dogs and vultures can have his bones. I can't let nomads eat him as I can't be responsible for the deaths of anyone else.

The journey there, was as trying as the journey back from the Acacia but with Mwoiny in tow he was less inclined and visibly tired this time to fight back too violently. She kept him occupied by chasing around his rear legs, snapping and barking at him when he played up. I picked a spot in some small dunes and led him into a small bowl. One entrance and therefore one exit. I spoke to him and told him what I was about to do, that it was for the best. I released him from his prison in a quick and efficient manner, my kukri driven directly into his heart. I waited until he had died before taking my tack and walked back with Mwoiny in tow. I hoped she wouldn't come back and would be dissuaded by the wild dogs which was the reason I chose where I did. Also that the vultures would see him highlighted against the sand, not that they needed any help. Subsequently, Mwoiny kept good health and I can only presume she didn't return.

I drift back to two other occasions when it has been necessary to take the lives of two camels and two occasions when I was present at the natural deaths of two elder statesmen. The unnatural deaths were, in the case of the first again, a camel with a systemic infection and extremely weak. I now knew that even with antib's he'd never make it and to prolonging his life was cruel. The owner agreed with my assessment when I later gave the news by phone. There was never a problem. The second, was due to an accident out in dunes. The sound of the breaking right ulna and radius (fused) of an otherwise healthy female was horrendous. Although far away, it sounded like a stick broken next to my ear. She too, was dispatched and left for the dogs and vultures. Her son was five years old, so no problem other than loss of his mother. The owner although upset at the lost future revenue, knew I had no other choice. Of the two elder statesmen I came across at different times, the process was dignified and calm. Not that the taking of the others lives wasn't. On both occasions I sat with their heads on my lap and spoke to them in English for the time they had left of their lives. The herds waited around and when both had died were nuzzled by two or three to confirm death, and the herds then moved off. A process filled with calm and dignity. Although I had no professional connection with the herds I believed it was my responsibility as a berger to be their for the end of their life. No tears, no regrets, nothing more than a simple farewell.

The process by which you slaughter your goats and sheep is also done in a dignified manner with respect for the animal that's about to feed you. The other stock have little awareness of their former cousin/brothers demise. I won't go into the process of describing of butchering the animal, as you soft souls in the civilised world go and collect yours at Tesco's or Gateway's in it's little plastic tray and cling film, with sell by and expiry date firmly attached. They don't look like that in the fields you know! Here you tend and care for, you slaughter, you cook, you eat. What could be simpler? Ah, the sanitized plastic tray version of course!

Believe it or not, but for 15 years I was a vegetarian in the UK. I was angry and uncertain as to what I really was putting in my body. The use of growth hormones, BSE, foot and mouth, steroids and feeding cattle the offal of other cattle! "They are fuckin' herbivores you assholes!" Battery fed chickens and farmed fish, again stuffed with hormones and steroids! Then again, Mauritania is another dark area of meat production but I buy from a butcher I know who doesn't buy from the abattoir at Teinweich but instead, buys from herders who have their animals raised in the desert. I certainly wouldn't eat a sheep or goat raised in town on a diet of household waste! As you know, I used to work out of the same camel market where the abattoir is situated, so I know a thing or two. So will you. In time. The fish I eat comes straight from the ocean at 1700, delivered by pirogue and I can for the moment, buy lots cheaply if I so desire. Not that I need to. Just enough for dinner or lunch and it's so fresh it's just stopped breathing! The crevettes you of course have to boil to kill and make . . .

## CHAPTER NINE

# A STATE OF WAR NOW EXISTS IN MAURITANIA

I T WAS TWO months later, and two job refusals, that I learned that Wahad hadn't gone home to Nema but had been taken by Leomine and was kept and used at his homestead just as Baba had said they would. The other thing was that the two cunts had meantime come and gone from my camp and had said they'd hadn't seen him but that they'd keep an eye out for him. I told them it wasn't necessary as he was free range but MY camel. I didn't need or want their so-called help it would only cost me an arm and a leg. In time, I said I'd pick up another mount and carry on doing what I wanted to do. Leomine always had a slimy grimace plastered across his fat ugly mug and this day I wanted so much to wipe it right off and stuff it down his throat. But I would always be diplomatic and smile the smile of an imbecile. Baba on the other hand it seemed would be trying to read my mind and was too desperate to please. He would use my association with El Mamy as a way of being pally, as if that association held any sway with me. Yet another arsehole who wanted as much from my association as he could possibly get. All the time asking about tourists, why couldn't I bring them out to see him at the homestead?

Money. The Bidan and the African love to talk about money endlessly. 50 000 or so Africans traverse the Sahara going north every year. They are way laid by drivers, soldiers, police and bandits and stripped of everything. The Mauritanians endlessly talk about sources from which to extract money, as if it grew on trees. Contacts to make money, when they didn't have any in the first place to begin a commercial enterprise, with the person or persons they were seeking to begin commerce. Numerous ideas on how to make more money from the first non-existent commercial enterprise that they've tried to empty your pockets into. See the pattern by which the Bidan lives by? It's fuckin' exhausting! Everything revolves around making money. Yours and everyone else's he can get his grubby little paws on, either by fair means or foul. Usually the latter. Perhaps it should be fowl, because another aspect of the Bidan character is that he has a fat yellow stripe down his back, ever fearful that you'll discover the truth behind his public intentions and apparent good manners and his fear is palpable. His reaction when discovered for what he truly is, is violent. As I have said, I have Bidan friends who are gentlemen and that makes them unique here. All have lived and been educated outside of Mauritania and have an eye and a regard for the world. Some have European wives. Some with American wives. The Bidan community of several hundred who live in Kentucky U.S.A. in the main I am told, work Illegally and for low wages. There are two who don't, who work hard, who live the American Life with Buds and Bar-be-ques. But the vermin in my story have no such associations with manners, good taste or an education grounded on other than banditry, and that hardly qualifies because it's genetic. Leomine and Baba are Bidan scum from the ground downwards. I'd rather have a sand viper or a scorpion as an associate.

So, for two months Wahad had left in the morning with the herd and returned at night, led by his mouth and carrying the berger's saddle, bidon and sac el badiya. He would be fed and watered every day. He was firmly entrenched by his appetite. So even if he did wander, he'd know where there was an abundant supply of food and water and go back. This information came from a former berger of El Mamy who had dispensed with this services two year previously. He had no respect when he worked for him and as he'd not paid out in full had every reason not to hold back information on him. I would meet through Mohamad, whose khaima Wahad had visited for lunch, at the camel market, when I had gone shopping for the day. The question of feeding would raise its ugly head later in court. Mwoiny and I took off a week later for the homestead at Teinweich Two, arriving at 0500 and laid up at the end of the piste, its exit point into the desert beyond, to watch the herd leave and go for the day's 30km stroll. The berger passed within 10m of us with Wahad loaded up and was being dragged along. At least he was making the berger work.

'Good man!' I thought it'll be a long 30! I let them pass and when they disappeared from sight we left cover and took a walk to find his house, by following the tracks of the camels. It's not rocket science. En-route I passed a limbur and was hailed. Nothing unusual there, I'm a stranger and often called in for tea and TV. It wasn't until I got nearer that I realised that it was Mohamad. Did I know where the house was?

"No, but I'd follow Wahad's tracks."

He of course didn't know if Leomine was in but assumed that now the herd had left he would have too. I said that I'd take a walk and see. I'd leave Mwoiny there, as she'd be a dead giveaway, he said I would too. He went inside and as I was saying good morning to his wife, who laughed when she realised who it was, Mohamad returned with his boubou and a piece of black cloth. He handed them to me to put them on. He said I'd now pass for a Bidan.

"It's the African combo," he said, "He'd know it was you straight away."

The piece of black cloth wasn't clean or particularly nice to smell but he was right, I'd stick out like a sore thumb. I'd have to wait for the return of the herd and go from there. I wandered in the tracks of the herd and immediately spotted Wahad's prints. Each camel has a distinctive print on the underside of his feet, something like a simple kanji. I have them too, on my both of my biceps.

My tattoos have caused me some grief in mosques and I was even grabbed once at my school's mosque and well not manhandled, because the stupid bastard landed on his face milliseconds afterwards, with my professor at the madrasa taking the culprit outside and giving him a mouthful as well as a slap. He then returned to give all the students a lecture and said I was free to beat them up should I encounter any more abuse. He'd stand by and watch, that the attitude of a minority of students was disgraceful. He didn't give me into trouble for my part in the fracas but he wasn't pleased either. I'd be forgiven this once. It happened not long after in a mosque in the capital and again at a roadside mosque. Every time I go to the mosque now, I wear long sleeves.

The established berger of a herd will know all of the camels footprints. It matters little if its twenty or two hundred. I know some, the head male and the elder females and babies of herds I've worked with. Loads of babies because I've tracked a few in my time. My speciality if you like. When I go back out for a stroll over the weekend I always look to see if I know them. I know some of those of Leomine's. One day they'll be seen in the minefield en-route for Laayoune, Inshallah. Here, for those of you interested enough, you can Google Earth the scumbag's homestead. N18° 04.784' W15° 49.263' It is located some 4km from the Poste Police Sortie Nouakchott, La Route L'Espoir. It would be here later that I would have to register before going into bandit territory. I knew the officer here from bringing stock into the market which is only two kilometres away. He would never dissuade me from going but clearly wasn't pleased at the prospect. But the onus here in Mauritania is on you to bring the culprit to justice. Not the police. It is up to you to deliver the warrants for court. This is where the bandit plays with the system, because he knows if he has numbers, force and intimidation on his side he will win every time. That was what Leomine thought he could use because he has no other options or imagination and the other options he has are too far away in the process that has to be played out, a recipe if you like. Negotiation. When it goes wrong, then there's the sick man plan. That too is expected and given serious consideration. You'd think they'd be a bit more imaginative being the bandits they are! It's a bit like the recipe for a Tom and Jerry cartoon now that I think on it. I'm trying to be enthusiastic on their behalf here, sorry, I just can't seem to find any, it ain't gonna work because this is no finesse attached here to any situation that the Bidan contrives to cheat, steal and connive. He truly believes at the end of the day that he has done a good and full day's work. Very sad. I could dream up dozens of scenarios, very complicated and cause utter confusion! Not them, no fuckin' chance! Violence after theft, and when it all goes wrong, "I'm sick, I'm old!" I have the line from a well known Sting song which runs in my head when confronted by Bidan scum such as these, "A gentleman walks, he never runs."

The next to last plan is using his 4x4 to run you over. The very last ditch plan is paying for a Haratin to cut your throat!

I wandered around the homestead and couldn't see either of the cars but the womenfolk and the Haratin were there, five Bidan women and two Haratin women. No dogs. That's good. A few children. I wandered back to Mohamad's limbur and waited the day out there. I was then given the nod around 1700 to look out over the piste, the herd coming back. I said that I would go after he had passed and wouldn't say anything of my association with him so as not to make life difficult for him. The only reason he had gone to live there was because it was cheap accommodation, that of the available two dozen houses or so, a third had occupants and only a quarter of them inhabited full time. And it was near the camel market. He would later have to leave as his association to me was known and Leomine made it uncomfortable for him and his family to remain. He moved some 60 km down the road onto another piste in a tiny village where he was welcomed and is respected by his neighbours. Some good at least came from this rancid episode in our lives.

I left Mwoiny there and took a detour to cut ahead of the herd and arrived to the surprise of Baba who was attending to his car. He was very nervous when he asked me what I was there for. I told him that I was there for Wahad. The 4x4 of Leomine arrived and he got out at the run shouting at Baba in Hassaniya and pointing at the herd a little way off.

"What do you want?" He screamed.

I told him I was here for my camel.

"He's not here!" Leomine said.

There was a heated discussion between Leomine and Baba as the herd arrived. I smiled and said, "Who's this then, the king of Scotland?" I added, "Do you think I'm blind as well as stupid?"

He starts screaming, "Fuck off or I'll get the police!"

It's the first thing out of their stupid fat mouths every time. Without fail. I'm here for my animal and he's going to have me arrested. Told you they are stupid. Without fail, every, fuckin', time! "All the time you told me you hadn't seen him and he's been here!" I said.

"You owe me for two months food and water!" He screams.

"Ah, so he's been here for two months!" I smiled and nodded my head as the realization dawned on him that he'd opened his fat stupid mouth without thinking.

"I've been looking after him, you owe me!"

He was livid and fast losing it. Baba was looking for a hole to swallow him up. More Hassaniya.

"You stole him and I'll have him back." I said.

The two then got really angry and came towards me, I moved towards them, after slipping out of my sandals. They froze and Leomine starts screaming. I look behind as the Bidan women I had seen earlier began to file out, with knives, an iron bar and a hammer.

"Ah," I said, "This would be reminiscent of the 'Great Battle' they had fought against the Black Mauritanians in 1989," when mobs rioted in the streets killing hundreds, the army led by the present President Aziz; then a Colonel, chased some 265 000 or so Black Mauritanians into Senegal and Mali. In two nights, 1500 Black Mauritanian officers and other ranks were tortured and executed. Their deaths barbaric. Men having their throats slit as they prayed, buried up to their necks and horses rode over their heads, steadily beaten to death with clubs, everything really except the most humane, death by bullet.

Baba and Leomine then stepped in behind the women. I laughed at this and everyone went mental, screaming and waving their assorted weaponry. I had already chosen who was going down in order of age as opposed to weapons, which never needs to be a concern, unless there's a pistol involved. The berger decided not to join in but hovered, he was terrified. I stood my ground, no fear no attempt to move for real until they did. The woman and the men continued screaming at me and I, phased out, I suppose you'd say, a calmness came over me and I took my phone out and dialed 17, the police emergency number. The disbelief was enough to make everyone step back from the metre and make it two, then three as they pushed back into the two men and pushed them even further away, weapons held out at full stretch, pointing at me. The wife shouted at me, "What are you doing?"

I knelt down and calmly said, "I'm phoning the police."

There was an outburst of talking, laughter and shock.

She shouted, "They'll not come, no-one will come here, everyone's scared to!"

I looked at her, straight into her eyes, "I'm not." I said calmly.

This stopped everyone ranting and raving. They eventually walked away and left me to it. The berger then brought Wahad to the house and he was tied up there. I was still kneeling when the light began to fade, still phoning. They had retreated to their house but every now and again, they'd come out to have a look. The berger posted at the door. Engaged or no answer. I put my sandals on, collected my turban and went for Mwoiny. At my departure a hail of shells and stones came my way, with all the women and Baba participating, the ladies with their weapons in hand. I picked up two large stones and threw one at Leomine's wife to hit her in the chest and the other bounced off Baba's shoulder. They stopped and ran inside. Round one to me I believe, as no-one went to hospital. I'd be back with the police.

I collected Mwoiny and made my way back to my khaima. In the moonlight I could see tyre tracks that I'd heard from a 4x4 earlier as I approached my piste. The tracks had come from the west and departed south west. Leomine I expect out to finish me off. On the way back, I was careful to keep to low and move in difficult terrain, and not taking a direct route so as to make pursuit difficult. The 4x4 had circled the khaima at 20m and there were no footprints. I made food, dug up my rifle case and slept out 300m from the khaima. For the next two days I did the same, until I left for town to rendezvous with the Keystone Cops at Commissariat de Police Toujinine Deux. Fun and games ahead. Why bother folks? Why chase after Wahad when I had set him free? There's a very simple principle here at stake. One of honour, dignity and respect, enshrined in the Talmud, the Bible and the Qu'ran. Where there is none, there is chaos. The principles of chaos theory reigns supreme here in R.I.M. I try to keep myself apart from the maelstrom by maintaining my own strict rules of principle that I have learned and honed throughout my life, although I am not perfect as you well know. The Bidan has no such yardstick to measure his by, as he firmly believes that his world is perfect and that nothing he does wrong is unpardonable. Robin Hood was a bandit with principles. If he were a Bidan, he'd rob from everyone including his own men and fuck all their girlfriends and wives too! Maid Marion would no doubt be selling mehlafahs; the shops here commonly known as a front for private brothels, servicing most of the clients herself including the Sheriff of Nottingham. This is the case in the vast majority of mehlafah boutiques, which are open right up until 0300. No-one comes into my life and steals from me and remains a friend let alone a well-known sack of shit. If I let him, the flood gates will open and my life would be full of confrontation.

I mentioned that it was the Keystone Cops at CdPTD that I was to contact. This was the first major hurdle to encounter. On finding it next to impossible to get a taxi, we walked to Toujinine. I asked where the Commissariat was. Which one, there are two? I had no idea and was directed to One. It\s a bloody long walk, it's hot, smelly and dirty, piles of rubbish everywhere. Mwoiny doesn't like town the myriad of smells confuses her and she wants to investigate everything, I keep her on a very tight leash. We arrive and I'm waved away because of Mwoiny. I shout at the officer that we're bergers and you can come out and talk here. I'm here to register a complaint about theft and violence from the Ould Sba family at Teinweich Deux. If the senior officer doesn't take my complaint, then I'll come back with the Representative of the British Consulate. He shits himself and disappears. He re-appears and indicates where I should tie her up. I tell him there's no shade and remain squatted against the wall opposite the station. He shouts back into the station and the Bidan officer in charge comes out having lost the rag, with KC 1. He waves me over. He then directs me to a spot where she can be safely left in peace.

I then go inside and sit down. I then hand over my passport and my details entered into the book, as other people wander in and out, giving their tale of woe, which he then directs left right and centre, answers the telephone, comes and goes and this process takes thirty minutes. I then leave and go and check Mwoiny, if you remember you have to move every half hour to keep shaded as the sun travels above. She's fine and I return to find a family embedded in the office and I have to squat on the floor, where he continues to question me from and the family crowded around the one chair simultaneously. The family then have the opportunity to listen in to my tale of woe. It strikes me that they might know Leomine, might even be family. I mention this, and the officer tells me to get out or continue I of course continue. He to and fro-ing from story to story. He abruptly stops the male representative from speaking as if tired by the family and throws them out of the station. They protest but to no avail. Out they go with KC 1 & 2. I at least get the chair back. He tells me they're bandits. I ask him if they are family of Ould Sba at Teinweich Deux.

"Teinweich Deux?" He asks.

I told him that I had said this at the beginning of the proceedings. He hands me back my passport and says "Commissariat de Police Toujinine Deux. Bon journee."

I ask where and get the direction as if in the desert. I leave. CdPTU is for the right hand side of La Route L'Espoir going towards Mali and CdPTD, the left hand side. No tells you this and everyone has their own opinion of where you need to go. The same happens when asking for directions. Even if they don't know they will send you off believing they do know. 'These Mauritanians are crazy!' Toc toc.

It takes another hour and a half to find the station, this even when I mistakenly ask two officers who send me in the wrong direction. It's now 13.30; I left my khaima at 0500, and it's hot, smelly and there's a dust storm. Turbaned up, I arrive at CdPTD and find a spot for Mwoiny as everyone's inside sheltering from the storm. She hunkers down and goes to sleep. There is anywhere she can't or won't sleep, except in the full glare of the sun of course. That would be simply stupid of course. I go inside and am confronted by one Bidan officer and four KC's all watching TV. There's a younger man in a boubou making tea and two others in boubou's sitting on the stairs opposite playing with their mobile phones. As it turned out the others were off-duty KC's. The phones are new. I give them the standard greeting and hand over my passport and give my story. He listens and then hands me back my passport.

"02, your passport has expired, get out of Mauritania."

He is deadly serious. I open my passport and show him that 02 is February and that it expires in 2016.

"We have plenty time to talk and drink tea, shall I begin again?" I say as I had over my passport. He is none too happy. I add, "I can come back with the Representative of the British Consulate if you think it would be necessary?"

He bawls and shouts at the off-duty KC's to clear off and dreams up work for the other KC's to perform. He has the sergeant switch off the TV and takes me to his office.

This station, like the other, is filthy, half painted walls, with the paint peeling off, with broken and missing brickwork, the front doors won't close and it basically resembles a war ravaged building. There's rubbish on the floor, numbers scrawled on the wall at the counter at the entrance and a single 2x4 m cell. Finishing just isn't important to Mauritanian society, even if the house is new, mis-matched tiles in your bathroom and floor, a percentage of which will have been broken and simply plastered in, paint on the tiled floors and blobs of cement left lying to harden on the same paint covered tiles. Quality just isn't regarded as important here. So a battle fatigued police station hardly raises an eyebrow. In the UK, you'd find addicts in the same conditions, shooting up! I neglect to make this point given that he doesn't want to deal with me. It would later transpire, via the corporal, Boubacar, I'd deal with on two occasions, that this KC officer was family to Leomine, a cousin.

"Now there's a fuckin' surprise!"

I patiently wait for the sergeant to bring the register from the same counter that the officer had been resting on, when flicking through my passport. He puts it down and opens it on the day's page and gives him his biro. It's black and he wants . . . . blue! It's apparently blue today, but yesterday he had or someone had used black and blue pens. I also noticed red pen to underline some Arabic script. The same colours funnily enough I'd love to paint this bastard's face, using the wall! The sergeant comes back and says he can't find one. There's silence and the officer shrugs his shoulders and goes to close the book. I smile and take out 1000UM and ask the sergeant to buy one blue pen, one red pen (now, he'll have all three colours available) lots of tea, sugar and mint, and 1L of camels milk, as I believe it's going to be a very long day. He then leaves after being given permission to do so by the officer. I then excuse myself, saying that I have to check on my second berger. "The responsibility of rank." I tell him smiling and check on her ladyship who's in the land of nod but ear poised, scanning, ready for action. I go back inside and we sit in silence as he hasn't yet asked me to speak, reminding me of the adage constantly told to me by Irene; my mother, when I was a child, "Children should be seen and not heard."

She'd like this man. Perhaps I could introduce one to the other and . . . the sergeant reappears to stop my conversation with myself. He gives the officer his new shiny pens which he immediately tries out, in the official register by scribbling on the front page, 'Obviously closed cases.' I thought.

I'm reminded of the curt treatment given to the family of bandits at CdPTU earlier. I have my Consular Britannique card to play though and would play it more than a few times before I would end my association with the Keystone Cops of Commissariat de Police Toujinine Deux. He looks at me as I open my first carton of milk and begin to drink, looking at the other as if I were to hand it over. I shake my head and wave my finger and say, "It's for the second berger, she drinks camel milk too, won't touch Rose."

Rose is UHT and she won't, which is unusual for a thief who will steal everything edible. She has some standards at least. I knew this would irk him and I add smiling, "Tea's on the way, sir."

He grimaces rather than smiles his acceptance of my gift as he knows the sergeant has used up all my money and bought a shitload of tea.

'Give me a fuckin' break pal!'

After he enters my details, he asks for my story. I tell him and am constantly interrupted by irrelevant questions and asked to repeat my self constantly. He of course isn't listening. This, as I've already mentioned, is a Mauritanian thang and he's a fuckin' expert! Has the lieutenant's shoulder bars to prove it. You are asked the same fuckin' question and ten seconds after are just as bored as they were originally. I repeat my tale from beginning to end four fuckin' times. On the last third repetition I hold up my hand and keep going until I finish. The last repetition I ignore everything he says and I speak slowly and deliberately. He then calls in the sergeant who then has to take down my statement in French as the top KC present, can't read or write French. He then begins to ask irrelevant questions and I calmly say, "Copy down what I say and ask the officer afterwards, as he has been told the story four times now."

The tea's shit by the way, really shit, very strong and very sugary. I drink only one glass. It's the rule. I can refuse after the first. It's now 16.20. We've been constantly interrupted by visitors or complainants, which thankfully he had others deal with, the KC's had lunch but not me or he simply got up and walked out in mid-speech of either him or me. I ask when the translation will be ready as it needs to be in Arabic to make it official.

"Inshallah three or four days."

"Give it to me, I know a translator at Marche Capital, I'll be back soon."

He looks at the officer who squints at me. I add, "It's my intention to go there right now after here, give him the same statement, have it written in Arabic, talk with the Consulate and come back tonight." I return two hours later after dropping Mwoiny off at the Sahara, then with my statement in Arabic, witnessed by Mohammad as the person responsible for the translation (because he tells me that the KC's won't tell me until I return that I need it witnessed) and it's then stamped, given a number and officially entered into the book and . . . underlined with the new shiny red pen.

'Aren't I a clever boy?'

"How long before the warrant's ready?" I ask.

It's now Boubacar who's dealing with me, and has all the pens now, the others long gone and no doubt exhausted by their exertions in dealing with me. He tells me to come back tomorrow at 0900.

"To go and get the bandit?" I ask.

He smiles and says, "Inshallah."

It's back at the Sahara that night, when I'm alone with Sidi Mohamad that he tells me I should have phoned 19 when asking for help from the KC's.

"Why?" I ask.

"Same difference, nobody will answer, ever!" He says.

So the next day at exactly 0900 I arrive at CdPTD and we leave at 1100. We commandeer a taxi, after four attempts and the driver's bitching about having to go to the Poste de Police. He doesn't want to have to pay baksheesh and not take a fare, a double whammy. Boubacar agrees he can drop us off just before and take off, which he duly does. I say hello to my friend the officer at the Poste and Boubacar and I walk the 4km to the homestead. We'd be seen over the last 2km and forewarn Leomine. His 4x4 is there and we're greeted by his wife.

"He's not here, he has gone into Nouakchott." She says.

I add, "He wouldn't go for a piss without his 4x4!"

Boubacar directs me to the Haratin's khaima and adjacent storeroom and he goes to check the house and adjacent limbur. I arrive at the khaima as the storeroom's empty. The woman there is smiling and with her four children gathered around her. There's a huge pile of material in the corner. I can see it's moving. I pick up a discarded baton and poke the pile and he surfaces and I shout out, "He's here Madame, he hasn't gone to Nouakchott!"

Out slithers Leomine, humbled by my discovery because he knows I haven't arrived alone. He storms out into the waiting Boubacar. He begins speaking in Hassaniya, I add, "French, speak French!"

He is complaining that he doesn't have the time and that he's got a hospital appointment.

"You can go afterwards." Boubacar tells him.

We go to his 4x4 and I'm directed by Boubacar into the back seat, which Leomine won't allow. I simply get up in the open bed as I often have to do with Mwoiny and is no hardship, saves me breathing the same air as the sack of shit.

We duly arrive at CdPTD, whereupon Leomine launched into an attack on me in Hassaniya, I add, "French, speak French."

He ignores me and I immediately ask for a translation which Boubacar gives me. He's demanding that I pay for fodder and water for two months, that I'm a thief because I won't pay it! I simply say that it is for the court to decide and anyhow, if he hadn't stolen my camel, we wouldn't be here now. Boubacar is enjoying the moment. The officer isn't obviously, because this is an elder of his tribe and obligated to help him, despite his banditry. The cousin takes Leomine's statement and they are in the office a long time. Eventually, the two exit very pally and give each other a very long, serious and warm parting goodbye. I can see that Leomine thinks he has me, hung, drawn and quartered.

"Pride comes before a fall, bandit!" I say as he leaves and he instantly moves to strike me. I make no move as Boubacar quickly steps in his way and sends him off. He then smiles at me, shaking his head and I shrug my shoulders. I then follow the officer into the office and ask him when I should return.

"Three or four days. The Commissar has to make a decision." He tells me.

I tell him, "I'll be back with my lawyer then, to register here that I will instigate a civil suit should the Commissar decide there's no case to answer for." I leave adding, "You have my number, phone me when there's a decision."

It's as I leave that Boubacar tells me of the family connection between the officer and Leomine. He's surprised that I have gotten as far as I have in the time I've been making my case.

"This might normally take two weeks or months." He says.

He's impressed. I have been speaking with Sidi Mohamad, who told me the same.

"Bluff them out and put pressure on them, they expect you to give up having obstacles put in your way at every turn."

Now they know Scottish stubbornness and they don't like it up 'em!

I go to the auberge, tend to Mwoiny, shower and eat. I was on the terrace with friend en passage for Mali and Mwoiny of course loving the attention from two pretty French girls as was I, when Khalifa arrived to say that there was a delegation outside for me, that they wanted to talk. I stood up joint in hand and looked out to see El Mamy and three others. My phone rings, it's El Mamy.

"Just give him the camel, you can buy another!" He said.

"If the old bastard wants a new camel, then let him buy one." I replied and cut him off.

He waved for me to come down and talk. I sat down and told Khalifa that I wasn't here. He then went out and talked to them. My phone rang again and I switched it off. They waited for two hours before going off.

They arrived the next morning at 1000 and asked to speak to me. Again I wasn't here I told Bilal (day security) and he went off to tell them so. After another hour or so the drove off. At 2000 they arrived again and my phone rang. I answered and spoke to El Mamy's boss a hybrid Bidan/

Moroccan bandit. I said that it was none of their concern and to go away. I cut my phone, to hear El Mamy call me. I stood up and told Khalifa to take Mwoiny out to them to talk to, she'd enjoy baiting them too. She doesn't like El Mamy and he's scared of her. Khalifa and I have the same sense of humour, he's a 30 year old Malian gentleman berger, who speaks seven languages. He wanders out, you can tell they like each other, he talks to her in Bambara and she listens, the five Bidan quickly disappear into the car and drive off. I can hear Khalifa laughing. He takes Mwoiny for a walk to make sure they're not stopping further up the road and comes back. This also is expected. Just let them have whatever it is that they've stolen, they're your friends, it' okay. They're not my friends and it isn't okay. The phone calls persisted and I blocked their numbers. End of story.

My phone rings at 0900 on Monday morning and I'm told to come and collect my second warrant but there's a catch, I'm to deliver it alone to have it signed. I take Mwoiny and my kukri, wrapped up in its cotton cover and hang it across my shoulder, hidden under my baggy African shirt. My mobile phone is put into a small bag and also slung around my neck, the photocopy of my passport is then put into my top pocket along with some money and 3 shiny new pens. We arrive at CdPTD and the Black Maure Commissar is there to meet me. He reminds me that I need to get him to sign or proceedings won't go ahead. I show him my shiny new pens;

"What colour sir?" I ask him.

"Your choice sir." he tells me.

Before I take off I ask him for his number which he gives me, surprisingly enough. En route I have the warrent photocopied, six times. I eventually get a taxi which drops us short and I go to report in at the Poste de Police. The officer isn't pleased but sees that Mwoiny is with me and this calms him after he finds out that there isn't another dog there. He likes her. I leave the photocopies in his charge and leave for the homestead.

As I approach I can see three 4x4's and Baba's 205. As I arrive there's a reception committee (no doubt forewarned by their cousin) of four men, five women, a scrum of children and Mohamed, Leomine's 13 year old grandson at the forefront. He alone comes forward to greet me warmly, as the men and women hurl abuse at me telling me to fuck off. I'm about 10m from the crowd and there are no weapons on show. They think force of numbers will suffice. I tell Mohamed that I have a warrant his grandfather needs to sign. He tells me he is his father. I then give him his orders.

"Tell everyone that I have the Commissar's phone number at CdPTD because," and I take out my kukri, "That he will personally phone the all ambulances necessary to come and collect all the body parts because he knows I have come with Mwoiny and this." Waving it for everyone to see I add, "You can also tell them that Mwoiny has been trained to hold or to attack and kill. It makes no difference whether it's an African wild dog, rabbit or Bidan."

As he turns away I shout out, "Also, I have a dozen photocopies at the PdP and can return day after day if necessary."

The abuse continues from afar and Mwoiny simply lies down in my shadow, watching everyone as the dance back and forward. She never was one to exert useless energy. I imagined her to be laughing at this point, coming from the attitude of her head moving from side to side occasionally and looking up at me. Mohamed re-appears without my pen but it's signed. He now knows when and where he's to appear. I tell Mohamed that it's a major surprise that Leomine can even write his name and that he can stick the pen up his ass and play with it all day as I am sure he is wont to do.

Mwoiny and I leave for the Poste de Police, accompanied by the 4x4's of his son-in-laws, who are driving around me like circling Apaches. I show them my kukri and pick up a large stone which turns out to be a meteorite, I grab another two and putting my kukri point down in the sand give them a small display of juggling, I'm no expert but it gives me some amusement and they now know I have missiles that I am prepared to throw. Anyone who walks onto their piste and confronts them isn't scared of breaking a window or head or two. Two stones in my left hand, my kukri in my mouth and one stone in my right hand which I toss and catch as I walk. They give up as I near the Poste de Police and drive back to their den. I immediately drop everything and re-sheath my kukri. I report in and make for CdPTD and hand in my signed warrant. The officer is surprised at my quick return and I wait until he signs the book, along with his not so new and shiny pens. Hopefully I won't need him or his pens. Oh how wrong can one man constantly be? Here in The Empire of The Sands it's so fuckin' easy as to be able to have an honours degree in it, without having to get out of bed! A student's dream eh?

The day finally arrives for the start of the showdown with Monsieur Le President de Le Tribunal de Toujinine. I arrive and present my paperwork to the junior secretary, with a scrum of people in his office and I'm made to recount my tale of woe, which is translated by a man in the scrum. I'm asked every two minutes if I speak Hassaniya and I keep repeating my self to the point of shouting my reply. Not a good idea but I persist with the smile of an imbecile and firmly and politely say "No!"

He then gives it to the senior secretary, with another scrum of people in tow and again I'm made to present my tale of woe, again with a translation from a man in the scrum. I'm acutely aware that there's no Leomine. Eventually I get to speak with the President in his big office. He too has a scrum in his office and it's while I'm being translated by yet another man, that a woman comes in with her baby strapped to her back and sits down. She then proceeds to demand charity giving him a long and detailed story of her life. I am standing like a lemon, because he's told me to give her my chair, and it goes on and on. He finally ignores her and turns to talk to a man to his left and she leaves. He then asks me to repeat myself, again translated by the same man in the first office. He then tells me through this man that I have to bring him Leomine here in person or the case will not proceed.

This is Toujinine and I surmise that this too may be a family member that I'm dealing with. The tribe of Ely Ould Val from which El Mamy and Ould Sba spawn from, hold sway from Teinweich One to K'sar (Luk'saar). This one region in my opinion, holds more scum than anywhere else on the planet per square metre. K'sar is dangerous for me, as is Toujinine as a result of my prosecution of the Ould Sba's and by association the El Mamy's. Toujinine is also the place you will find most of the Bidan drug dealers of Nouakchott who live and operate there, ably assisted by the KC's. Teinweich Two is okay as long as I keep my wits about me and by-pass the village by going around it into the desert. The camel market is across the road where I have the protection of Ol Loli and my past bosses who come from different tribes, who will have no truck with these lower forms of life. Taking their money is one thing, helping them out is quite another. Since the Al Qaeda attacks started there have been two Guarde Nationale in place at the market and has not silenced my critics but it makes it very difficult for them to bait me.

I immediately phone the Commissar and tell him that the President of the Tribunal has said for me to bring Leomine in, single-handed, I am of course being translated, and that should I ask the President for a warrant for his arrest? He asks to speak to the President, who's shitting himself. He listens and talks and hands back the phone. I am to arrive at 0900 and will be accompanied by an officer to have Leomine brought to the Tribunal. I asked if it were not simpler to have the Lieutenant phone his cousin and have him come in without being arrested. I am trying to show that I bear no malice in the court room, which is basically an office with a huge desk and eight chairs arranged in two rows at four at right angles to the desk.

"No we'd do it officially." He said. I smiled at the President and left.

The next morning the Commissar is there bright and early with Boubacar who has the third warrant and a side arm. 'Serious stuff.' I thought and we commandeered a taxi once more to be dropped off short, reported in and walked the 4km. Leomine was standing with his wife and began pleading. Boubacar has him sign the warrant and motions to move to the 4x4. This time Boubacar opens the back door to strong protests from Leomine and he's told to shut up and drive. Leomine tries to engage him in conversation but Boubacar won't speak. We drive in silence to the Tribunal and Leomine's escorted directly to the President's office. He interrupts the proceedings and hands over the warrant and retires to the back of the room. Leomine immediately erupts into Hassaniya, they know one another I thought, and then everyone looks at me waiting for my reply. I recognise that it's the compensation thing for board and lodgings for Wahad.

"I don't understand." I said.

Boubacar steps forward but is waved back by the President. A man translates and confirms my suspicions.

"If you hadn't stolen my camel we would not be here now." I said.

This is translated for the President and Leomine, who goes ballistic and seems to be supported by the President, funnily enough. I'm then told to find a translator and Leomine gets up to leave.

"It's not necessary for you to leave Leomine, I know a Gendarme next door I'll be back shortly."

That stuns them! I then spoke to my last translator that Leomine can speak French. He denies this of course but later slips up when his temper gets the better of him and bursts into a stream of French. I had met this sergeant I knew, whose father' camels I had once looked after, on the previous day's foray into the den of justice. He told me that the President and Leomine are cousins. The Gendarmerie is next door and off I went to find him. He instantly agreed and came with me and would do on each successive visit to the Tribunal. This particular meeting is only to get to the next layer of Justice to determine if there's a case to answer and involves the Procureur de La Republique in Nouakchott.

With Ahmed's help I get to go to the next layer of frustration and Boubacar and I are taken there in Leomine's 4x4. He's fuming as his plans to stall and circumvent the proceedings go awry. Leomine tries again to get chatty and he's told not to discuss the case and drive. He really doesn't like him one little bit. I've now got a fan club of two as Ahmed doesn't like him either and knows of his sleazy reputation. He's only too eager to help. The game starts with going through three secretaries and eventually onto the Procureur de La Republique. This process takes an hour and a half and the building is jammed packed with people and there are dozens of offices and without Boubacar's help we'd have been there all day. He simply keeps going until he finds the office's necessary by butting in everywhere. We're up and down and Leomine's flagging fast and Boubacar has no sympathy, when he claims he's ill. Finally into the office of the Procureur. He listens to me as the complainant and when Leomine starts in Hassaniya he tells him French. He says he has no French and Boubacar tells him this is not so. So without listening to his side of the story he immediately grants me my hearing, signs the paperwork and wishes me luck. So not impartial then or just submerged in so much of this shit he's gotten hardened to it. I don't care, I'm on my way to having my day in court at last. We return to the Tribunal and hand over the paperwork to the President. He's speaks with Leomine in Hassaniya and I don't ask what's being said until that is we get outside. The President had assured Leomine that everything would be alright and that he wasn't to worry this was why he had looked so smarmy talking with everyone as he left. He didn't probably know any of them, he was on a high and thought he ruled the roost. I'd give him his two minutes of fame.

The proceedings started off the next morning with me being asked to give the court my statement. I said that he had my statement and that it was in the file, written in French. Ahmed was livid but kept his cool as he translated. The President tells me that it is the police statement and he needs my statement for the Tribunal. I simply said that I would return tomorrow with my statement in Arabic. Short meeting and off I went to see my translator.

We drafted exactly what was written in the police statement, I signed it and it was witnessed by Mohamad. I arrived the next morning and presented my statement. He read it over and said that it was incomplete that I had to present my case in full, my demands, my proof of ownership etc. I simply stood up and asked for a piece of paper for both myself and Leomine. You must also understand that there are two other cases being heard at the same time which adds to the confusion and anger on my part! I asked Leomine to draw his brand and the ten that Wahad had on him. I drew Leomine's then the ten Wahad carried, circling my own.

"I have photographs if you like." I told the President.

Leomine scribbled away like a lost child totally confused. The old bastard had no idea. I signed my piece of paper and had it witnessed by Ahmed, who then witnessed Leomine's, making him sign it too, smirking as he does. He's also wearing his dress uniform everyday in court, which adds weight to his presence. No this would not be sufficient but could anyone collaborate the ownership? Yes, plenty of people. I told him I could virtually empty the camel market and bring everyone here, about forty people at a rough guess. As well as their children and wives if he wanted. Then there was the bosses that I worked for, I drew their brands and he passed them onto Leomine, who went pale. Ahmed said that his father would be delighted to come and speak up for me. I asked without waiting to be told to speak "Are there any of your tribe who'd like to dragged in here Leomine? Perhaps the brother of Ely Ould Val?"

Silence and open mouths followed my question. He told his cousin that he knew about this connection and he would only be too pleased to testify for me. Ahmed translated this as was said. The two men looked at each other and knew that they had been rumbled. It finally came to pass that just names and phone numbers would do. Leomine was flagging fast. There would be an adjournment for three days and proceedings to begin on Monday morning at 0900.

I left there and went directly to the camel market by taxi and gathered two dozen names and phone numbers, left for a cyber café printed out the list and gave them to Mohamad, who then wrote up my statement and my list of witnesses who had added the ususal formal Arabic greeting to the court and end the statement in very elaborate and ancient legal form. He said it only occurred to him after I had left and hoped what I had asked for would do.

"Leave it with me and come for it on Sunday afternoon." He added.

This I did and returned with a tagine for lunch. It was a fantastic document and he took no money from me for it. I of course use him for any translation and direct everybody who needs a translator to him.

Monday morning and Leomine hasn't arrived and we've waited an hour already. I begin to phone the Commissar and I'm asked who I'm phoning.

"No," he tells me, "I'll see to it that he's here tomorrow."

On the way out, Ahmed and I say goodbye to a junior clerk and say we'll see him tomorrow.

"Why?" He asks.

"Proceedings." I reply.

"The President's not here for three days then it's the weekend." He replies.

We turn tail and go back into the office without knocking on the door and everyone's having a jolly time, cousin's on the phone, so they're not their for legal purposes and I'm simply TV again. I ask him directly and calmly.

"Why didn't you tell me that you wouldn't be here for the next three days and exactly where is it that you're going, because I'd like to make a formal complaint, that an officer of the court has lied to me and I have a witness to the fact?"

He's shell shocked. He can't speak and I carry on.

"If that's Leomine you were speaking to, you'd better tell him to be here as soon as possible or I'll have you both dragged up in front of the Procureur on a civil suit. I know you're both cousins!"

He asks me to wait outside and I sit down. Ahmed stands beside me. I stare directly into cousin's eyes and he swivels his chair around to use his phone, Ahmed can't hear and he obviously can't move from his present position. He finishes, swivels round and asks the others to wait outside.

I add, "It isn't necessary because it's common practice here, is for everyone and anyone to come and go, listen in and give their 20 ougiyas worth of opinion even when they have no knowledge of the circumstances that brought me here." I carried on, "Your system of justice is a farce and I will go directly to the British Consulate today and give them a statement and also write a piece for the BBC on the Internet. If necessary, I will sit outside your office everyday until justice is served. If my money runs out, I'll beg charity from people in the street, I'll sit in here dirty, disheveled, smelling like a dustbin!" Ahmed calmly translated. There was silence in the room. Everyone present looked at cousin, whose mouth had gone very dry all of a sudden. He licked his lips and said that he could postpone his journey and we'd resume tomorrow.

"Will it be necessary for me to have him arrested by the police again?" I asked.

"No," He said, "I'll have my clerk phone him."

I added very quickly, "You'll not do it yourself then?"

He simply shook his head. I got up and left, no more said. Ahmed took me next door to the Gendarmerie for tea and debrief, he was on a high and thoroughly enjoyed the moment as much as I had. He asked if I was serious about telling the BBC. I said that I'd tell the world about Mauritania, its corruption, it's unjust justice system. He couldn't stop talking or laughing, translating for the other Gendarmes. I don't think he's had a better day in his life! I can honestly say that it was very special for me too. I managed to speak to a judge openly and honestly, as warrants speaking to the sack of shit that he actually is!

I realised that my taking on a senior member of the legal system could probably get me investigated and set up with a kilo of coke or guns or both, imprisoned for a long time and red flagged. Or simply run over or shot. This is Mauritania. The reason I titled the book, Rien Impossible en Mauritanie was that one day after returning from a frustrating meeting with Bidan, I stared at the registration number on the car in front . . . 2367 ABOO and R.I.M. and the national flag beside it (Republique Islamique de Mauritanie) and it arrived . . . you can simply do anything here you have a mind to . . . except deal with the Bidan on a level playing field because he is fuckin' impossible!

The next day with everyone in place and for the next two hours it went like this. Leomine kept demanding that he deserved compensation of 60 000UM for looking after Wahad. I replied that if he hadn't stolen him that he wouldn't have to have looked after him and that hell would freeze over before 1UM would leave my pocket for him, that I did not ever and would not ever reward a thief. He exploded into French and he ranted and raved that I lived alone and that the desert was a dangerous place. His cousin calmed him down and then asked what the problem was about compensation exactly. I replied that his cousin had suddenly found his French after losing it for so long, that he was a thief who was relying on his cousin in the court; indicating to the President, to get him out of the dark place that Leomine's greed, ego and stupidity had put him. Leomine was up on his feet and his progress towards me fists clenched, cut off by Ahmed who reminded him that he was a Gendarme, pulling on his uniform shirt and would arrest him if he tried to assault me again and that he couldn't be paid off like the Surete. Leomine's cousin asked him to sit down. I then countered with my own compensation claim for use of my camel, costs incurred at the auberge, translation costs, taxi fares, lost work etc. It amounted to 1 000 000UM ! It was a girlie scream of monumental proportions that came out of his mouth. He was on the verge of virtual collapse, clutching his chest as if was having a heart attack. Oh how I truly wished he would at this moment have one. He rambled on in Hassaniya for ages. The thread of which was, that I was a thief trying to steal money from a hard working old man, who'd never done anything bad in his life, that he was ill and needed hospital treatment. Except, I added that he had stolen my camel, which his cousin had now agreed was mine and was witnessed in front of others as such. Leomine went ballistic and Ahmed stood to warn him from moving off of his chair. Leomine sat back down. So back and forward we went. He demanded and I demanded. I knew it was never going to materialise and I added that I'd use the tribal system to broadcast to his family the bandit he was and publicise also, the shame he had brought down on them.

I was given my camel back by his cousin and Leomine was told to deliver him to the market the next day. The question of compensation would have to be dealt with in either the tribal system or in court. Leomine would later exact his own claim in the desert and I, well, I wait to exact mine, now that I have definite proof of his theft of my encampment.

The next day would see me and Mwoiny go out to the piste and take possession of a weakened Wahad from the homestead of Leomine. I surmised that Leomine hadn't been fed Wahad throughout the time of my discovery of him. He was in tears, Leomine not Wahad as I walked away. As we left to walk the 4km, Leomine drove around us intimidating me with his 4x4 and he was unable to negotiate all the little dunes that we walked over. I got to the Poste de Police and said my goodbyes and made off for the market 2km away. Leomine charged up one way and drove back down straight at me, again the small dunes by the road side made it difficult for him and as soon as he drove past again on the opposite side I crossed over and did so all the way to the market. Wahad hates crossing roads. Mwoiny never took her eyes off the road for one minute. I went into the market by the back route and went straight to the limbur of Ol Loli who had been phoned and told of my arrival. We went straight to the abattoir, there Leomine was ranting and raving, surrounded by a few die hards. Ol Loli was dismayed to see Wahad in such poor health and vented his anger on Leomine whose friends suddenly abandoned him. He spat at the ground in front of him and never again spoke to him. Leomine then fucked off in his 4x4. Ol Loli told me that Leomine would now want me dead, that his loss of face was immense and my death would be the only way to redeem it. I told him of my short journey here from his piste.

"So, it's begun already." He said. The price from the abattoir is poor for Wahad but he's in such a physically depressed state. The men there say that they'll attend to him later and that I can go. I shake my head.

"If you don't kill him now I'll do it for you." I tell them.

They laugh. But neither do I or Ol Loli join in. Ol Loli tells them to get on with it. They take him into the slaughter arena and quickly and without fuss end his life. Leomine I would later hear, said that it was unforgivable to kill his camel, that I was a criminal. For once, I've nothing to say.

So, eventually we come to the finish line in this marathon with the Mauritanian legal sysytem, as I began to pursue the tribal system of compensation against the advice of Sidi Mohamed. I was directed to the first sub-chief, who knowing who I was refused to begin the dance. I sat outside his office for five successive days, 0800 hrs to 2000 hrs watching for him to arrive, which he did at 1900 hrs on day five. I walked directly into his office complex and introduced myself in the midst of a small soiree. He shit himself, he promised everything I asked him to do, knowing that he had no intention at all of doing anything. This process could have taken years before I eventually got to the top, through six layers of sub-chiefs and thousands of hours of negotiations and tea drinking. No, I'm a stubborn cunt and woe betide you if you fuck with me. I'll cut you bad. That's a promise.

## CHAPTER TEN

# THERE'S AN ICY WIND THAT BLOWS IN THE SAHARA

I T SNOWED ONCE in the Sahara, in Southern Algeria on the 18th February 1979. The storm lasted a half hour and the snow was gone a few hours later. I made my way back to my khaima after eating with Ol Loli and discussing my immediate problem. He'll relay any information he'll get at the market, to me by sms, which I can receive easily enough even when it seems, I have no signal! That's bloody Mattel for you! The walk back is done at night, so that I can pass unseen and see any 4x4's easily enough. None arrive from any direction and it's good to be home. I'm on alert as never before and decide upon my last ruse before setting out for the CdPTD of setting up my bed to look as if I'm there and sleeping out, with my rifle up to 200m from the khaima. For the next two weeks I have no contact with anyone and have settled down into my usual routine of walking my 15-30 km everyday, without my rifle, my judgment is that he'll prefer to do anything by night. Oh how wrong I'd be!

This day, I'm about 8km from the khaima and I come across some archeology previously hidden by sand. This happens all the time. You can walk over the same piece of desert day after day, month after month, year after year and never know what's beneath your feet. I met a berger of goats who lives at Teeavee. I like it there, it's pretty and the nomad are friendly. Around his neck is a piece of string with a grenade pin attached. I motioned at my own neck and nodded at him. He then told that he'd found a grenade out in the desert and had no idea what it was. He had carried it around all day and when he got back to his khaima at night he decided to investigate. He mimed exactly what he did; his wife screaming with laughter throughout, no words just mimed. He put the grenade to his ear and shook it. He then shakes his head. He's now looking for a way to get inside it. He then hits it off a stone mortar. He really gives the huge stone a good seeing to . . . . he squeezes . . . the safety lever and . . . pulls out the safety pin . . . and lets the lever fly off . . . he puts it to his ear and doesn't like the sound of the delay fuse cooking off so he throws it away . . . he kills several goats (his wife screams out laughing: "Okid yesser el ham!" "We ate lots of goat meat") who are beside the khaima and takes three pieces of shrapnel on his face and neck. These he proudly points out and displays them, smiling like an imbecile. He says there are others and then draws out on the in exact scale, 81 and 120 mm mortar rounds. I wave my finger and tell him not to touch, not to beat like the grenade. I ask his wife for red material which comes in the form of red wool. I indicate that it should be larger. I make a flag with his baton and another small piece of material and stick it near, not beside the mortars and then draw a grenade in the sand, putting my own baton beside it. I then ask him to phone the Gendarmerie. He nods and smiles that stupid smile that tells me absolutely nothing. There are mines too in the northeast. The locals know where they are, I doubt the military does and the government certainly doesn't give a fuck.

So, back to the day in question, I had found a necklace of tiny white stone rings, scattered over a 10m² area. It's about 14.00 and hot, bloody hot, not 50 but damned close. My bidon has about a little less than 1L and Mwoiny's stationed as always at my back getting shelter from the sun. Little parasite. She's then up on her feet giving me the signal that a 4x4 is on its way as I can't yet hear it. I grab my GPS and drop the handful of beads into my bag. I don't like anyone to see either of these. As it gets nearer, I see that it's Leomine. I've about 500m of piste to run and he's already started to accelerate as he's seen me and I take off my sandals and run like the wind. He's driving like a man possessed and on reaching sand I use trees, small dunes and bushes to make life difficult for him. Difficult for him! I'm running uphill underneath the baking hot sun! I've still got my bidon and sleeping bag carrier and ducking quickly behind the shade of a bush I take off my turban and tie it around my waist. I then guzzle water and ditch it along with my sandals. He's getting close to the edge of the rise and my fear is that he'll get out at some point and use his ancient single barreled shotgun. I have very little choice here and I need to keep going and weave this way, using the desert to help me, it's also going to kill me if I can't find a solution, either that or Leomine will.

As I run, Mwoiny's doing her best to get in-between him and me, barking her head off. I'm cutting back and forward as he tries to manoeuvre into position but the terrain is working for me more than it is for him, but I'm drenched in sweat and you of course realise that I can't keep going indefinitely. I duck in behind bushes, like Mwoiny when we're out. She'll run ahead to shade and wait for me to arrive because the sand's hot underfoot for her. I cut back towards and away from him, making it hard for him to get a line on me. He's being thrashed by his driving and the desert, the arsehole isn't wearing his seatbelt. They never fuckin' do!

I'm reminded of an accident at Carrefour Nouadibou Deux when a top of the range Merc saloon, hit the roundabout at speed. It did a Hollywood five roll spectacular, coming to rest some 100m from point of impact, resting on its chassis. The wheels splayed outwards and its engine block, 20m ahead. Inside were two men and a toddler. The toddler had been standing in between the seats. I could see the five impact points of her little head inside the car. The adults too had impact points on their side windows, roof and windscreen. Of course you couldn't see where they had clashed heads. All the airbags had deployed everyone dead of course. They never ever use them. They put their trust solely in Allah. Imbeciles. I asked someone one day, "Doesn't it occur to you that Allah gave you the intelligence to protect yourself. Why are they there in the car in the first place?" He had no answer, other than smile the smile of an imbecile. I know of another imbecile; it's not difficult in a country full of them, this particular specimen lives at the camel market who says that Allah will protect him against HIV/AIDS. He has a penchant for African whores and will not use a condom. No-one will shake his hand, eat or drink tea with him. His face is wrapped up in his turban and he sits excluded in company. "Allah will protect me." He said to me and held out his hand. I took it and told him, "No he won't, you're a dead man walking!" No one laughed.

I am too busy watching this particular imbecile in his 4x4 and I suddenly sprawl full length my bag flying, as I trip up over a clump of grass. The clump of grass has cut my lower right shin. He's getting a line on me and Mwoiny moves to intercept him and he gives her a cursory swipe but she's too small and quick for him to see. I get up and move to the right and move directly towards another bush and an adjacent small dune as he cuts round behind, hitting the uneven terrain hard and bouncing his 4x4 rather than driving it. Mwoiny's still barking her head off, chasing his ass, sorry flank as I cut back towards him and can see that anger has taken over all of his senses. He's jolted again and his head hits off the side window and he screams in anger, thrashing the steering wheel with one hand. He's being constantly jostled and thrashed by his driving and the desert and I continue to run circles around him, smiling and laughing, which he can see. He doesn't like it and it makes him angrier. I eventually find my bag, as I'm running I'm searching and it's about 80-90m away, a black lump on the desert floor. It has my kukri and it's time to attack. I don't want him to think I'm going for it so by running here, stopping and running there to hide behind a bush, I eventually get back to and grab it at the run. I open the drawstring and wrestle the kukri out, stopping just short of a huge Acacia that had suddenly appeared in my way. I know this tree; I've cut batons from it. I throw the bag into and under it. I'm laughing my head off as I run on, as I hadn't taken any thorns. 'It's a good day to die!'

I give the desert and Mwoiny my call. He's close again and I change direction going for another small dune, a little taller than me and about 15m long, to use its cover to hopefully come around behind him. The sand is far too soft here, but there's no time to rest, there's no time to plan, and the terrain is too complicated. Guerilla tactics only. 'Fine, if I had an RPG or AK, I'd be going home for tea and scones.' I thought, adding, 'These, can be made by using a biscuit tin oven and superb with jasmine tea.' It's amazing the shit that goes through your head when your life's in the balance. I look at my feet, they're a bloody mess. I look around the edge of the dune and see him turn away and go left to manoeuvre to come behind me, I wait gasping for air, my lungs burning, sweat literally running down over me as if I had just stepped out of a shower. I know I haven't many reserves left and I need to make my move. I wait until he straightens up and take off the kukri's cotton cover. I slowly stand up and walk towards him, Mwoiny sees me and runs to me, I bend down and give her a kiss on the forehead and caress the side of her face. "It's time to go. Bon chance cherie."

She is walking beside me, no fear, head up ears alert looking straight at the 4x4, then we jog, he's trying to line up on us and getting jostled this way and that, we start to run and at less than 100m, to go at him full pelt. As we get close in I raise my kukri and intend to throw it at his head straight through the windscreen. The realisation of the moment of his folly arrives and he's pissing and shitting himself to get away. He swerves after hitting a clump of grass and bouncing over another he comes down hard, we are leaping over clumps of grass, getting closer and closer and I think I can still throw it in the side of his head, he moves off right and disappears behind a tree then a large bush and after going forward 50m almost does a 180 accelerating hard, leaving another cloud of black exhaust fumes. His 4x4 is protesting by screaming in pain with more black smoke pouring out of his exhaust. He's working his transmission hard and he's crashing gears in an attempt at getting away as fast as he can. If he grinds to a halt it'll be knife against shotgun I expect. I let Mwoiny continue the chase alone as I can't catch him and fall to my knees. I'm at the point of no return and can only breathe, just. Sweat is running off my nose and making an indentation in the sand. That's bad, very bad. If he comes back . . . I'll go down fighting that's for certain, and one or both of us will die here today. Then I can't hear the 4x4 anymore. I can't hear anything as my ears are ringing, cramp begins to rise in my right calf and I try to get up but exhaustion and the cramp has already taken hold and it's inevitable that I fall onto my face. I'm screaming with anger mostly, at not carrying my rifle but also from the pain in my calf. It'll be the last day I leave my khaima without it. I didn't want to come across like Rambo. 'Fuck him! Rambo's what he'll get!' Mwoiny arrives as I am getting my cramp under control but I'm also shaking from the adrenaline coursing around my body and fluid loss and I still have 8km to walk. She sits down and leans on me. I fall over, she's only little. I give her five minutes as a pet again and take a look at my feet. They're all cut to buggery. It's only now and later that I can visualise all the objects I had run over and were responsible for the state of my feet. I have a large paper cut on my shin caused by a leaf of grass. I've run over hard piste with shells and sand strewn with anti-personnels and had not noticed the difference. I wandered around disorientated as to where my sandals are, my head pounding. It's more by chance that I find them with my bidon and I guzzle the last 100 mls. The bag's easier to find as I know the Acacia. I laugh again as I don't take any thorns, sandals in hand. 'See, my day's already better!'

The walk back is surprisingly quick and I even find the energy to run 500, walk 500, run 500 . . . but as I approach my valley, I'm flagging fast and getting more and more exhausted. It's the bloody walk up the rise onto the ridge that drains my reserves as the sand's softer here, and I can feel my feet sinking in deeper and deeper. I'm still barefooted, my sandals in my bag but I'm carrying my kukri. The sand has a strange medical quality and your feet are never dirty. I can seem my khaima a kilometre away and it seems like ten but eventually I collapse inside and lie like a fish gasping its last on the deck of a boat. I fight the urge to sleep and my leg is about to go off again. I drink endlessly and pour out a large bowl for Mwoiny and push it towards her, it's just inside the khaima and she won't touch it. Hysterics takes over and I push it out for her to drink. She empties it and I pour another and drink more myself crunching a large rock of salt along with it. My head's racing to make a list. Drink, rifle, food, drink, rifle, bed, hide, where do I sleep tonight? My fingers too are locked in an arthritic pose and I force them to open. My intercostals are aching, every muscle is locked it seems and I can't hear a fuckin' thing! I throw Mwoiny some dried sausages, which she gulps down and later throws up to gulp down again. Been there, done that and got the ugly T-shirt.

Dragging my carcass out into the desert I dig up my rifle, load the two mags and set about cooking. The chore is good for my spirits and a determination sets in with a new burst of energy that arrives like a text message. I am like a sand devil, a little tornado of sand that skips around the ridge now and again. I have watched them dance this way and that, thinking they'll pass and WHAM! It slams into the khaima sending everything in all directions! I cook dinner for three without chili, I can add mine later, not the same but I have Mwoiny's health to consider. I make a double helping of potato scones and whilst all is cooking I rig up my bed, to look as if I'm sleeping. It has a large mosquito net surrounding it and will make it more difficult to see inside. They'll think it's me alright; we're not dealing with intelligent life forms here. Bacteria have more sense than these imbeciles. On reflection my feet aren't too bad and I wash them as part of my ablutions for prayer, wincing here and there. My mind raced at what he'd be telling his family, his boasting, no! Probably on how I tried to kill him! Let him come with the KC's and I'd show them the ugly scars on the piste where he'd turned this way and that the clumps of grass he'd dragged out of the desert floor as he negotiated this way and that to run me down. The fuckin' state of my feet and shins would further add to my defence. If he tried again I'd kill him. No mp3 tonight but I'd have a joint to two, yes I know, foolhardy but I needed to celebrate. To make it a little more exciting for Leomine and his family of thugs I'd leave a candle burning in my khaima protected from the wind by its plastic bottle. There was a three quarters moon tonight and it would soon be full, not the time I'd choose but I had already miscalculated what he'd do. So for the indefinite future it was my plan to set up at different hides at no more than 200m from my khaima and wait for the inevitable visit.

It was to be a week later a 4x4 came out at night and stopped about 10m from the khaima; I didn't recognise it but put the cross hairs on the door anyway. If it was him I'd wait until he shot the khaima up and when he exited I'd nail his fuckin' ass. The window didn't open and after a few minutes it went away. A week later, El Mamy came out to see me, alone. I was preparing lunch and he stopped some 20m away and gingerly exited his 4x4. "Salaam aleykum." He said. Mwoiny had already stationed herself between me and the 4x4, about halfway, keeping him at his door. "Fuck off and die!" I replied. He laughed the laugh of a very uncomfortable man, who had no way of knowing if he was going to live or die. "Leomine said that you weren't happy to see him." He squeaked. "He tried to kill me, chased my ass all over the fuckin' desert with his 4x4 for seventeen minutes. Seventeen fuckin' minutes!" I added very quickly, "How long will you last if I now chase your ass with your 4x4?" He instantly shit himself putting both hands out in front as I exited the khaima with my rifle putting a mag in and then putting one in the chamber, cradling it in my arms. "How long arsehole?" I waited for a reply but none was forthcoming adding, "One, two, five minutes?" He started shaking and began muttering, "Look, wait . . . you know he's angry because you took him to the Tribunal . . ." I interrupted, "And that merits trying to kill me, when the Tribunal found him to be guilty of theft, which he was?" He nods. I add, "That's the Bidan way, using your 4x4 to get even?" I see a pigeon in a nearby tree and I shoot it. It falls to the ground and Mwoiny doesn't move, as I've said she doesn't like him and with her recent experience she has no reason to trust any 4x4 in her garden. Though she does now know where there's a snack. I've put the safety back on and put another in the chamber. "Dance." I said. I've always wanted to do this, "Dance or I'll shoot your fat ass . . . it won't kill you but it'll be as sore as hell all the way to the hospital." He smiles and shakes his head and starts to move from foot to foot, trying hard not to whimper. I'm enjoying this too much. I shout out in English, "BEEP BEEP BEEP. I've started so I'll finish." He asks me what I've just said. I translate and he begins to blubber and pisses himself. My face registers no emotion and no pleasure. "If you, your bands of thieves or family (meaning Leomine) come out here again,

I will wage war on you, on your family, on your children. I will come into your homes at night, when you wake up in the morning I'll be sitting in your 4x4; I might even go to Marche Marocaine and buy all I need to make explosives. I have a contact in the Gendarmerie . . ." He stopped dancing. "Did I say to stop dancing?" Motioning with my rifle, he shakes his head and carries on, in his pathetic two step, barely lifting his feet off the sand. "If you or the other scum see me in the street you and they had better keep going, because I will take it as a personal threat against my life if you or they as much as cough in my direction, is that clear?" He nods his head. "Move!" He makes to go into his 4x4, I tutt tutt. "Walk, you need to lose the weight, you're a fat bastard!" He's mortified and I aim directly at his chest. "It's a two stage trigger and I'm already at the second . . ." I tell him. "All I need to do now is sneeze and because 1.8kg of pressure isn't very much it's, WOODANAK MULANAA!" (Bye bye!) He's crying now as he slowly moves away and periodically looks over his shoulder my rifle trained on him. I drop it when he disappears over the edge of the ridge. I wait for ten minutes and we get in the 4x4 and drive down onto the piste. There ahead on the 'road' is El Mamy, I blast the horn at him and drive straight at him, he scrambles to his right and instantly falls over, he's now on his knees as I reverse, his hands clasped together, "Pardon, Mohammad Ibrahim, please, don't kill me, I've family, I've camels." I burst out laughing saying, "And none of them will miss your fat ass!" I drive off and let Mwoiny out, I belt up and thrash the 4x4 on the hard piste, handbrake turns, reversing and doing a 180, accelerating hard and thrashing it every which way I can. I eventually burst a tyre, which ain't hard because he's running on condemned rubber, the vast majority of car owners do. I won't say, drivers, because they buy n'drive. Pay their 100 euros for their licence and get in to their car without any lessons!

I abandon the 4x4 on the piste and carrying my rifle go back to El Mamy, Mwoiny breaking cover. She's never seen me drive before, she looks impressed! I shout out, "Get that piece of shit off my piste as quickly as you can or I'll use it for target practice." I then sit in shade to watch him toil under the hot sun. He changes the tyre and goes inside to find that I've got the keys. He then has to walk the 200m back to me and ask for the keys. He's flagging fast and has abandoned his boubou. I hold them out low, making him bend down. His breath stinks and he's sweating. I tell him low and calmly, "Remember, a state of war now exists between us. If you cross my path again, I WILL kill you." Negotiation isn't possible with a single celled species. They have one function, which encompasses the following disagreeable genetic traits: to steal, to lie, to cheat = success! He runs as best as he can, starts up his 4x4 and drives away as fast as he can, with the customary black cloud of exhaust fumes trailing behind. I look forward to at time when there's no oil left. Then there will only be camels here in the Sahara. It's my dream. I later find out that an oil reserve of about one third of the world's supply has been found in the Empty Quarter! So much for that dream!

There was one moonless night, as I lay up in my hide, when a 4x4 arrived around 2230. Mwoiny was posted, that is, tied with a short cord to a post, dug one metre into the sand. Message received and understood she had done her job by wakening me. It stopped some 10m near the khaima, it wasn't Leomine's, could have been a son-in-law's, could have been perfectly innocent. Nonetheless, I put my crosshairs on the driver's head and waited safety off, the window rolled down and perhaps, 'Salaam aleykum.' Nothing. They waited. I could see there was another in the passenger seat. Perhaps again, 'Salaam aleykum.' Yeah, rest in peace more like. Then the 4x4 started up and took off. And it would be so until I left the pistes. Never again would I welcome night time guests personally and always with my crosshairs on their head.

For the next month all's well and the only visitors I get during the day are potential bosses, whom I cannot work for, as I have no camel. Most, if not all have heard of the state of war that exists between me and the El Mamy's and Ould Sba's. Some apologise on behalf of their fellow countrymen or family. I tell them it isn't necessary, that their concern is to keep good relations with me as I with them. I'm a berger who simply wants to do his job, which I can't do, when I have my animals stolen and my life threatened too. My rifle was on permanent guard duty and anyone who asked has never gotten to touch it. I denied them flat. I decide that I need a holiday and Mwoiny and I take off. I go to Scotland and Mwoiny goes to stay with a friend, and once more she's driven all over Mauritania like a tourist! This fuckin' dog's seen more of Mauritania than I have!

I spend quality time with my sister Lesley and her family and my friends in Scotland. It's also a bad time as my nephew Robert's sentenced to four years. "You're a stupid cunt Robert, shortcuts never work! Never! And as for smuggling a mobile phone into prison from your weekend visits so soon to parole! FOR ONCE I'M SPEECHLESS! I hope you've been enjoying proof reading for me Robert, thank you for your input."

You might say, I've a captive audience there! I put on about 4 kg and loved going out in the rain with Jack a crazy white West Highland Terrier, who doesn't believe he's the size he is. I thought Wahad was a grumpy bastard. I would treat Jack with same gentleness as a camel and he seemed to chill out with me as I gave him no quarter, unlike Lesley who allows him to dominate. It's fair to say that he was abused by a former owner, 'But Jack, that's no reason to be a complete old bastard.' He's named after my sister's godfather, who taught me how to shoot when I was a child. It's his skills that have kept me alive one way or another. Jean, his long suffering wife I love dearly. The Mother Theresa of Scotland is a sobriquet well earned and deserved and I wouldn't know of anyone who knows her in Kilsyth who would disagree with that. I also had an MR2 to scoot about in. Well, I'm doing my best to help use up the oil and have a dream come true!

The journey from Nouakchott to Glasgow takes five days for a little under 5000 km. The cheap route is a Moroccan fruit lorry from Marche Marocaine in Nouakchott to Marche Inzaghi, Agadir. Agadir to Marrakech by Supratours. Marrakech to London via Atlas Blue. The Silver Star coach from Victoria Bus Station to Buchanan Street Bus Station, Glasgow. The driver had to switch on the heating and cooked everyone on the coach. I borrowed a jacket as I became colder and shivered like an epileptic. I had to buy a big warm jacket at a service station and sat wrapped up all the way to Glasgow and throughout my stay, with walking boots, jeans, shirt, T-shirt and sweater, on everywhere. The journey in tickets costs a little over 220 euros and is a holiday in itself, allowing gentle transition from wild to, ahem, cultivated society.

The journey back south in reverse by the exact same route. Losing my European clothes at Marrakech and reverting to African dress, I eventually get back to familiar dusty, smelly deserted Nouakchott. It's not the tourist season so it's virtually empty save a friend on passage with a car to sell in Mali. I waited a day or two to reacclimatise and took off for my khaima. It's the tail end of July and bloody hot, it's early morning and I have 1L of water. There's nothing there. Not a scrap of paper, not a discarded piece of household waste. It's the first time I've seen a struck camp completely devoid of waste. Other than the brush wood walls you'd never know there was any camp there. 'Compensation,' runs through my head. 'I'll cut his fuckin' throat as slow as I possibly can. I'll make him drink his blood drop by drop,' is my thought for the day. We sleep all day under my favorite tree, moving every half hour. The water's soon gone. As soon as night falls we leave the piste. I know exactly who has stolen from me. I will wait my time and seek proof. My rifle that was stored under the 600 kg of food in my store khaima, a metre down, is also gone (I was too predictable here) but I have three components that make it inert and as useful as a club. There are some African friends and an officer at Brigade Mixte on the lookout for it. Brigade Mixte are the untouchables of Mauritania. It comprises of plain clothes Police, Customs and Gendarmes under the direct control of the Procureur de La Republique. Matters little that he has it as I now have another, a 7.62 x 39mm AK47 with 60 rounds buried out in the desert. There's a man I know who will sell me an RPG should I so desire.

It would take seven months for my suspicions to be realised and here I was helped by a former student at my madrasa, who I had persuaded to separate from his association with the group of Salafist sympathisers there, and found in a great many madrasas. The malcontents from my madrasa were later arrested by 100 Gendarmes who arrived at the roadside mosque they were taking prayers at. My professor had kept me away for eight months because of the problem there. The Gendarmerie had one belted .50 cal, mounted on a Chevy on the main door and one belted .50 cal mounted on another Chevy on the side door, as well as every Gendarme carrying an AK. They knew exactly who they were coming for and the four were thrown into the back of a 4x4, the mosque searched, the student houses were also searched and these imbeciles haven't seen the light of day since, until Sidi let them out and The General put them back inside. Two escaped before the arrests to Morocco and the one who came back, lasted three days before being taken.

These Salafists are mainly the youngest sons with no camels, no future and no money to marry their first cousins, to stand by and watch her taken and fucked by another cousin. They feed each other's misery and vent their ill-educated anger against those who would, 'wage war on Islam.' They are simply unable to separate politics and religion. They believe Bin Laden and Saddam to be great warriors, 'It's not them who kill innocents, but the Americans who masquerade as Muslims and use the media to say Muslims kill Muslims.' What can you possibly say in the face of such, shit. The madrasa teaches them nothing except the Qu'ran, it does not prepare them for the world or even life in Mauritania. The madrasa are used to get rid of male children who would otherwise hang around the parental home eating and sleeping their life away. I'll discuss the talibes in the next chapter This is the particularly criminal use of boys to beg money on behalf of the Qu'ranic teachers of some schools, something akin to Fagan's use of orphans in Charles Dicken's Oliver Twist, set in 19th century London. So when these malcontents become soldiers or Guard Nationale, they have direct and easy access to weapons and other Salafists. The country is awash with illegal arms. They are as common as the sand of the Sahara and often buried there!

I returned to the auberge and started to look for work, by advertising through contacts. I had gone out to see Ol Loli, three days and gave him my news. He tried to give me money and I refused it. He hadn't heard anything about my encampment and would keep an eye and an ear open. He told me about the rumours that had surfaced about my supposed attack on Leomine and El Mamy and that I had gone home to France because the police were chasing after me. I recounted the tales of both incidents, admitted that my abuse of El Mamy was true, that Leomine had used his 4x4 to take me out and that I had family in the Scotland not France. Surely anyone could tell that French wasn't my first language! He immediately set about telling everyone in his limbur (eight bosses) that the truth of the matter was that it was the wounded pride over Leomine's admission at the Tribunal de Toujinine of theft from me that had driven him to attack me. Why would I attack a 4x4 on foot except in desperation over extreme exhaustion at being chased down by a madman in the mid-afternoon heat? He said that none here could have done the same for two minutes and would now be lying out in the desert, the sun bleaching their bones! Now my encampment had been stolen and it was assumed that Leomine had done the deed, when he had pursued compensation wrongly, in Ol Loli's and everyone present's estimation. From him I borrowed a camel and saddle, and an ex-officer's pistol from one of the bosses present that I had no choice but to accept, and took off to patrol around my campsite. I found nothing and lost Mwoiny in the process. I returned to the market and would hire a 4x4 three days later as the Harmattan was blowing hard making progress slow and difficult. I returned the pistol to its owner who wanted me to keep it. I asked if I could return to collect it, if need be. I was shown the cabine and the berger responsible for guarding it. He was told to give me access without question at any time of the day or night. If he didn't he would have his ass flayed.

I went to an agency I had used in the not so distant past to hire 4x4's. The driver I knew, a Black Moor, took me out to scout 2km around the former site of my encampment and look for any signs of my baggage being stored, until it was deemed safe by the bandits to return and collect. This is common practice. The periodic tracks we found were of a charette that had passed close to the encampment and headed back into Teinweich Two, safe to assume that he had perhaps collected the booty for his employer. We drove up to the encampment to look for tracks and found Mwoiny. She had come to the place she knew best and had waited faithfully for my return. She was parched dry and the driver gave her all his bottled water; we had more out back, but he insisted that it would be better for her health. He then gave her his dish of rice and meat that his wife had packed for his lunch. He insisted she eat out of his dish! That was a bloody surprise! He said that he would eat later. She wolfed it all down within minutes, despite that I knew she would have hunted. She's not stupid; she knows all the best places for rabbit. We had a drive around but to no avail; I had found Mwoiny so was happy enough. I had eyes and ears out looking for all my gear and listening for stories of items for sale. I knew it would be a long shot in high winds. We then drove back to the auberge and he took off.

I had been asked often enough to teach English and so began giving private lessons. I very quickly through my many contacts found a place at a language school but soon ran into what would become familiar territory, working and not being paid for the work undertaken. This is Bidan habit. For instance, A Bidan will ask two Africans to paint his house, he will pay for half of the paint and the two men will toil all week under the blazing hot sun. They finish the job and need to be paid for the other half of the paint as well as their salary. The Bidan walks around his house, tutting and shaking his head. "No, I won't pay you, the job's a mess. It's terrible, fuck off." He simply withholds their money and they can do nothing. They now have to find the money to pay for the paint and do without their salary. I left this Bidan's employ the second time he paid me short and have dissuaded anyone else from working there. I have had the same problem as the painters in that there are three Bidans who hold 120 000 UM of my money and the Cote D'Ivoirien director of a primary school withholds 50 000UM in salary.

I have worked for the present school on and off for four months now. A mixture of one class and private students should see me just tick over as I prepare to leave. In the next chapter you will get an introduction into Bidan town society and all of its ugly facets as well as the prediction of Mauritania's future, in the face of climate change. My feelings at present are that I will simply be documenting in my blog, the future demise of a culture that has only just stepped out of the Stone Age and will go back to the Stone Age. The Bidan has spent the last fifty years, squabbling, stealing, coup d'etating and fighting amongst themselves, abusing their slaves and the Koli citizens and quite frankly they deserve everything that's about to befall them! Being the minority is never good when the shit hits the fan!

I have a P.S. to add here in relation to an incident at the camel market. One month after my departure from the desert, I took some French tourists out to be introduced to some personalities and photograph the market at work. I met a man at Ol Loli's limbur; he wasn't there, who introduced himself by standing up and walking outside the limbur to have me shake his hand. He's a bull of a man and he makes fun of my size as compared to him. He's fuckin' huge! He said that he was finally pleased to meet me, that this a special moment for him. "Why's that?" I asked. "Because I will be given 20 000 UM when I cut your throat." He smiled at the crowd in the limbur and at the tourists. There's always a crowd in the limbur. There's silence. I take out my Spanish pen knife with its huge blade open it up, sharpen it on the small wall of the limbur and hand it to him. I walk away saying, "Come with me now and we'll go into the nearby dunes and discuss this man to man." I stop because he's not following me. "Is there something wrong, don't you have the time? I can spare five minutes to go there, talk and come back, as I've these tourists to look after." They're in total denial but one man readies his video camera and comes to stand with me. His wife is going mental. I nod saying, "I'd like top see this later at the auberge." I motion to the huge Haratin (a freeman) to follow, who's completely dumbfounded. I shout at him, "Is there a fuckin' problem here? You have a job of work to do and so have I, so come on and let's get this over with." I add, "I've 17 500UM in my pocket if you succeed, so you'll get 37 500UM for the job." He's rooted to the spot in utter disbelief and hands the knife to the nearest boss and walks away. The bosses erupt into a very rapid chatter and the tourists and I are fed, watered and treated like lords. I ask the Frenchman with the video camera if he got it all. "No." He says, "I only have a little battery power and was keeping it for the fight." My moment of glory passed into history unnoticed except for now that it rests in the minds eye of a few French tourists, the bosses and myself, who all for a moment or three; except me, were stunned into disbelief. The Bull; as I now call him when I see him at the market, I was later told would have waited for night before doing the deed and with a least two others. He doesn't stop to talk and only if cornered with others or in Ol Loli's limbur. I always run my finger across my throat and point at him, no smile, as a farewell. He really isn't sure about me. C'est ma vie! Toute est normale! And only 20 000UM, Leomine's a cheap skate bastard! I'd do Leomine for free!

It was also my intention; a project I had pursued whilst in Scotland, to invite astronomers out into the desert. I'd have liked to set them up in a camp and keep them supplied with food, water and have a cook look after them. I know of lots of spots unaffected by the light pollution from NKT but sufficiently near enough for them to come and go, by camel of course. I wouldn't of course live there with them but would have visited every now and again. A 4x4 could bring them out with all their equipment, which I wouldn't be paying for. They'd be supplied with goats for milk, plenty of rabbits for the pot and an amazing vista by night and day. The invitation would be for as long as they considered it necessary to stay there and work. I had four camps picked out, and was going to have another khaima made and stock it. I hoped in the future that I could install a solar panel and European batteries; not the Chinese shit that you find discarded everywhere, to enable the guests to use sophisticated equipment. But alas, it all came to nothing. The short term greed of a spiteful and jealous arsehole would shoot my plans down in flames. But where one path ends another begins.

## CHAPTER ELEVEN

# 'MAURITANIA IS A NATION OF MOSQUES AND SHOPKEEPERS . . . AND HAIRDRESSERS . . . AND SLAVES'

I BORROWED AND adapted this quote from Margaret Thatcher. The most despised woman in Scottish history, next to Elizabeth I, and quite frankly I'm shocked to be quoting this bitch, but it best and fully describes Mauritania. I would also add, that it Mauritania is also full of special people. This last reference comes from the myriad of opinion of African, Black Moor, Haratin, ex-pat Euro's, ex-pat Arabs, and myself who have our daily lives interfered with, run by and dictated to by the connerie of the Bidan. Everything that goes wrong is solely by the hand and interference of the Bidan, who always knows best even when he doesn't know or understand a fuckin' thing that's going on! The story arrives in his Tardis sized head, searching for the h-bar sized brain, bounces around until the only way to proceed, apparently, is to exit through his fat ass as reasoned and deliberated speech! I make no apologies for being belligerent and verbose, throughout this journey you have decided to take with me. I'm driven to it by frustration and I hope a temporary state of madness. Thank you for that observation on my character Mr R, a non-resident, resident of Mauritania, who wishes to return to his mattshaggingafricatrip. comdon, but sadly, is making piles of money in London at an American conglomerate or other US financial institution. He could be R.I.M's next

President! There's a coup d'etat every two years, hell I could be, but my vote's (AK) for Matthew. His reasoned and educated opinion from his Tardis sized brain; on almost every subject on the planet, and the direct manner in which it is delivered, with a colonial Ozzie humour of course, is what I like about him the most. Mostly and annoyingly, is that he is always fuckin' correct. Just like me. He must have some Scottish blood in him! My dear long lost brother, I love you lots.

Matthew came through The Empire of The Sands on passage going south; with surprisingly little gear, to Ghana on his KTM. Needing to do the desert thang, he disappeared off to Atar and developed a mechanical problem and another and another the day he left to go south. He spent 2000 euros on spare parts DHL'd from Germany, a shitload more euros on a bike mechanic, Toujani who's ace by the way, lots of expensive beer at Schenker, where yours truly sporting his African combo had difficulty getting in. Matthew stayed what, two months in all. So with the small fortune on parts, board and lodgings and a week spent shagging in Dakar, he didn't even get a free T-shirt from DHL, which surprises me because even the girl that cleans the floor there gets one! He's they're top West African customer! His KTM now rests in Togo, because Matthew had to return to the UK to satisfy visa requirements, because he's a colonial cousin, and is now earning a HUGE salary capable of paying for the next coup d'etat here in Mauritania. If he wants to pay me I've said, I'll collect his beloved KTM and bring her home. Well, he is resident here. AT LEAST I HAVE A FUCKIN' LICENCE MATTHEW!

Mauritania and not the tiny island of Mauritius, where I believe some of my mail has been delivered to, for those of you who have no clue, is in between Senegal, Mali and The Western Sahara and a little bit of Algeria. Here are the bare facts. It has a population of 2,906,000 comprising of 40% Arab-Berber (Bidan) and 60% others: Arab-Berber Negroid (Black Moor), Haalpulaar, Soninke, Wolof (Black African Mauritanians) Gentlemen, stay away from these girls, they are deadly. The national flag is a green background with a gold crescent moon and star (as signifies the end of Ramadan, which you'd assume makes the recognition by Mauritanians rudimentary, not so!) The motto: Honneur—Fraternite—Justice. These don't exist here in Mauritania. I know the title of the book is, Nothing's Impossible in Mauritania, but this state of being at the present time, is.

Never again will I jump through Bidan hoops designed to safeguard what isn't theirs to safeguard in the first place. GDP $1.6 billion. Per capita income $13 a week. 50% of the population live on $1 a day. 1 million Mauritanians suffer from chronic malnutrition. Ask Save The Children and the World Food Programme if you think I'm shitting you! Infant mortality rate of 77/1000. Life expectancy, because they will not, even when they can afford to, and 50% who cannot afford to, eat fresh fruit or vegetables or brush their teeth is, 51 years. Exports earn Mauritania $623 million. Imports cost them $1083 million. Mushkila kibir! Big problem!

The Empire's natural resources are: oil, fish (the fishing grounds are fast becoming over fished), phosphates, copper, gold, salt, gypsum, gum Arabic, iron ore and uranium. This high grade commodity is to be found in the Zednes region at the 100% owned mine Bir En Nar of Murchison United NL. You can find Murchison on the Australian Stock Exchange and in the Alternative Investment Market at the London Stock Exchange. This is typical of the Bidan. He hands everything over to others to do the work and pockets his commission. The others are simple in the extreme of dig, scoop, pour and send away. Just like making tea. They have handed over their oil to Repsol, Total and China Petroleum Inc to extract 18 500 barrels per day. The earth's plates make extraction with the bendy straw technology difficult and expensive. Mauritania needs the USS Enterprise to help get it out. The gold mining at Tasiast, Ahmey-Tijirit and Karet are 100% owned by the Canadian company Red back Mining Inc. The Bidan's only necessary technical ability, literally stretches to putting on the TV, their mobiles, starting the car, playing on the Internet and turning on the gas to make tea. Oh sorry I forgot, turning on the radio too and all of the above items, off of course. Why should he have to work when he has slaves, paid or unpaid to do it for him? I've also included in this list natural resources an unnatural resource list because it makes a hell of a lot of money for the Bidan: a flourishing cocaine trade and there's as much cocaine as there is sand, illegal guns, tobacco, stolen cars, slaves and young girls for marriage to old Arab men. Something for everyone here in R.I.M!

Politics are heavily influenced by personalities, whose family has the tribal and family considerations (wealth) in order to pay everyone off, as well as the perceived ability and erm, integrity, to be seen to able to exercise the control of power. At the time of writing, it is The Military Junta who holds sway again. In 2005 Col Salah Ould Hanana was sacked by President Taya and the resultant coup was simply his anger over being sacked. There was no political agenda attached and he was aided by the then Colonel and now General Aziz; the present big cheese, along with the President, Col Ely Ould Vall who then, in the first 'fair and honest democratic elections' (kiss my toubab ass) voted the puppet, Sidi Mohamad Cheihk Abdellahi as the next President in 2007 who has now; on the 6th August 2008, been retired prematurely. The General now runs the State Council and once again will re-instigate 'fair and honest democratic elections.' It matters little what all of the interested parties, either for or against, have to say on the reasons for yet another coup. It is the Mauritanian response when bickering amongst themselves to over-react; like blaming each other for a pot of boiling milk overflowing because you weren't paying attention, and make themselves look even more stupid than they did before. The political parties exist on the whim of whoever's in power. If he or in the case of The Junta, don't like them then they simply ban the party and arrest the leaders. Taya's regime publically condemned slavery but prosecuted SOS Slaves and any journalist who investigated stories. Vall imprisoned many Salafists and Sidi then let them all out again! Or was it the other way around, who gives a fuck! Sidi released the Minister for Oil in the Taya government, imprisoned for his theft of millions of dollars of oil revenues to help out in his political campaign. So the theft of my encampment by Leomine is nothing really and I should also give him the clothes off of my back and thank and pardon him for doing so! Most political parties simply don't have the funding so form alliances in elections. The was a Green Party two years ago but fraudulent use of their funds saw them discredited. The only thing Green was the people who gave them money!

The General's use of, the supposed effect of Sidi's flagrant misuse of the office of the President and the effects it has had on the poor of Mauritania as the reason for the coup, is a gross criminality of the wretched situation the most vulnerable find themselves in due to the corruption of the ruling classes, when The General has done nothing himself to alleviate their situation. There was also the question of Sidi's wife, Khatou, being asked by The Senate to answer for the financial accounting of her charitable foundation, the discovery of millions of dollars in House of Saud donations, 12 brand new LandCruisers and the immediate sacking of the General and several officers, by Sidi just shortly afterwards, with Sidi apparently demanding that The General answer for his part in the Race Riots, who then arrested Sidi, making the actual truth of the matter very confusing to ascertain. I'll try and keep this simple as I and I expect you begin to get dizzy at this point. For us, this is normal everyday life here. I'm smiling and content, so should you be, because you aren't here!

The Bidan's continual conflict with everyone, including his own kind, is the major stumbling block to national unity and growth. This arises over an ancient system of racism which the Bidan deny. 800 years of slavery which they deny. Corruption which they don't deny! 'If it's alright for the Bidan to steal, then it's alright for me,' is the view of the masses who are desperate enough to make some, any money. Just don't get caught if you're not Bidan. The World Bank Governance Indicators for 2005 are: Voice and accountability, weak. Political stability and the absence of violence, weak. Government effectiveness, middling. Regulatory quality, middling. Rule of law, weak. Control of corruption, middling. Mauritania ranks 153/177 in the Human Development Index of 2006. In the Doing Business 2008 category, given their enthusiasm you'd think good, think of the no tone for Family Fortunes here, 157/175. Therefore, could do a lot better boys!

A border dispute with Senegal in 1989 wasn't the reason given to expel thousands Black Mauritanians and murder thousands more. It merely facilitated a plan already being conceived to clear the Black Moor officers, NCO's and soldiers from the army and were murdered as the fear was that FLAM; the black rights group, would use their access to weapons to fight back. Over the years, 20 000 or so have trickled back and live near to their former homes and land or have had to re-located due to intimidation. Conflict over land tenure and property seizures from these Race Riots and the remaining, God knows how many in actuality waiting to return, will I believe reawaken old animosities and the toxic spite of the Bidan will rise to the fore as he will not relinquish his ill-gotten gains, under any circumstances. The Human rights abuses the Black Mauritanians have suffered, makes you sick. Torture, beatings, murder, intimidation of women and children, rape. As yes, the Mauritanian soldier is a fine warrior!

Next on the list of "Things I hate about the Bidan," is slavery. The Great Denial. Yet another subject you had better not discuss. I will of course. The trafficking of men, women and children in and out of Mauritania to use as a beasts of burden, to freely abuse either physically or sexually as you see fit and simply give them the left-overs on your dish is as much care as you need to show. The Bidan places his goats, sheep and camels as being of far more worth and fed a damn sight better, and the slave placed on the same level as a dog. Therefore, the slave's health and welfare is of no consequence to him. Punishments can be as sadistic as the owners warped senses dictate as being correct for the crime committed against his peace and tranquility. Mostly it's a slap around the head, belted with perhaps electrical cable, it has so many uses here, the head slaps would give you concussion, such as the slapping Aminetou gave to her younger brother. In many cases it results in death.

This next story I've had immense trouble with. When as I tried to include it before I couldn't, it was too painful and I could hardly see the screen for tears. I then couldn't stop shaking from rage or sadness or both. Its inclusion has taken four days for me to add, two of which I didn't sleep and only last night did I sleep reasonably well was because I smoked more than a few joints. My resolve is set and I am going to use this opportunity to tell the story of Mylo, so that if I am to die afterwards, I leave his story for someone to read, even if it's only my sister. I'll be happy to breathe my last knowing in that it has been committed to USB. Mylo is the name his mother calls him but his real name is Mohamad Salem. I'll use Mylo if you don't mind.

Mylo is an eight year old Haratin. He works from 0700-2300, everyday. He runs back and forward from the store room to the house, to the corner shop to the house, to the kitchen to the house, to carry this and that. In one breath he's told to go and get something and to then come back because 'he's' forgotten something and of course he's slapped, hard. This could be stepped up to being belted or whipped with a flex from a phone charger or the ubiquitous electrical cable. There are 101 different uses here in R.I.M. for that particular item. This goes on all day, everyday, week in week out, month in month out, year in year out. You think your life is difficult! At least you get the fuckin' weekend off! His family, is spread over four families in the same village of this tribe of Bidan, all related through intermarriage. They rank in-between the El Mamy's and the Ould Sba's. They are the first family to inhabit the village and so hold a position of superiority but fuck all else! The village in question, is on the Route L'Espoir and I won't mention it's name, there are so many, Mylo's, in many villages and town houses. I can't remember the family name but the sour-faced matriarch of a beached Orca, is called Aicha. It was by her hand that reduced Mylo's face to a slab of meat one day.

As is his daily chore to run back and forward, he was in-between coming or going or coming and going all at the same time and slapped back and forward, from the Orca down to the smallest child who is indoctrinated to slap Mylo, who has to come and get on his hands and knees for the child to do so. He stumbled and fell and in the process, knocked over a jug of bisap (a drink made from dried hibiscus, water and sugar) onto an elder sister's mehlafah and of course the filthy carpet. Their prayer rug is also filthy. When I was there I would go out into the dunes to pray, where the sand is clean. Bisap stains everything it touches. Their carpet is a fuckin' mess, stained with this and that and the bisap actually added some colour to it! In a Bidan house hold everything is on the floor, scattered all over the fuckin' place, in other words a tip! The Ugly sister then starts slapping and shouting at him as does the entire family and not being enough for Aicha, she then demands his presence, to which he goes to her to be savagely punched around the head and face repeatedly, until as such time as the oldest son steps in to rescue him and hands him over to his mother by the scruff of the neck, asking her to then give him a slap or two.

I arrive four days later, en-route to a nearby road side shop for some supplies and see him collecting water. He has his back to me and I call out with my camel call and it is only when he turns round, that I see his face. I leap out of the saddle run full tilt and ask him what happened. He can't speak French and my Hassaniya's shit but I know he didn't fall. And we have an understanding like Moulay and I do. He's trying to smile, shaking his head and saying he's alright. Tears are running down my cheeks and I see a visiting Bidan male and ask him what happened. He naturally tells me Mylo fell and asks Mylo what he said; in Hassaniya of course. I immediately interrupt and tell him that he said he fell. I can barely keep my scowl to myself and of the entire family, it is a 15 year old girl called Maryam who can gauge my simmering anger, kept in place by the merest sheen of a smile. She can barely look at me her guilt so heavy.

His mother was in the kitchen cooking and I go on the pretext that I need salt, which everyone knows I eat on a regular basis. I manage to speak to her for five minutes before I'm called by the next rank of brother. I tell her that I will be back in two or three weeks time as I'm taking a herd into market and on the way back will come and ask if I can take Mylo as my berger. I can say that I'm having a boss drop off his goats and that I can't look after them my self as well as camels. She's grabs my hand and kisses it repeatedly. I stop her by kissing hers, we're both in tears. A minute or so later I can hear Brahim calling me again and I shout out that I'm in the kitchen. He arrives to see us wiping our eyes. There's a huge pile of peeled onions and we claim that this is what's causing the tears. They had been done ages ago and had lost their potency. What the fuck does he know except to stick them in his fat mouth and lose them out of his fat ass! I leave with him and can barely drink their tea. It is while we're there that I ask why Mylo is still working after his fall. The reply is that it will keep his mind off of his injuries. I mention that perhaps he has difficulty seeing due to his eyes being mere slits and have a headache from the repeated banging of his head off the sand. The uncle translates for everyone and it is agreed that perhaps it would be better if Mylo could be given a few days rest.

After tea I go outside and take out my phone put it on 'Fuck off and die.' mode. No ringtone, no vibration, no backlight flashing, nothing. I don't want to look stupid when 'talking to a boss!' for it to go off. I play my little theatre and am joined by some younger children who call me to eat. I wave them away and talk and talk. The uncle calls me and I signal to go and eat and then signal that I need to go. I finish my call and walk into the house and tell them that I have a rendezvous with the boss who would like to meet up. It's work and I can't refuse. I don't want to eat their food let alone drink their tea and my mind had been racing from the moment I got there. I move the camels back in the direction of the market where I know of some good pasture. Its about 30 km from this village and near a well, uninhabited because the well's deep, 60m plus before you touch water and the families moved on a long time ago, allowing the pasture to regenerate. I also used it because the smell of water will keep the camels nearby, whereby I could come and go. Who's a clever boy then? I then wait two hours or so and go back to the village and ask Aicha if I can have Mylo for a berger as I have a boss bringing out a herd of goats to my camp in about eight or nine days time and I need help. I'm stationed nearby and can come back en-route for my camp, in four days time. She agrees and I leave.

Another D-Day and I arrive Chez Aicha 0700. I've waited outside of the village for one hour. There are smiles and cordial greetings and an atmosphere you'd need an oxy-acetylene torch to cut with. I ask straight off if I can have him for the goats. No is the reply as both he and his mother have gone into K'sar to stay at another house. I walk off and get my phone out and have 'conversations,' rolling a joint and act busy. I eventually go back and say that I can use another boy from the market and that I'm going to buy some supplies. I tell them I'll be back later. A sister has replaced her mother in the kitchen and an older brother has replaced Mylo. Everyone disappears to go and do what they do best, lie around and talk. I snatch a few minutes outback with Mylo's brother. Mylo had become depressed after Aicha told his mother that they would be moving to K'sar, he simply laid down and wouldn't eat or drink, no matter how much he was beaten. His brother didn't know if he would ever see him again. He thanked me for trying to take him away. He said he wasn't staying long, he'd made up his mind to go. I gave him my number which he has never called. He is no longer in the employ of the family as true to his word, he ran away three days after talking to me. On my return there, I wasn't made very welcome and I haven't been back since.

Mylo was a happy-go-lucky chap who took his beatings and when alone, disappeared into his own world. How do I know? I've talked with him and watched him for hours. He could detach himself from their control no matter if it was only two minutes. His sister too. I'd see her in the afternoons when the families were asleep. She'd dance and sing all around the back of the village, free for two hours to then put on her slave face and carry on working until she's told to go away. When I was there, the punishments were less severe and there was some respite for Mylo. I have no idea if he is alive or dead. He is just one of some 500-600 000 slaves in Mauritania, who have no recourse to justice, a day off, a decent meal, attention given to their injuries or accorded one grain of respect. I need to go for a run and cry under my turban again. His TV programme is still too vivid and more painful than I could have ever imagined when I started this particular chapter of the events of my life here.

Imagine you are a 17 year old Haratin girl taken to court by your owner for the loss of a goat which he says you have sold. You have no right to representation or voice; similar to the UK Section 5 of The Public Order Act that drove me here in the first place, found guilty of selling your master's goat and are then thrown into jail for a month. This being of the quality found in Japanese World War II camps. Here you are beaten daily. Sexually abused at will and given little or no food. No water to wash with. How as a Muslim are you to perform your five daily prayers? You are now a 15 year old boy found at the side of the road, accused of trying to run away. So slapped all the way back, you are then hung over the hump of a camel on your stomach and your hands tied to your feet. The camel is then given water to swell its belly and the ropes tighten and your Bidan boss will have the camel run around for a while. Or like Mylo, you are simply beaten for not bringing the tea quick enough or because the Bidan beached whale is a little upset at being wakened from her afternoon nap too soon. The use of free-born children, I will cover under commerce. But for the moment, if you don't believe in anything I have said since page 1, I refer you to SOS Slaves, run by Boubacar Ould Messaoud, a former slave who now lives in exile in Dakar and runs an underground system for passing escaped slaves onto freedom in Senegal. Please read it. If you go to Dakar for a holiday, try and make his acquaintance and listen to him. Slavery isn't an abuse locked in the past in documentaries and films. It exists now.

Malouma Messoud, a former slave.

"We didn't learn this history in school, we simply grew up within this social hierarchy and lived it. Slaves believe that if they do not obey their masters, they will not go to Paradise. They are raised in a social and religious system that everyday reinforces this Idea." [1]

Amnesty International.

"Not only has the government denied the existence of slavery and failed to respond to cases brought to its attention, it has hampered the activities of organisations which are working on the issue, including by refusing to grant them official recognition.' [2]

The US State Dept, affectionately known as Foggy Bottom, came out to Mauritania in 2004 and could neither confirm or deny that the traditional form of slavery exists in Mauritania. Foggy Bottom, at the time of writing in September 2008, have Mauritania listed as a Tier 2 Watch List. That means, that Mauritania is failing to provide evidence of its efforts to combat trafficking. Neither is it committed to abolishing slavery despite it being outlawed 27 years ago. In 2003, the President Taya ran a radio, TV and newspaper campaign in French, Arabic and Pulaar in July and December. The government has not prosecuted any case against traffickers under the new law.

The abuses of the Haratin are many and manifold, although it is also true to say that many are not. The 800 year old history of an ancestral owner/slave relationship, of an obvious unequal status, has a familial relationship. In many cases, staying put is the only option as the slave has no education, personal or marketable skills that will allow him or her to have a chance of economic independence. That it continues to exist is very very wrong. If it were ever to be truly abolished, then Mauritanian society may just erupt into civil war. As the member of a race of big-mouthed belligerent verbose bastards, I will continue to shout out for the rights of those who have no avenue to do so. I will not include a list of Internet sites as you are, I assume, more than capable of sourcing the material for yourself, it's hardly quantum mechanics folks. Kick your underage teenage son off the computer from his nightly foray into Vice City and read for an hour or so. See how calm you are afterwards, perhaps you too, will end shooting a few bandits and whores!

Famine as I have previously mentioned has hit hard here as it has done in many third world countries, in a country of gluttony for the Bidan and 250UM if you're the unlucky part of the 50%. What can you buy here for that? O.25kg of meat, half of which will be bone . . . 0.12kg of meat/bone 130UM and 0.5kg of rice 120UM . . . remember the student stand-by, 0.5kg of macaroni 100UM and a tin of sardines 150UM . . . 0.5kg rice, small bag of oil 50UM and a stock cube 20UM, 8 custard creams 50UM and one sweet 10UM . . . 100UM for a baguette with 20UM of butter and 20UM for jam, small bag of powdered milk for 20UM, a boiled egg 50UM and four cigarettes . . . or you could do tea, sugar and mint for 200UM and half of a baguette. This is why the life expectancy is low for all Mauritanians. Even when the Bidan has money to burn, his diet is generally mundane and nutritionally poor as his health education is non-existent. With an improved income in The Afro-Mauritanian, Soninke and Pulaar households, they at least eats fish, rice and vegetables but in low quantities, when shared out amongst a large family.

The entrenched system of abuse continues unabated to denigrate and degenerate further what little quality of life there is for everyone, except for the Bidan. For everyone else it's hand to mouth. Of course he's happy with his lot, overjoyed on being waited on hand and foot, having his huge ego fed day in and day out, as well as his arteries stuffed with cholesterol. A Bidan wife does nothing around the house. She doesn't even look after her children, that job is delegated to the youngest housekeeper. Her job is simply to bloat out like a beached whale. Gavage, is what farmers in France do to geese to make pate de fois gras. Here it is a display of wealth and beauty. Mmmm. C'est pas jolie! Or healthy, clinical obesity that's actually encouraged. Though the girls around the 16+ age group are taking a stand here. No thank you they're saying. I enjoy being slim and pretty.

So, with the actual players in government firmly rooted in place, makes little difference, as they simply continue to ignore and magnify the general population's misery and I won't go into the machine here in any great detail. You can read that for yourself on the Internet should you be inspired to do so. Of those members of the present machine of government, the Ministers, the 13 regional governors, the Senators, the members of Parliament and the Mayors, there is a combined majority gaggle, who have been well compensated for their support of The Gen . . . sorry, The State Council in assuming control for the good of the country, wrested from the incompetent and glutinous Sidi. There are a significant number who oppose obviously. Does it really matter, when everyone simply emulates what has come before? The last President's family out, the next president's family in. Same old same old! What Mauritania needs, is a Martin Luther King to take on the establishment and the same will probably happen to him as happened to Mr King. The Junta regularly releases statements of its intentions to prosecute Sidi and Khatou before negotiations with the World Bank, the EU and the US. They will promise them the earth, with their fingers crossed behind their backs. This comes from Scots children who promise to behave and cancel the promise by crossing their fingers. The Bidan does the same in his tiny brain. In all negotitations he is not to be trusted under any circumstances.

Let's have a little wander around the streets of Nouakchott, you as a tourist and me as your guide. On every street corner in Nouakchott; as well as being filled with beggars from every tier of society, thieves and whores and probably outdoes Vice City, you espy the crouched beached whale in her mehlafah and look at me in horror. Whispering, "Mohammad is she having a piss?" You ask. "Would you like me to ask?" I reply.

"Perhaps not." I add nonchalantly. You shudder all the way down to your feet and shake your head and we carry on a gentle stroll past the man standing facing the wall of a house pissing. "He's having a piss." I say. Nouakchott you quickly surmise is one huge public toilet. There are piles of rubbish everywhere and it stinks. Cesspit covers are left open and broken and it is not uncommon to see Bidan and African leave their big houses and piss and shit in the street. As well as this, there's an abundance of small grocer's shops, hairdressers and mosques surrounding each quartier. Within a four minute walk from the school I work in at the moment, there are seven grocers, four hairdressers and six mosques. Can you imagine for instance, if you lived in Bishopbriggs, Lenzie, Kirkintilloch, Lennoxtown or Twechar and that in each and every quartier of each town, they'd be the same number of Pakistani shops, hairdressers and churches? No fuckin' way you're saying! I've even got you doing it now. As you can imagine, the call to morning prayer is very noisy and there's no way you can sleep through at least two hours of call to prayer and the actual prayer itself, this of course five times a day. Then during Ramadan, it can start at 0300 and finish at 0600. During the last two days, it starts at 0200 and finishes at 0600. Only here this year; ha ha he he ho ho, they got off to an early start and then decided that it wasn't the end of Ramadan, to begin the process all over again.

Two days ago, at 0300, a large group of Bidan en passage stopped outside in the street near to the school and debated the end of Ramadan. I naturally woke up, and went to the edge of the terrace to get them to move on before I started throwing lumps of concrete at them. "Excuse me gentlemen, what's the problem?" I bellowed out. "It's the end of Ramadan." Another "No it's not!" Then another and another begin and the hullabaloo's at full tilt again. "WOOS TYFAIL!" I shout, meaning 'Silence children!' (Variety, male.) I point up at the crescent moon and ask, "Where's the star?" There's mumbling and shaking of heads and I'm tired. I add, "There's no star, therefore it's not the end of Ramadan, go home or just fuck off from here and let me sleep!" They take off and continue to argue way off into the distance. The phrase, 'Couldn't organise a piss up in a brewery!' comes to mind. Not just because they're Muslims, because lots of Bidan drink alcohol, smoke hashish and snort coke. They just really couldn't organise themselves if their lives depended on it! That list again. There was a pre-Eid party, Eid, post-Eid, pre-Tabaski party and Tabaski. It's official, Ramadan is a joke in the R.I.M.

Every new President who takes office throws 2-3 major parties at the Stade Olympique. The Stade was built and paid for by the Chinese, with Chinese materials and workers. They simply; as they do with all their projects, pay for, build and hand over. At no time is there any involvement with the Bidan community. The Chinese are by the far the most switched on when dealing with them. The last shindig there was The General's that he threw after Sidi's retirement and comprised of the same six or seven songs for Sidi's bash, a griot or two and some Black Moor rap for the youth. I asked a friend for a translation of the rapper's lyrics. "It's a fuckin' noise Mohamed, I haven't a clue what's he's singing about!" There's a new Malaysian Boite (where ex-pat Euros, Arabs and whores hang out) in the old Woodside offices, a former hotel and throws a party on Friday nights from 2200 to 0430 with the same six records and some Youssou N'Dour occasionally, which must mean that there are Wolof whores present. It blasts these same songs out endlessly.

Bidan marriages of which there are a great deal, as well as lots of divorce, are first advertised by the stationing of camel outside on the pavement for the dinner party. They will drive around in a cavalcade of cars blaring their horns and perhaps this will go on for two-three hours. The music will be of a traditional Bidan flavour and comprises of a vocalist and perhaps a guitar. She will shout the praises of the Bidan patron throwing the party and it's basically for everyone within hearing distance, which is considerable given that it's at full volume, to know how rich a Bidan he is. You thought I was going to swear! There is no melody and the occasional twwanggg on a guitar is as electrical as it gets. It can go on for hours and you have no choice but to suffer. There is no licence required for a do and there obviously no noise laws. If there were, the population except for myself, the ex-pat French and Arabs would be in jail and we would have the town to ourselves! The African population freed from their penal servitude would also be in prison for noise violation, for constant and unbridled partying. I think they could be given some leeway here and allowed a week of celebration before incarcerating their noisy Koli ass!

The most recent 'democratic' elections held in 2007 were a cacophony of noise from morning till morning. In Toujinine, the two Presidential candidates Sidi and Daddah had villages of khaimas lining both sides of the road, each with their P.A. systems turned to maximum volume. I swear you couldn't hear your own thoughts. This too repeated all over town in smaller head to heads. Sidi would set up and Daddah would set up opposite and the two P.A.'s left to battle it out with perhaps one or two people in each khaima, as was the case throughout the huge array of khaima. You can't actually discuss the finer points of political debate with the representatives attendants because a. it was so noisy and b. there wasn't any. Cars driving by with P.A., khaimas stationed at every available piece of ground and blazing out their message which was indistinguishable from the other and the same three songs from Sidi, who played Bidan, Koli and Indian for some reason, it was sheer and utter lunacy. This was also the first time the general Bidan community was involved and everyone proudly exclaimed they were going to work! Cars pass you, their horns blasted in a continual show of support for God knows who and a hand held bull horn attached to a small Dictaphone? "You've no fuckin' poster on your car you twat!" They are simply adding a cacophany of momentary madness to the orchestra of the madmen and everyone's doing their own thing completely oblivious to everyone else and the conductor!

On Sunday 24th August 2008 I was at my computer writing in my blog at 0500 because I couldn't sleep. A nearby mosque had began the call to prayer and there was feed back for one hour and ten minutes, at high volume. I was indoors at this point and had my mp3 on and it was still audible. The list again. Technology and the Bidan understanding of its complexities would be something akin to the problems encountered by the Wright Brothers when flying a shuttle pod from Star Trek Next Generation. Does it not occur to him that the pain he's experiencing in his head might have something to do with the feedback from his P.A. system? Or, is he so inured to noise that he simply ignores it? Or stone deaf? Or simply stupid? This capital is never quiet. At night, the donkeys take over braying out their heartfelt misery to the previous day's beating and hard toil, the gangs of dogs gang up on them and give them a mouthful and anyone else who passes by. Cars drive around going nowhere in particular and make liberal use of their horns, even when it is illegal to do so, as if that matters a fuck! The KC checkpoints continually whistling at drivers to stop and extract 200UM for some violation or other. Gangs of youth play football at 0400 and give no quarter. If you ask them to shut up, you're the one causing all the noise! It simply doesn't enter the Mauritanian psyche that he's ever in the wrong or making life impossible for others, again simply inured to the noise around them. This has been one of the hardest things to deal with since I left the desert in August 2007. They are among the most selfish race on the planet who haven't one ounce of respect for anyone else. So much for Islam. That list, it's getting bigger and much longer!

The grocers shops open around 0700 and close, well, sometimes never but generally around 0300. The hairdressers tend to open all day and night. The other markets are generally 0800-1700. It's by far the noisiest city on the planet. Opposite the school is the home of a wealthy Wolof couple (Senegalese) who have eight house slaves. Brahim the Black Moor teacher here tells me they aren't any slaves in RIM. When you work 288 hours a month for 69UM an hour, it's fuckin' slavery no matter how you want to paint it. The couple scream night and day for the two youngest house workers, Hawa and Waga both 18 or so, and if they're not available, Boubacar the berger who looks after the resident herd of 10 sheep, that live in the garden, gets the call "WA'HIGHLA!" "Come here!" What? You don't have sheep in your garden . . . no of course you wouldn't! Silly me, or goats either for that matter. No that would be stupid, all that free milk and not having to cut the grass either. I've seen the price of goats milk in Scotland, IT'S A FUCKIN' FORTUNE! The Madame was shouting on Waga at 0330 the other morning. I got up from my underneath my mosquito net and gave her such a mouthful, as if that'd surprise you any. She kept it down until mid morning and continued throughout the day bellowing at the top of her voice.

This might seem contrived but as I write there is of course a life that goes on in connection outside of this house and the city, it doesn't just stop because I'm not there! I don't have to make anything up, this country does it itself without any prompt from the private madness of a Scottish berger. The eldest son of the house opposite continually arrives at 0030-0100 and blasts his horn to have Waga open the doors to the garage. I've asked to no avail to have him phone ahead, so only one night ago, he arrived at 0100 and BLAAAP BLAAAP BLAAAP. "WAGA, WAGA . . . WAGA!" BLAAAP BLAAAP BLAAAP. I shout down "Please, enough. It's well after midnight" He totally ignores me and again BLAAAP BLAAAP BLAAAP . . . "WAGA!" BLAAAP BLAAAP BLAAAP I then take off for my bag in the room on the terrace, where I have eighty bangers that go off three times each. Chinese goodies. I light and throw for an air burst which ain't hard because I'm up on the terrace. BANG BANG BANG. He and Waga shit themselves! Four minutes later the household is at their and our door. Again, just my luck, he's fuckin' huge! He gives me a mouthful about having a gun and he's going to Blah blah blah blah. You're only little, you're the shitbag who's making all the noise." He's screaming his head off and all I've done is say "Please, enough, I'm tired" and throw a banger. "It's illegal to use your horn after the hours of darkness, but I can throw bangers all night long if I want to and I can every five minutes for six hours!" He goes ballistic.

His mouth goes off in Wolof, French and English. I add calmly, "Go for the police, but as you're a Koli, they won't listen to you, no matter how much money you have and as I'm toubab they consider me a Bidan and in the right even when I'm wrong which I'm not because I'm right in this case!" He adds, "I don't need the police, you only had to ask!" "I did and you ignored me until I threw the banger!" His mother agrees with me. He's leaning down into my face restrained by Waga, who like me is little and has seen me practice with Niagy and Diallo is laughing, as he's seen me practice with Niagy too, who's a big guy and I throw him about the street, apparently, without touching him. 'Blah blah blah blah blah,.' as soon as he takes a breath I say, "Okay, phone three or four friends about the same size as you and we'll talk then." The guy's giving me another mouthful leaning into my face, Diallo says something, he apologises and I apologise and everyone goes back indoors, the bigmouth being bergered by Waga and his mummy, Waga's winking at me over his shoulder and mummy's all happy her boy's safely home and not en route for Clinic Kissi which is only an irimi nage away. Thank you Diallo, I've now seen a mathematical model for this throw . . . interesting. The next morning at 0730 mummy is sitting outside with Boubacar and the goats and asks me if I slept well. Then at 1915 the younger brother arrives to invite me to break the fast. Tea, zreig and an assortment of small eats, served by a very attentive Hawa, you really must read the blog page, 'Gazelle at thirty paces . . . and you thought they were extinct here in R.I.M!' She did hear it!

If I wanted to, I could set up a rave on the terrace and blast the quartier all night and day. "AACEED!" I'd simply give them the excuse to catch up on a little sleep during the day. Not that they need to of course. I do believe that this chapter will give you the biggest headache, in trying to manage to come to terms with the real Mauritania, as well as have an enormous amount of foul language edited out. If he does so, the publisher will get such a slap! I can pay an awful lot of people; not an awful lot of money, to do the job for me, all day and all night if I want to! Ask Mr R, he's knows I have numbers in my phone.

Let's look further into the business side of life as seen by the tourist and his faithful unpaid guide as we continue to stroll around heaps of rubbish, being narrowly missed by a charette, whose load snags your shirt but doesn't cut your arm this time, as boubou's on a mission cut across your path, another stops to take a piss, squatting at the edge of the pistes, schools of slow moving whales push past without wanting to touch you and drivers oblivious to your presence as they drive at speed straight for you, "But we're on the pavement!" You scream. I take your hand and stepping out into traffic, weave across the road on to the central reservation which is high enough to deter even Kamikaze 4x4's, the charettes remember have no brakes and so what if it's doing a little parcours without its driver! So we stand and let it pass. "Why is that driver driving up the wrong side of the road?" I simply reply, "Because he can!" You are dumbfounded to have seen the KC on traffic duty (this you know from his white Sam

Browne) wave at him simply in recognition, not in fact to stop him as you would normally imagine. Archie's laughing, you'd like Archie. This is the heady life of Mauritanian commerce which is arranged in Marches or markets. Marche boubou, 10 pharmacists, 40 + mehlafahs, 20 + D.I.Y., 15 + building supplies, garages all in a row . . . fuck me . . . there are literally hundreds of car mechanic's workshops in sand soaked black in oil in K'sar, so you're fucked if you live in Tevragh Zeina. You also need an NBC suit and respirator there. You need to get towed or go there by taxi to bring back a mechanic. Please don't equate UK towing practices with those practiced here. Attendez-moi eh!

I was once in a train of four quads tied onto a Merc 190D. There was a piece of thick but frayed oily rope from the Merc to quad 1, a piece of webbing from quad 1 to quad 2, a piece of electrical cable from quad 2 to quad 3 and a piece of oily rope from quad 3 to my quad. We travelled a distance of 4km through heavy traffic. The three in front of me were aged 12, 17 and 14. None of them had ever been on a quad before. We are freewheeling but you'd guessed that, right! We slewed across round-abouts, cut across busy intersections on the wrong side and weaved in and out of traffic and up onto the pavements and pistes. When you read the section on driving you will either rush to the bathroom to be sick, as in the case of my sister, simply piss yourself laughing when you think back to my trip on the quad train. Just another normal day in Nouakchott. Foggy Bottom recommend getting a locally 'trained' driver. Nice touch gentlemen. Slick humour from the men in black. Arseholes.

Another Marche Photocopiers 10 of, Marche Kitchen, I can't remember, fuckin' loads as they go up both sides of the street and around the corner! You name it, there's a market for it. Marche Capital is where we are walking over flattened debris, around pools of effluent, Marche Viande to our right, selling fly infested meat on their cabin style and extremely unhygienic wooden stalls, seeped in years of old blood and fly-shit. In the UK it would be a simple firing squad at dawn for a trader such as this! The mehlafah boutiques you already know about. I lived in Premier for six months. Along the street called Ah-ho, which means middle, there are forty-two here. That's a lot of mehlafahs! A new one which opened on the other road leading in from the moneyed quartier of Inor and eight km from my room, had a mother and her three daughters in situ. I walked this road because it cuts through desert where you can buy fresh camel milk and I know one or two bergers there. Marche Leben

Naga. (Camel milk market) This night when I get back I discover a new, solitary boutique at the road side and the mother asks me if I need a pretty mehlafah. 5000UM. Code I surmised. One is 13, the next 15 and the third 16 and all fresh she says! "Bon nuit Madame!"

There was a mehlafah seller attached behind my small courtyard of two rooms and a toilet, well a hole in the ground, French style, not. You couldn't hold your breath long enough to get out in time before you were on the verge of collapse. At night I could hear her working, there would be twenty-five minutes of talking with her client, he'd climb on and climb off two minutes later claiming to be huge and a wonderful lover! She'd agree naturally enough, take the money and kick his ass out the door. Thirty minutes. Exactly. This would happen four or five times a night and she was really really fuckin' ugly! I couldn't last two minutes talking with hear as her mouth was a fuckin' graveyard!

There is a woman in my quartier now selling mehlafahs. She sells from a garage attached to her house. Her prostitution is very en cache, very discreet. This is yet another layer of this side of life. It takes many many months to be able to access, perhaps not the phrase I should be using, but gain access to her services which will take long and careful negotiation. She has a husband and family, who are within talking distance and she watches TV in the salon through a huge lattice grill but can bring across, folding doors can be drawn to talk with potential female and male clients who may be interested in her goods! You must cultivate contacts with the guardians here. The real Secret Service of Mauritania.

If you are an enterprising Koli, and everyone here is, and you open a mechanics workshop in Tevragh Zeina, you can bet your ass that within a month there will be another six workshops opened up all around you! You are, an enterprising Bidan and decide to start a business, 'I think I'll open a boubou boutique, now where . . . I know, beside the other twelve at Marche Boubou that don't have more than three customers between them during the day!' Great idea! The Bidan has no idea about commerce and wanders from disaster to disaster. Shops open and close overnight to relocate and do the same, over and over and over. There are dozens of barrows all selling the same crappy Chinese goods in Marche Capital, that you can buy the same goods in the dozens of covered shops, two seconds away. There are dozens of barrows at Marche Marocaine selling tiny bags of peppercorns, spices, stock cubes, rice, beans, lentils, vegetable oil etc that you can go into the nearby covered market and purchase from dozens of stalls all selling from huge sacks and huge barrels of vegetable oil. Marche Salt, Marche Dates, (the kind you eat but a very interesting idea has just occurred to me) Marche Rope, Marche Leather, the same thing. The repetition of commerce is staggering in the extreme. Marche de Tentes behind Marche Marocaine, Marche des Chevres at Toujinine, Marche des Moutons at Carrefour Madrid. Marche des Femmes at Tevragh Zeina is where you go to choose your cook or housekeeper or girl for a few hours cleaning but secretly hoping the pretty young one's will fuck you and your friends. Marche des Hommes for gardeners, guardians and drivers are a little more unique.

How do the smally people make enough money to eat let alone buy more goods and sell those? How do they afford the rents? In the case of the Bidan whores it's simple enough but the others? It never fails to amaze me, the blind stupidity of these people. Is it that family and friends buy from family and friends only? What makes you go to one very small stall with its limited supply of goods and not the other six hundred nearby? It's not about choice because they all have the exact same goods for sale. They make probably sufficient profit to buy a 0.5kg bag of rice. It's not about prices either because it's all the same fuckin' price! Ah, there I'm wrong, because as you leave the precincts of Marche Marocaine, where all the goods arrive at for distribution, the further you get from there the prices increase. So, a kilo of mangos at Marche Marocaine is 100UM, in Marche Capital it's 300UM a kilo. I can walk from one to the other in less than five minutes.

These jaunts to get what you need can take hours if not all day. The process is tiring, not just in terms of having to negotiate piste in the side streets, as there's sand everywhere, the traffic, beggars, street hawkers and would-be bandits out to contrive to have you give them money for some scheme or other, there's the constant negotiation for prices and if he doesn't have what you want he will go to say, another stall or shop, 2m away and then negotiate commission for going there! One man increased the price of a knife by 200UM. "What, did you take a taxi?" I asked and left. It takes time to find out the prices but right off if you're a toubab, then it's three times the price. That's standard. So price accordingly if you decide to come here. Then again I don't think the Tourist Board of Mauritania will want me to publish somehow, as I believe I will have chased away hundreds of potential tourists. If just ten people buy this journal of a mad man, they'll spread the word and the FO will red flag Mauritania, if they haven't already! It must say something if I'm the ONLY UK national to have registered at the British Consulate here. So twice now I have been unique in R.I.M.! Aren't I a special person?

The same Marche exists for the majority of restaurants, (and I use the term loosely) which are arranged by and large along four streets, all selling much the same cheap; and I struggle here to best describe the food, well shit would be fair. There are some gems in amongst them but you generally pay for what you get. A sandwich for example is half a baguette filled with a handful of cold chips, mayonnaise, some salad (don't expect too much) and a very small amount of meat of some description, all for the handsome price of 300UM. (Current rate is 485 to the English pound I believe.) The majority, 99.999% and even some of the best, would be closed down by Health and Safety in the UK and it is to my constant wonderment that I haven't ever had food poisoning. I now firmly believe I could eat nuclear waste and have nothing more than a full stomach feeling for two hours. You will not believe some of the small Senegalese restaurants I've eaten in where you'd think you'd die of at least four notifiable diseases. The food funnily enough; in the myriad of the restaurants in Cinqieme, the African quarter of Nouakchott, is in fact bloody good. Just incredibly dirty, squalid fly infested and cramped places to eat. The standard offering is Tiboudienne (chey-boo-zhen) a fish, vegetable and tomato flavoured rice dish for the universal price of 300UM though you can have a 200UM plate or considerably more for as many people as is needed for. My favorite is poulet yasser, (lemon chicken) and this dish can be varied with either meat or fish. This quartier is densely populated and it's where the African population who toil for the Bidan live. The sand is black. The many heaps of rubbish are fetid, flies everywhere and every building looks as if it's ready to tumble and at night, pute alors gentlemen, the streets are filled with thousands of perfectly clean and immaculately dressed gazelles and giraffes. These being small pretty girls and tall pretty girls. It's a feast for the eyes. Just stop to talk to her and if her first language is Wolof, keep going. Don't look back, I know she's beautiful but just keep going . . . think piranha. Think piranha. It'll pass, and as you stroll on, 'Oh my God's she's delicious too!'

Of the best restaurants in town, these are in my opinion for quality of food, prices and cleanliness of a European standard: Pizza Lina, an Italian owner, where once, you could roll in the toilet and spliff on the terrace but can drink Italian wine. Asia Restaurant, where you can drink cold beer and spliff in the garden and be entertained by extremely beautiful Chinese girls. Le Prince, the first restaurant in Nouakchott which was situated on a piste and run by Lebanese, though at the bottom due to cleanliness but pristine compared to the 99.9% who aren't. Sadly Café Brussels no more. 100% European standard of hygiene, quality of food and service, where you could spliff inside and on the terrace and roll discreetly under the table at the back. Fiesta, an excessively expensive Mexican restaurant by my standards. There are other more expensive and discreet restaurants to go to but way way out of my price range. Somewhere the French businessman is persuaded by his whore . . . sorry girlfriend, to go for that special dinner. El Khaima is the restaurant in town with the view of the city. I couldn't afford coffee there, but it's where Mohamad the co-owner of Café Tunis is taking me for his English lessons and lunch of course and free sheesha at Café Tunis. I have waived my fee as the three times a week feast on top of the world and sheesha, more than compensates my time teaching with my friend. Then there's the three cafes frequented by the whores but they do serve good fare and the whores go there because they are filled with toubab. These are Café Sahara, Café Savannah and Petit Café. Of the three, I stay away from Petit Café because the whores are younger, 14-18 and always more of a pain in the ass there. I eat in two Senegalese restaurants, one behind the Chinese Embassy and one in Cinqieme but you'd never find it and it would be condemned instantly by H&S as would the first one but clean for a Senegalese eatery. El Karama does excellent falafel and not far from Menata. My favourite café is Café Tunis on Ave Kennedy, for coffee, sheesha and the best crepes in town. It's full of Tunisians, Algerians, Lebanese and of course Bidan. I'm on good terms with Mohamad and Raouf, the Tunisian brothers who own and run it. Of course I am, I'm running an advertisement on this page for them. Open from 0700-0300. See you there, oh by the way, did I mention I have my own table.

Then there's a gauntlet you have to negotiate on the south side of Marche Capital. The black market money changers. I have passed this way often enough with my distinctive turban and after one year of telling them to "Imshi!" before they've even thought of crossing the road to interrupt my peace, think it makes a difference? So one day, I engaged two Bidan men, who have made a habit of chasing after me, weaving in and out of traffic. "I'll change ougiya for ougiya, you can do this?" I asked. The two Bidan nodded enthusiastically. "Okay, if I give you 1500UM you give me 2000UM. That's okay?" The two took twenty seconds to discuss the transaction and nodded, smiled and then shook their heads, completely lost at sea. I attract a lot of imbeciles, mainly one, because Mauritania is full of them and two, because I elect to walk most places. Why I perform the second, this will become apparent later. Back to the two men of business. We wait another fifteen seconds for the two to decide what to do. I repeat my request and it suddenly dawns on them and they smile that smile and shake their heads, that says I'm lost. I then ask, "Is it because you don't understand what I'm asking you or that you don't agree with my request?" That smile appears again and I say slowly, "If I give you 1500UM . . . you give me 2000UM . . . because . . . you said you'd change ougiya for ougiya!" It eventually arrives somewhere in their Tardis heads, complete with the miniscule brain and they laugh. There's neither the shaking or nodding of their heads at this juncture and matter of factly I say, "Okay, thank you for your time, good day." And I leave. I've passed these men of business and asked them the same question hundreds of times since, to be confronted by that same smile. Lost in time and place, as well as being normal for Norfolk.

Mauritanian commerce is practiced by everyone at every level, of every layer of society but the recipient of the king's ransom of the total amount of money garnered is the Bidan. The use of children, is forbidden by law. Code du travail 2004. Loi no. 2004-017 (July 2004) Article 153 and 154. It sets 14 years as being the minimum age for employment and a minimum 9 year period of education, and according to the said document the worst forms of employment are: slavery, child exploitation, activities that exceeds the physical capability of a child or can be considered degrading, trafficking of children, activities that require children to handle chemicals or dangerous materials, work on Fridays or holidays or outside of Mauritania.

You now have a small idea of what's allowed and not allowed. Again you can easily access the information via Foggy Bottom. Despite this being in place, you will see boys aged 7 and upwards driving charettes delivering water, bricks, transferring household waste to a local tip, scrap metal or as taxis. I saw three boys with an average age of ten, at 1445 in temperatures of 40°C + with a huge pile of battered rusty gas canisters tied onto the charette with tatty old cargo netting. I've seen a boutique in Marche Capital selling these same rusty battered canisters and a Bidan smoking inside. I of course smelt it before I saw it, did an immediate 180 and took the long way around. The smell of gas from the charette was noticeable even at 5m! The boys were of course intoxicated. Street vending is highly popular and relatively easy and safe work. Talibes, are boys out on the street for 12 hours a day begging on behalf of some of the marabouts who run Qu'ranic schools. These boys generally have insufficient access to food or housing to compensate for the long hours standing in heavy traffic at intersections and walking around the cafes at night. They are handed over by poor parents who simply cannot afford to feed them. They have to make 300UM a day or be faced with being chained up and food and water withheld. There are other Qu'ranic schools which don't send the boys out but are in a very small minority. Children working as car mechanics, unpaid work carrying out domestic duties from 0700-2300, construction work, working in small family businesses, country girls working in the rural homes as unpaid domestics, out on the streets selling small bottles of bisap, or being sold for sex, or being physically and/or sexually abused whilst working as an unpaid domestic. In rural areas there exists an economy of bartering children and exploiting them in slave like conditions due to the sheer poverty they find themselves in.

The Ministry of Employment is the primary agency responsible for enforcing Child Labour Laws and regulations. It has an institutional mechanism in place to receive complaints. Yup. The inspectorate has eight inspectors for the whole of Mauritania, but lacks the capacity to investigate and address potential violations due to a lack of resources. "Surprise Surprise!" Thank you Cilla, This is claimed by not having the vehicles, telephones and the equipment necessary to carry out their work. Yup. Yup and yup. Everyone here HAS a fuckin' mobile phone. Everyone here, except your truly generally speaking, uses taxis because every car IS a fuckin' taxi. And the necessary equipment necessary of course missing is, A FUCKIN' BRAIN! One could buy an exercise book for 80UM and a pen for 50UM and pound the streets and within five minutes document several possibilities. Motivation to change the status quo is the fuckin' problem methinks. Then again what the fuck do I know? I'm just a verbose and belligerent Scot's bastard, is that not right Mr R? The man selling the gas in the shop has his ID card in his fat ass pocket, photocopy it 20UM and take his details down. Photo 1 minute his fat ugly ass 250UM! There are thousands of them all over the place. Thank fuck it's not a Marche! Find out the person responsible for building the building using children labour and prosecute his ass. OOPS, he's your cousin! Tear out the page and walk on! These inspectors may have Haratin at home, may have family who use children in their businesses and there's where the conflict of interest arrives. He's part of the same abusive Bidan system and can't prosecute someone from the same racial group for the same thing he and his family do, odds on he knows him anyway even if he isn't family! I could also quote the penalty's from Law No 075/3003 (17th July 2003) Against Human Trafficking and the improper use of children in the employment sector and the use of fraud and violence to abduct minors, but what difference does it make to you if it doesn't make a blind difference to the children being exploited? You'll only get as angry as I am and spoil your day. It's not your problem.

Prostitution here is an urban phenomenon driven by social ills, extreme poverty and a high rate of divorce, with a great many households headed by women. I know of villages along the Route L'Espoir where 90% of the villagers are women and children. Girls from the country side are brought by parents or acquaintances to look for work. More than a few are lured into the seamier side of life and by default become prostitutes. Their parents are very often ignorant of their daughters real life and of course welcome the money sent home to them. Why do you think I have been asked so many times to take daughters from nomad camps. To inject money and new blood into their impoverished families and for those in the know, to save their daughters from being abused and used. In rural areas children perform tasks necessary to the survival of the family, it's the African way. Town life is far wilder and ten times more dangerous than the Sahara could ever be.

On our way to and from Marche Capital, we will be badgered by street hawkers selling, mobile phones, phonecards, food, cheap sunglasses, cheap watches, T-shirts, sandals, a camera, beads, jewelry. The woman with the five children at the traffic lights has simply rented these children and babies to hand them back at night and pay 500UM. There are street hawkers for everything you can imagine. Lots of beautiful African girls sell their bodies on a part-time basis when out of work, lots of girls do it full time and many many others don't. The girl you meet at the café or restaurant who engages your eye and subsequent conversation, will hope by the night's end that you can give her a 10 000UM or less, gift, without having to fuck you. She's now your girlfriend of course. On no account hand over any money. I don't care if she's the most beautiful creature that you have ever seen in the entire world or a delicious life form from a distant planet on Star Trek, simply because you're a computer geek and don't have contact with girls. The fact that she has asked makes her suspect. Are you listening? Taxi fare is ok and perhaps paying for her sandwich and coffee but leave the rest of your money and your libido where it should be in a public place. Kept out of sight and under control. These girls are savage, and can strip you of your money and pride faster than a shoal of piranha taking apart the baddie in a James Bond movie.

Construction is done by hand here. Well, you're thinking, isn't that the case everywhere? Consider this, a team of four Koli toiling from 0500 to 1700 six days a week making bricks. A pile of sand, a pile of sea shells, because there is no aggregate unless it's imported and only for the very rich Bidan, four shovels, concrete and an ancient electrically operated brick mould or the unmechanical variety. A water supply either by hose or oil drums. All day everyday, with Friday off. It's back breaking and the salary, shit of course but the bricks sell for a fortune. There are hundreds of these teams all over the capital. Should you be less than gentle with a brick it will break and crumble apart. A round from an AK will pass through a house no problem and still have enough momentum to kill your neighbour in his salon as he drinks his tea. These bricks are then handed over to the next team and made into houses, high rise constructions, singled roomed restaurants, mehlafah boutiques, a single roomed house at the roadside, whatever. The sand and shells of course contain salt, so decay sets in from day one. The single roomed dwelling you see at the road side out of town being reclaimed by the desert, fall apart four walls at a time. I heard a building behind Marche Capital collapse one morning, three stories that simply fell like a house of cards, killing all the occupants. I arrived to see a massive cloud of dust and for once, there was silence in a market place that you can't normally hear yourself think in. There are no hoists or are very rare, so the cement needed to put the bricks together has to be shoveled onto successive rickety wooden platforms or hoisted up in battered 20L paint cans, with old rope. The bricks are passed up hand to hand. They are huge.

Scaffolding, hold on. NO NO NO, you misunderstand me. Sorry to mislead you there for a moment but these structures would look more at home in the Amazonian jungle rather than to be used to build a major construction with. These are rudimentary wooden planks, and supports that are ready to fall apart, nailed and tied together with electrical cable or string or cord fashioned from your new beautiful girlfriend's mehlafah.

They simply punch a hole in the already constructed wall and slot in a 2x2 or 3x1 or what ever the hell size it is, and nail or tie on the platform. God knows how they manage to stay together. So as the building rises you will see holes everywhere resembling an artillery attack on your new house! Even if it's six stories up, you can see them using the same type of wooden ladder your eight year old and his best friend next door slung together during the summer holidays, from two long but different lengths of wood and a few struts nailed in place. For you it's wood you'd burn whilst talking with your male counterpart next door whilst doing a bit of male-bonding or, throw it away at the recycling centre conveniently situated a short drive from your home. You of course know, that they'll only fall a metre or so onto the nice lawn and therefore aren't too concerned, other than making holes in the lawn and on reflection, direct them up to the back, where there's more mud than grass. The men haul up cement and bricks using them. There's no compensation should they survive the fall and no Social Security if they can't work as a result of their injuries. The Black is dispensable. Just as there won't be to look after a child crippled for the rest of his life by working there. They can be replaced from the slave's baby factories of Cinqieme. Don't think me blasé about the lives of these men and boys, by this last caustic comment. I have many friends from this quartier and it both saddens and enrages me to see them have to risk their lives day and day out for 104UM an hour. The boys much less of course, simply because the ruling class won't pay a decent wage, simply because the Junta won't ensure that all children are looked after. It wouldn't of course make the work any safer. At least the house slaves are getting fed, these men buy their own food and during Ramadan, work without water or food. The Bidan can't cross the fuckin' road without a spot of gavage!

As for the finishing of these new houses, the quality in a majority is abominable. Of course here, there are pretty interiors and there are extremely lovely interior but on closer inspection, it's still the house that jack built. There are no blueprints for one thing. Electrical cable nailed to the walls, incomplete sockets, jerry rigged bathroom equipment. Plumbing's a complete farce and there's no sewers. If you turned up to see your Barrett house in a similar condition; and I chose this example as the best of the worst of the UK's offering, you'd be in complete denial. I know I am every single time when I see new houses. I smile and nod my head enthusiastically at the awe and wonderment of it's new proud owners. "Yes. It's beautiful." I say, thinking that a khaima would be a much safer option. Which a great deal of people put on their terraces to sleep in at night or as an alternative venue for tea, even if they have two salons to do so. You can take the nomad out of the desert but not the desert out of the nomad apparently. So the proud Bidan wife will move in with her team of assistants to help her with her busy life of drinking tea, resting, afternoon naps, stuffing snacks down her fat neck, having tea prepared by the house boy when you so wish and eat tagine prepared by the cook at the appointed hour and the clothes washed by and the children looked after by the new 14 year old country girl, that your husband would love to fuck and eventually does, along with his brother and her 16 year old son. And all the time you are staring everywhere thinking, 'When are they going to finish it?'

Okay, driving. Driving in Mauritania is extremely dangerous. I've already mentioned an experience of out of town driving. The overtaking on the brow of a hill of an overloaded brousse taxi meeting a huge green lorry on the Route L'Espoir. Here you will come across dozens of brousse taxis loaded up with eight or nine people and luggage, 4x4's with an enormous amount of baggage and six to ten people up top, White vans; with mentally handicapped versions of the White Van Man in the UK, top heavy with baggage and perhaps twenty to thirty passengers. Because even White Van Man wouldn't fuckin' dare get into one, making him Alladin Sane! Sorry David, it's a bad joke. The huge green ancient lorries that would be better placed in The Museum of Transport, also top heavy makes moving stock alongside the road a nerve racking experience. And the tyres, fuck me, I once saw a huge green lorry with huge gaping holes in the three of the trye walls and no tread to speak of on any of the tyres. I declined to take a lift and walked the 15km instead. Don't drive at night please, never ever! In town it has to be seen in the raw to be believed. I hope I can paint a vivid enough picture for you here. One day I hope to put it on YouTube if someone don't beat me to it.

Imagine if you will, a nation of untrained drivers without a standard driving test on the road and in the classroom, before you decide to drive down here. If you do, come in a gas guzzling NGO standby, the Toyota LandCruiser. If you go desert, carry GPS and a satellite phone. It's Buy n'go here. ID card and 100 euros. That's all there is to it, next! You can drive HGV, PSV, PAAF (Pissed As A Fart) and every other form of road going vehicle. There are signs but it's not necessary to follow them and most importantly you should know that there is one rule, there are no rules.

It's mediaeval jousting gone motorised. Robot Wars would be a better description. Quite part from that, there are donkeys strolling around with or without charette, herds of goats and sheep, mad fuckin' crazy Kamikaze dogs, four kids on a quad cutting across your path at speed, Kamikaze charettes with driver, drivers on mobiles and drifting sand everywhere. Did I mention it's fuckin' treacherous? Maybe I started off gently, ah I said dangerous, no that would be banging your head off the dodgem car pole at the fairground and not wearing the strap. You can at any time drive where you want to at any speed, either forwards or backwards into or away from traffic. Thankfully most accidents tend to be small affairs. If not, then it's a complete wipe out. No survivors, all the eggs in the box are broken. There's a car graveyard at the edge of the camel market, for the Sahara it's a little cold there.

Or in the case of my accident, completely farcical. I was in a taxi with Mwoiny in the front seat and we come upon a blocked route where two cars had T-boned. Nothing drastic but a little road rage had taken over proceedings and the taxi driver got out to have his 20UM's worth. His handbrake isn't working and there's a slight incline. We sit and wait. The car then decided to roll, ever so gently and Mwoiny true to form starts to act up because she wants to get the fuck out of it because it's smelly and hot. The car slowly picks up momentum and I can't get my foot over to hit the brake because I have her on the floor stationed between my legs, there's a small bump and the immediate tinkle of glass breaking. It's the car that's T-boned the other we've hit and now the taxi driver and the other man come and give me a mouthful. We're about 2km from the auberge. They rant and rave occasionally, then gave me a mouthful on how I had crashed the car into his! At this I get out and tell them to talk to my dog and go to untie her cord. Both men then take off into a nearby shop and close themselves in. Both cars would have been condemned in the UK and you would normally only see them in a scrap yard. I imagine what Archie, my imaginary Glasgow cop friend would have said had he been called out to this accident. 'Sirs, hello. Please tell me that both these cars fell off of a flat bed truck, en route to the scrapyard and that the same flatbed truck, has now been stolen or perhaps spirited away by a UFO?' The two imbeciles would have smiled that stupid smile that Archie instantly would have known their whole story without explanation. As for paying him a small gratuity . . . 'I think you and I need to go the station, sirs!' I begin laughing my head off as I walk over to the shop and tell the driver that

I've hurt my neck as a result of the accident and claim compensation. 5000UM! I'm trying to keep a straight face. He's dumbfounded and I again ask him for the money or I'll send for the police. He won't come out because Mwoiny's giving him her 200's worth. I ask again and he tells me to go away. I then take my bag out of the taxi and walk off, saving the 1000UM I would have had to have paid all the way from Teinweich. He didn't come to the auberge for it.

I was given a lift one night by a very rich young Bidan, as I walked through a residential area where I wouldn't get a taxi, who had a laptop on his lap, watching 50 Cent's videos and using his mobile and chatting to me in Frangalais. As it was a brand new Merc I immediately put on the seat belt on as I do when I can. He laughed and said that as he had airbags front and side the belt wasn't necessary. Thank God it was an automatic. Diving on the main Route Nouadibou in Nouakchott is like the real life version of Dungeons and Dragons, well all the roads are really, but this is town madness. It's more frenetic than simply hammering it from A to B, where there is more order but obviously not any safer. You have drifting sand to cope with, all the fuckin' checkpoints and not many stops in very hot, smelly and cramped conditions. Crossing intersections you roll the dice and make a dash as the driver opposite decides against your better judgment to cut inside the nearside to turn left into the on-coming traffic, when you are trying to do a normal right turn and there's someone coming onto your left and another cutting him off. It's the reason I walk everywhere if I can possibly help it.

I was out near Las Palmas going to visit Mame, Eric and Yusuf their new baby. A driving school car slowly passes me, I'm actually capable of walking faster than this woman's driving. In the driver's seat is a small fat Bidan woman who can barely see over the bonnet of this battered Honda Civic, with its hand painted sign in Arabic, welded to the roof, she's swathed in her mehlafah, her eyes barely seen . . . and . . . and . . . a paraplegic middle-aged Bidan lying full length in the front passenger seat on a mattress with a 13 year old boy sitting up high on a heap of material, cramped up in the back passing on advice given by the driving instructor to the woman and darting his head left, right and back surveying the traffic. You and I know that this is merely a chance element and will make no difference if they return home or not. There's constant chatter except for the woman who looks neither left or right as traffic whizzes by her on Route Nouadibou as she hugs both piste and tarmac. I butt in and walk along for 20m or so and the instructor's happy to talk and touts for business. Never is an opportunity wasted here. Everyone is a potential customer, even one with an UK driving licence. I wish them luck, 'Bismillah.' It's the only time she has taken her eyes off from dead ahead, driving at 6km/hr. It would take even Archie sometime to compose himself before stepping up to the plate for this one!

Archie, my Glasgow cop friend has a soft but commanding Glaswegian accent and a rugged not handsome face. He's a tall chap in his 30's, not yet with the stomach but it's on the verge and he's seen a thing or two. He has a girlfriend, Heather, whose not so very pretty but has a fit body and like him has a sarcastic sense of humour but never, never in his wildest dreams has he ever seen the likes of the daily events that cross my path . . . his laugh always sets me off. It's a berger thang. I have another imaginary friend, with a West Midlands accent and he's a real loser. He talks to his reflection in a window at night and thinks it's a real person! Stinky and Bloaty were the same dead dog lying in the street, until Bloaty went away! Ahhh! We're a lonely lot. I have spoken to other bergers and bergeres from France and Spain and we all compose poetry which is not for publication! It can be a little too dark and bizarre, I wouldn't want anyone doing a Sylvia Plath on me just because of something I happened to put into your head!

Cars exit and enter the main thoroughfares from small exit or to entry points or wide pistes with speed, pulling out in front of moving traffic, with a concertina effect and it's almost but not quite most every time just a miss. There's no circulation and out walking, NO mp3 please, you have to be ready to take emulate the dive over the touchline at Murrayfield to score the winning try against England in the last two seconds and send Scotland into a massive united roar all over its 78 000 sq km surface. They will drive at you with speed on piste blasting their horn for you to move. As I've said before it makes no difference on your age, ability or sex. Road rage is frequent and in most cases short-lived but anything can happen and it's always good to know where a block of concrete can be found in an emergency to dissuade the more fervent imbeciles from getting out of their cars. Or use the door approach, my favourite. As you sit with friends in the Menata you can all hear far off, the long screech of tyre on tarmac and . . . wait . . . wait . . . ah no! Missed again. 20UM coins are pushed across the table in different directions. By way of comparison driving in town in the Scotland is like, Scaletrix. Orderly. Here it's Dodgem City without the regimented order of dodgems at the fairgrounds in the UK. At the end of your trip here, you'd have chronic whiplash, have battered your head off the fuckin' pole about a dozen times, clashed heads with your new beautiful girlfriend even more and never again does she want to speak to you, just as much as you never want to step inside another fuckin' dodgem, for the rest of your natural life. Even if it were free and came with a new beautiful girlfriend! Archie's pissing himself, again! By the way when my UK licence expires, it doesn't here obviously, but by the time that happens, Inshallah, I'll be sailing a yacht here! I'll be doing that with Jonas, he's a Kiwi sailor who has a dream . . . don't we all?

Wildlife in Nouakchott. "Oh no Mohamed, not another reference to those Wolof girls again!" No no, calm yourselves my dears. This is your actual honest to goodness account of the animal population of Nouakchott. Okay, we've done the Bidan, the Wolof girls, the packs of dogs, herds of sheep and goats free range or bergered by dogs. Camels, cows and beautiful Arab horses tethered outside their owners houses. Goats, the bastards! Olivia, the owner of Maison D'Hote Jamilla, arrived one day with her new car covered, bonnet to boot in deep hoof scratches from six goats who had used her car to get to choice foliage overhanging the wall, where she had parked under for ten minutes, for the shade. I once saw four goats sitting in a car next to Agence Mattel. There was a driver and three passengers having in-car snacks. These being, the upholstery, a newspaper, a box of paper tissues and a Marlboro packet! I do believe I've seen her before, a discerning specialist as perhaps the upholstery was a little too tough for their constitution! Putain! They eat all the rubbish of the day, found heaped all over the capital. Plastic bags, nappies . . . I can't go on or I'll be sick! Donkeys, much abused and a bloody disgrace that Muslims should do so. Or anyone of any religion for that matter. Here as in Spain it's institutional. Cats by and large are accepted by Mauritanians but aren't pets. A Bidan is s likely to caress it as they are to throw it against the wall or out of the door should it give the Bidan a claw or two. There are no pets here except for the ex-pat Euro's. Obviously not me as I'm a savage bastard. There are the same birds as you would find in the UK. One bird I love is like a small Chinese kite from underneath and has such a soft sweet voice. Luminescent greens and blues. They range in large flocks and can be seen and heard every morning and evening feeding at Col Ghaddafi's campsite at the Libyan Embassy just next door. It's fuckin' pigsty. It has a huge football pitch, well, goals and sand really but enormous for a pitch.

You'll see the occasional falcon, hanging around, though I've never seen them in action in town.

As dusk begins to fall during the hot season, huge bats appear and swoop high and low in their search for mosquitoes whose numbers dramatically increase at this time. I was in the Menata's garden one evening sitting under the small canopied table with a friend. There are six French tourists sitting at a nearby table under the canopy of the trees. We're talking to Dylan and one girl shouts out, "Oh it's raining!" In throes of an orgasm I believe as it was rather hot and she thought . . . "No," I pipes up, "It's bat piss!" Everyone scarpered for the toilets and used every available sink, including one girl who half stripped off and tried to get into the not so large hand washing bowl in the garden! Great TV! If you stand on a terrace you can have them fly around your head. Another flying beauty, is the vulture, and can be seen mostly in two's or four's circling high around town surveying the many choice morsels of carrion available. Of course you see more out in the desert. One of my guardian friends Buckery phoned me and asked to help transfer Birdy to a new home. "I'm a fuckin' berger of camels," I said, "what the fuck do I know about vultures?" He of course had a smart-ass answer, which escapes me for the moment and I couldn't see him doing it alone. Birdy was an huge emaciated vulture with attitude attached to a concrete cover with a length of electrical cable. Never again. I carry a little memento of Birdy on my leg. These Mauritanians are crazy! Toc toc.

Again from the Menata and since, here at the school, was my meeting with two Moroccan monkeys. A couple. I had a fever and had come to the Menata to see Dr Cherif, a French doctor who specializes in tropical medicine. Armed with a bag of medical goodies I decamped to the khaima on the tree covered terrace. I burned and vomited and burned and slowly cooked my brain. At about 0200 I had to get up to go to the bathroom. There sitting on the terrace were two monkeys. Naw, no fuckin' way. I dismissed it as an hallucination and went to be sick and have a shower to reduce my fever. When I got back they or my hallucination had gone and I went to sleep. I surfaced in the afternoon to talk and eat with Amadou. "Of course there are! They come here all the time!" He said. Then when I moved temporarily into the room on the terrace of the school, I was resting up before class and saw lumps of concrete raining down onto the terrace floor and left to see, the same male running taking the flak as the female hid behind the terrace wall. I immediately threw the missiles back at the kids on next door's roof and sent them packing. The female had a very small kitten in her arms that she cradled. He came back sat on the wall near her, she reached up and kissed him on the lips, looked at me, she then put the kitten in her mouth and the two took off across the Libyan Embassy wall, moving towards the French Embassy, crossed the road and went into the French Embassy. The Embassy is shrouded in very old trees and ideal for monkeys to live in. They are regular visitors and I leave old bread, roll over the occasional apple and throw a banana. I have woken up in the morning with the two of them sitting close by. I know it might seem I'm a little Doctor Dolittle at times but I'd rather sit and talk to animals over the vast majority of Bidan in this asylum. On the subject of monkeys, I have been told there are chimps from Central Africa here in the capital, but they are very secretive. I cannot confirm this as I haven't personally seen them. I have seen the occasional Moroccan monkey chained up here and there, babies. They're shit scared of course. The kids bait them by throwing stones at them or poking them with sticks but only when there's a toubab around. If Lesley were there she'd hand over the dosh and then have a maniacal baby to feed and house. "No! It would be yours truly left holding the baby! No fuckin' way sis! Phone them!"

And to finish off, again from the Menata. There are two resident, well I used to think this but on reflection not, two tortoise. One huge, just a little over a metre in length, the other slightly smaller. A customer once reversed over the biggie and he was perfectly okay except for the red paint scrape mark he still carries. There is a tunnel at the left hand corner of the garden next to parking. I was with two French drivers I know and a short-long term resident, JP. I've not long finished class, it's 2130 and they've been inhaling a little French red and a petard or two. I'm stone cold sober. JP being the smallest decides he can go down the tunnel and see if he can see the tortoise. The other two immediately get a length of rope not wishing to miss out on free entertainment and immediately tie it around his left ankle. They continue to give him good advice, except for the look out for snakes and scorpions and JP is now stripped down to vest and rolled up jeans, and is sporting a gay Kamikaze type bandana; it's so French girlie, puts a little pen torch in his mouth, primes a camera and crawls into the tunnel. It's tight fit but he keeps going. The other two continue with a little red and I roll a petard, and we wait until the rope's at it's at full stretch. JP's persuaded to come back only when he's dragged back a metre or two, and I'm thinking he'll be eating a ton of very dirty sand. He has and of course he's completely covered in dark damp sand. No bites then. Apparently it goes like this and I've seen the photos too. It goes in a metre moving west that's right facing it, into a large chamber that JP can just about curl up into a ball and sit in, then moving down wards south at a gentle slope for four metres you come to a tunnel moving east and downwards, continuing to move down and south-east after another three metres there's a tunnel moving west and downwards, the tunnel carries on in the direction of the Canadian Consulate. Where he ran out of rope, he assumes he was five metres down. And he wants to go back down! I've a lot of catching up to do as far as Dylan is concerned and I nonchalantly ask, "Was there anything else down there?" He's smiling and shaking his head, searching for the image of a stray dog or cat, still smiling he says, "Nothing!" "Nothing like, scorpions or snakes?" I add. Shortly afterwards, he's watering the garden with French red! My two chums are doubled up with laughter and I'm talking with Dylan after a very difficult class. "Happy days are here again . . ." 'Just for once it ain't me, Hallayfuckinluyah!' "Archie, there's a daft French cunt here who needs a Section 24!"

[1]   The John Hopkins News Letter SMIR talk exposes modern day slavery. Brendan Schrietar and Maria Andrawis. 5th December 2003

[2]   BBC World News 13th December 2004. Slavery: Mauritania's best kept secret.

## CHAPTER TWELVE

# A BLAST FROM THE PAST
# AND INTO THE FUTURE

THE RALLIES THAT once came through RIM were all inspired by the Saharan dream of conquering her. Not possible. The were banger (B) or professional (P) or the organised privateers going to Dakar or Banjul; of which before the Salafist madness, there was: the Amsterdam, Twente and Nederland Dakar's (B), the three German, Dresden Dakar's (B), Lisboa and Valencia Dakar (P) and the Plymouth Banjul (B). As well as the French lot, who being the first to pull out in 2006, gave everyone the easy option of cancelling theirs. They marched off to pastures new, everything in place. The 120 vehicle Slovenia to Dakar (P) turned back at the Spanish border when news of the murders reached them. I like the Slovenians, they are generally laid back, very wealthy and are a gentle race of well balanced and interesting people to talk to. All in all, there is little benefit to the local populations of the country's they pass through, other than a handful of guides, auberges and officials.

In between the 'official' rallies, there were the privateers who are mostly professional in their outlook and equipment. In 2006 Scot's 'Grays' arrived on 14 GS1200's and a 4x4 support truck. It was somewhat of a surprise for them when a French speaking African combo dressed turban clad man and Bidan guide to approach them and after the usual greetings, 'Salaam aleykum' and 'Bonjour, ca va?' shake everyone's hand say "How's it goan?" in broad Glaswegian. Hoots and screams of laughter and utter disbelief. Lot's of "Fuck, me! I'd never of guessed! Fuck me!"

"No thank sir, you're not pretty!"

Well naturally, it's the clothes, the language and the place we're meeting in, it can disturb the senses somewhat.

"Fuck me! Ya bastard!" He says. I ask, "What did you do before you retired?"

He replies, "I was a police inspector."

"Fuck me, your mouth's dirty!" I reply.

Dahide fell in love with every Scot's girl (who I asked to say were lesbians) on the Plymouth.

From these rallies I have met a great many interesting and decent people and quite frankly, a lot of clinically insane sons of bitches, who should have had arrived secured in a straight jacket and be permanently sedated. Foremost amongst them a minority of Dutch, whose reputation has tarnished the majority, would make people pack up and leave for the desert, prior to their arrival. They arrived at 60 cars per weekend for one month Dec-Feb. Like a plague of grasshoppers, they arrive at 1700, disgorge and immediately if not attending to their car's mechanical problems, unload essentials, beer and hashish and to and fro between toilet, kitchen, drinking, rolling and pashing de shpliff. They party all night until 0300, get up at 0600, make coffee and joint or finish beer and joint, pack up and drive of in a massive convoy, going south. The terrace in the Sahara was a sight to behold. How is it possible to leave your boots or trousers that you wore last night? The Joseph's Coat of Many Colours trousers are by far the first item that strikes the eye, even through eyes as bloodshot as mine were! I remember him leaving wearing shorts, a T-shirt and big yellow clogs. Torches, magazines that you don't need to be able to understand Dutch to read, shoes, beer kegs, sleeping bags, shirts, sweaters, the list is endless and I've gotten some nice gear out of it. Bilal and Khalifa simply scoop up the clothes, shoes, sleeping bags and odds and sods to sell them at the market at Cinqieme. I can't allow them to have the magazines, which would be inappropriate as the elder Muslim present to allow them to be subverted in such a manner!

Come onto the terrace of the Sahara for an evening stroll, as the occupants are getting down to serious discussion after imbibing and smoking as if it were going out of fashion. One man has decided he's going to chat up Mwoiny, because she's quite pretty apparently. He didn't understand that he was baiting Mwoiny with his big yellow clogs and she ripped into the gentleman. Then the children continued to run around the playground leaving the recently chewed imbecile to lick his wounds in the bathroom. I couldn't possible smoke all I was offered to pacify me by his school chums. Mwoiny too was given a blob and wouldn't partake in any case. She doesn't like people who are drunk wearing big yellow clogs. On his return, I told him that he, "hopefully had all of his injections prior to coming to Africa because I wasn't going to pay for another."

One year, a Dutch wreck, no, an abortion of an estate car arrived. On the bonnet was a plastic baby, painted black with an erect phallus, a poster of a naked girl in stockings, sellotaped inside right for the benefit of the checkpoints. Theshe Dutch shpasticshs had performed featshs of unbridled lunacy at every shtop and NKT wash to be no eshcepshun. Sho, after fuelling up on shmall beershs and shpliffs, Shpastic number 2, took off left from the Shahara . . . I'm sorry I can't continue like thish . . . turned around Carrefour Nouadibou Un and drove shtraight for Rondpoint Nouadibou Deux. No . . . no he drove straight for RND! At speed!! As he hits the high kerb of RND, Dutch Wreck glides a little and slams down on all four wheels, near enough dead centre and there's a crack that says this camel's broken his leg. He guns the engine, sand spewing out behind him moving forward off of RND turns 270 showering the near vicinity in sparks because the car has grounded into on-coming traffic then the other 90 as he slews around RND with it's firework display from the rear, to come shuddering to a stop, 30 m away. After ten or so minutes or so, he's towed back to the auberge and works well into the night re-welding his chassis and repairing the shocks until it was time to go. Good to go, Shpashtic number two, took over driving the next leg.

My last offering from the many rally tales I could write another book on, concerns again, natually, the criminally insane side of the enthusiast out in the desert in his banger. Sitting outside the front door of the Sahara, it's early afternoon and plays like a scene from the Good the Bad and the Ugly. The Magnificient Seven Pot Bellies, dressed in new black heavy metal gear and sporting graying ponytails, slowly dismount and survey their home for the evening from the empty expanse out front of the Sahara. They get themselves organised in a relatively calm manner. Naturally they speak English and it transpires, that they had left associates in another car out in the desert, after they had stopped. The rally's end the goal and the most important aspect don't you think?

"Here in Desert Travel 101, what did I say a million years ago folks? If you see someone . . ." and everyone has their hands up.

"The girl in the red top."

She's lovely and as she smiles, she's biting her lip because perhaps she's not quite sure, "You walk towards them." She says shaking her small firm breasts from side to side as I clap my hands silently to give her a little reward for her efforts.

"Yes. Sooo . . . In this instance?"

Everyone's got their hands up again but I don't give a fuck as yes, pretty girl with the skimpy top's arm's straighter than anyone else's, waggling her slender fingers at me.

'Under control as always, berger of one.' "Yes . . . ?"

"Alison."

She clasps her hands around her left knee, with her slender left lag wrapped around her right leg.

'That's an ever so short skirt you're wearing Alison.'

"Okay . . . Alison, you do what?"

She smiles a big wide smile with her big beautiful eyes and full beautiful mouth.

"You stop and see, if there's anything's wrong."

She's now pushing her breasts outwards and staring directly into my eyes.

"Correct!"

I nod my thanks and acknowledgement to Alison, whose top has now been re-arranged slightly to indicate that a lecture on desert etiquette is absolutely necessary after class. You can access Sahara Overland for yours. The Slovenians would have simply radioed and found out that Dushka needed a piss. I love their dedication to detail!

Back to the Magnificent Seven then. The next morning they are up, showered, well breakfasted and packed up by 0800 and parked out front, facing south. The Pony Tail with the biggest paunch and therefore the man with experience, as nominated boss, is pacing up and down slowly and deliberately with the others inside the cars silently waiting. Mwoiny and I are sitting in shade as a small herd of goats pass bergered by two dogs. The berger's give each other the once over and it's then back to watching PT1 walking up and down. Three gazelles walk slowly by as camels would, each step measured for elegance. 08.10 PT1 turns to survey them and then the road back up towards Nouadibou. 08.14 He moves to stand at the open passenger door of Jalopy One, checking his watch. I do too. 08.15 and he pumps his fist up and down, gets in and slams the door as clouds of black smoke erupt out back, as the jalopies move off south. If there was a custom's tax for both gear and testosterone, they'd have been stopped in Morocco. The cars will be sold for charity in Banjul. The German's then fly back to wherever they are going with lots of excesse baggage. Dickheads.

It is then at Chey-bou-jen Time; 13.00, that the four similarly dressed occupants of Jalopy Three arrive by brousse taxi. They are short of baggage and temper. They ask when their rally colleagues arrived and left. Arrival and departure times are confirmed and they then go off with Hermann at a brisk pace. They shower, coffee and hail a passing taxi to take them direct to the Senegalese border. They had said that very soon the others will be in a hospital in Dakar. I don't blame them. I know Alison would have stopped; short of actual school qualifications as she is, she isn't a malicious person. The handbook for the Plymouth is a fuckin' disgrace. There's a copy at the Sahara should you stop there. The triangle from Nouadibou to Atar to Nouakchott was littered with wrecks during the season, which were wrecks long before they became inert wrecks. They have been in many cases, scooped up, reprocessed and perhaps former rallyists may find themselves in a familiar looking taxi. Thankfully, these cretins are few in number but if only one life is lost through actions such as this, then hospital should be the least of their problems.

"What should have happened to them Alison?"

"They should have been taken far out into the desert and left to walk back, teacher. But give them sufficient water."

"Well done Alison . . . Class dismissed."

As you all filter out, "Alison . . . can I see you for a moment, it's about your homework."

'That's a little too eager Alison!'

I would like to introduce you to a few people who have passed this way. First off is an intrepid Frenchman, Cyril Ribas. He has single-handedly GPS'd the whole of Mauritania (takla-makane.com) in a myriad of 2CV's. One quite frankly didn't look as if it would get him to the nearest corner shop for milk and bread, never mind go into areas I wouldn't go with a fuckin' camel! A thin, wiry, gentle soul I met three times in NKT. On his last stay he departed looking something like a WWI French pilot. The information on Mauritania he carries around in his head is quite astounding. We both know the same blue training shoe!

Anders, a Dane, an intelligent handsome swine and a gentleman documentary film maker, arrived in 2007 traveling with two Frenchies en-route to Mali with cars to sell. He stopped over in NKT and we met at the Menata. Why did I say yes to him and not the other three documentary filmmakers who asked for an interview? That I can't answer but I'm glad I did because I now consider him a very dear friend. Perhaps I can persuade him and his camera to come with me on a little stroll around Mali, Niger, Chad, S Libya and S Algeria, Morocco and RIM . . . more on that later.

We did my interview at Café Brussels the last night it was opened. Alex looked like a ghost and was physically and mentally exhausted. A year of intimidation from the Bidan owner of the butcher's shop next door, simply because he coveted his successful business had taken its toll on Alex. It started off by not announcing that the water bill had arrived and it would take days for Alex to find the truth of the matter. Then there would be trouble with the electricity bill and again days would pass before the truth of the matter would arrive. It is of course difficult to run a restaurant without either. The Bidan would send round African heavies to order food, cause trouble and not pay but Alex always had enough help and would eject these types as soon as it became apparent what was happening.

The next level of intimidation was breaking windows at night when the restaurant was closed. Not once but many times. A hedge was planted one day and pulled out at night to be thrown far away. Nothing for weeks then the offal from the butchers would be strewn across the terrace. Then, offal from the fishmongers which the Bidan had set up on the other side of Alex arrived. Rumour and bad publicity never did do much damage to his business but the stress was always there. It was surprising that his so-called ex-pat friends thought this was all normal. That he should just give up even though he had a family to look after. Blood one day, fish guts the next week but Alex kept going. He thought by buying meat and fish from his shops would help, of course not, no fuckin' way.

On the afternoon of the interview, we arrived to see a mountain of rubble nearby, the remains of the wall Alex had built around his terrace. Anders and I stayed the afternoon and night with Alex as he said farewell to his livelihood. They had a beer or two and I and Alex a few joints, with the employees of the Bidan sitting outside and the Bidan walking up and down in front of the restaurant. Anders and I got up to leave and we climbed over a non-existent wall. The Bidan were mystified and I went back to have another word with Alex as if I was about to give him into trouble and mimed banging my knee on the wall. Alex slid off his chair in hysterics and suffering from nervous exhaustion. We helped him indoors and left going back over the wall. He has decamped to Belgium to work there for six months and intends to come back for six, as Maryam and his son Sidi naturally have family here.

Vincent who arrived with his sister Severine and her boyfriend Yves-Marie in 2006, are three mad but gentle French nationals who had left Brighton on three Vespa's, sponsored to go on a 7000 km voyage through France, Spain, Portugal, Morocco, The Western Sahara, R.I.M. the Gambia, Mali to journeys end in Burkina Faso! (vespafreaka.com. mysite.wanadoo-mebers.co.uk) Vincent and I talked saddles for hours as I was unhappy about the Tamashek and Mauritanian saddles. He guided me in diagrammatical form on how to cut the leather and fashion what was basically an old tractor seat. It was of course designed for the maximum comfort of the camel. He has substantial experience making traditional saddles. I modified this into a sack form. You sit in and not on the camel. 19$^{th}$ Jan 2008, "Hello wee baby Margot."

Bizou pour tous

Zachary, is the American Jane Goodall. His track record in Africa is second to none, as he monitors the demise of the habitats and lives of the chimpanzee. He revisits all the chimp areas outwitting the authorities in his efforts to make contacts with the chimps. His depth of wisdom far outreaches his age and it is entirely possible to talk with him for hours. I asked him to come to speak with my English students one evening and he had them spellbound with his stories. I wish he'd write a book! His observations are astounding.

Matt an OCD sufferer came to RIM for a three day trip and stayed with me for months. He came to a country of inhabitants who'd make dumping illegal nuclear waste look like child's play! Putain! During his stay, he near-as-dammit bought NKT's supply of industrial strength wipes, he'd use AFTER his ritual 20 showers and subsequent same amount of arm washes to finish off with four wipes. He had great fear of eating from the same dish as everybody and I tried to take him to the cleanest cheapest restaurants to eat. He can't eat sugar either, which is difficult in a country whose diet includes one tablespoon of sugar PRN. Out walking in town and we'd have to re-negotiate the heaps of rubbish if the gap was less than 4m. We would walk four times the actual distance required.

Matt; through me, met Ould Bou, who was the major influence in disrupting Matt's serenity. This is a Class A1 Bidan Space Cadet who has a shorter fuse than my Chinese bangers. I had the misfortune to work with him for just over a month on behalf of his French partner Axel, who supposedly had gone to France for ten days. He never returned nor has anyone heard of his whereabouts since. Ould Bou deals in just about anything from fake passports, stolen cars, drugs and alcohol. Due to a difference of opinion over who's got who's money, I made declarations at the British Consulate and Surete National saying that if I have as much as an accident, or was found in possession of drugs and guns, that they should go looking for his Bidan ass.

Here's an example of that short fuse. He arrives at the Gendarmerie checkpoint Sortie Nouadibou and gets into an argument with an officer. The next second the officer is on the ground, his nose broken by a Glasgow Kiss. The Gendarmes arrest him and find 12kg of hashish in his car. He is taken in and held for three days after which, a fine of 1 000 000UM is paid for his release; without his ID card and passport. These will be returned after six months, by an associate who is no longer an associate. This man makes the simplest complication a gargantuan task to overcome. He knows nothing of the business of running a B&B and his only goal is to fleece as much as he can in the time available from the guests who have the misfortune to stay Chez Lui. He has an enormous appetite for hashish and is an alcoholic. The Aberge Awkar will have a representative at the Poste de Police sortie/entre Nouakchott. Decline the card from the spindly geek on the red Crusader quad, sporting a placard with the name of the auberge. If he shakes your hand, count your fingers and look for your watch should you wear it on your right wrist. Think I'm joking? At this point in time do you think there's a smile on my face?

The first time I passed the Poste Gendarmerie going to the camel market, I had 24 animals with me. I was stopped and asked for a camel. I smiled. "Sir, you know the brand, so why bother ask me for something that isn't mine to give?"

'Imbecile!' I said.

"Get your bag down!" He shouts.

"It's a bidon and food bag!" I shout back.

The stock is beginning to wander and he's keeping me from going after them.

"Give me 2000UM!" He shouts.

"For what?" I shout.

It dawns on me and I begin to take my trousers off. Inside the row of parked cars, waiting to be processed, the occupants begin to cheer. The women are going mental and I'm dragged off, my camels rounded up and I'm told to "Go away and don't come back!"

I shout, "Every time you ask me for money, I'll give you my trousers!"

Sooo . . . the next time I arrived, two boys immediately came to take the herd and keep them nearby and I, was taken into custody for tagine and tea. Take no shit from these thieves, try polite and if that doesn't work, try mad . . . it always fuckin'works!

On a short break waiting to be picked up by my boss, I met a young Dutch couple in the Sahara, en-route to South Africa by bicycle. The auberge empty for the three days we were together. On the morning of day two, I'm given two Franklin's to inspect. ($100 bills) They're brand new and different from the green versions I'd seen. Lots of security and I believe them to be real. I suggest that they take them to a bureau de change to verify them. Their story is: that whilst crossing NML they spy a white bundle just off piste and walk over. There's a huge package, cellophane wrapped and has $100 000 inside it, all new Franklins. They then take it and stash it deep in the sand and GPS the location.

"Would I like to go and get it?" They ask.

"NO!" I reply, "It isn't my cadeau and besides you buried it in a minefield!"

I suggest they carry on to South Africa and they can decide to do whatever but it would give them a good start for what ever should follow. They can line their clothes, bags and stuff it in the tubes of their bikes. They duly arrive back at the auberge and have smiles from ear to ear.

"They're real then!" I say and that's the end of it.

We spend another day together, they take off southwards and I go back to the desert. I wish them well.

Another cyclist, Fraser an Ozzie of Scottish ancestry had left Australia three years previously to my meeting him at the Sahara. He had cycled all of Russia, China, India, the Stans, Europe and down to R.I.M. He was en-route for South Africa and would decide if he went back to Oz or hop over to South America. In Kazakhstan he had been holed up with a family, stuck in between two snowdrifts for two weeks and had no way of communicating with the family. He simply sat in the corner and was fed. Cabin fever drove him to get his gear and bike and haul it up the mountainside to summit to find perfect conditions on the other side. The day that I met him he'd had eaten only couscous for three weeks, breakfast, lunch and dinner.

Before I go into my next shpeel, I must share my two Michael Palin 'Saharan moments.'

I saw only once, the trailer . . .

"Quite by chance I met an Englishman out in the Libyan desert . . ."

'Michael, it's we darling! You and your eleven assistants and no-one, no-one meets anyone by chance with lunch for sixteen people out in the fuckin' desert. You arrive with a huge mountain of salad in a fuckin' huge Tupperware box, two tea-ladies, a large camping table, plates, cutlery etc.'

In reflection Michael, I'd like to apologise for all the disparaging things I've said about Sahara. It comes directly from my ego the size of the universe, simply 'cause I lived there and believe myself to be special.

'Ain't fuckin' so!'

Many people live there on a level of subsistence that would kill you and I. I believe you had an infinitely more difficult time that I have ever had out there just on logistics alone. There's a wee something I'd like to ask you . . . would it be possible for us to do a four month, 3000 km, three Saharan country walk together, with the inclusion of nine documentaries as well as the making of, of course? There'd be a chariot or two and a shitload of camels. Three of the documentaries have a Scottish connection, two with a direct connecetion to my clan lands. This just goes to prove how similar we all really are, no matter where we began life.

My first Michael moment was . . .

"Quite by chance, I met an English couple out in the Mauritanian desert . . ."

Out on Wahad one afternoon, and from our lofty view up in dunes, I could see a short-wheel based Land Rover. As I got nearer I could see it was a right-hand drive. The unmistakable Paris/Dakar sticker on the door but of its occupants, there was no sign. I can see tracks and following them thinking, 'Stupid c . . .' as I pass from the back I can see a gray couple eating lunch. Folding table, chairs, table cloth, glasses, napkins, proper cutlery of course, glasses, a nice Bordeaux, salad, bread, cold meat. I am now about 5m from the Land Rover and I call out, "Bonjour, ca va?"

There's an instant, 'He's speaking French dear,' written across their faces.

Then a very polite, "Oh, hello," from the woman.

I sh sh sh Wahad who's not having any but after a few whacks, decides to go down. I'm certain Mrs South-Eastern Counties wifey isn't pleased but she continues to smile her lovely smile. I secure his cord to my baton and drive it into the sand. I then take off my turban and say, "As you have no French we'll talk English!"

The relief is obvious, with "Ohhh, you're Scottish, doo come to lunch!" In a very polite feminine voice.

We eat and talk at length. Before they leave I'm given a small Tupperware box with goodies. After Dakar it's onwards around Africa, no set plan. True nomads. Bon chance.

The second moment was a French gray couple. Where I found them in their 4x4, is en route for deep desert and good grazing but of no consequence to tourists whatsoever. Besides with the seven or so different grades of sand, you need to know yer sand! The wife was ever so pleased that I managed to persuade Blockhead to turn back, after he, she and I did the Pastis and snack thang. Well, I did the rolly thang. He'd refused to hire a guide as he had some notion of doing it himself without prior experience. Fuck the GPS!

Bet you're all sick to the back teeth with climate change and of its mentioning. For those of us who live on this planet, that should never be a consideration. Already at a disadvantage by proxy of the peole entrusted to look after her, of the total km² of Mauritania, 75% is desert and 25% Sahelian. So therefore, vulnerable to increased desertification. You don't need to be a scientist to know what I know you know! The winds that arrive here are marine trade wind, continental trade wind and monsoon. There are two climate zones. Out in the Sahara there are greater variations in daily and annual temperatures with low rainfall and high evaporation and in both the coastlines of Sahara and the border of Sahel, there is a smaller variation in temperatures, and higher rainfall humidity, naturally.

In the 70's and 80's severe drought had a devastating effect on all aspects of life here and a mass exodus from the desert to the rural areas took place. In the case of drought, it is the women who have to walk further to find and carry as is the need to secure firewood and water because the Bidan male won't get up off of his ass and lend a hand. So now, as everyone pours into the towns and cities, there's an increase in pollution due to the increase in the use of old cars and poor quality petrol. There's still an erratic access to a water supply and sanitation, whatever that means here, which all have given greater increased cause for concern in the matter of public health. As you now know, every town is a public toilet. The Hassaniya language course at the French Cultural Centre has three books. The third on ill health is as thick as the first two combined! Health education is non-existent and every illness begins in the stomach.

Deforestation has occurred both for natural and anthropological reasons and further complicates living standards and the ability to grow crops. Of course, in the natural world there are balances and flora and fauna had adapted to the severe drought conditions but, the effects of climate change have begun to reverse this process. It was already a precarious balance being an arid zone so further desertification is a simple one way trip. The projections are the southward expansion of the Sahara at 5km every year. The rising of the seas and variations of temperature have begun to alter the balance in the marine ecology off the coastline, with grave visions for the future in both financial and ecological terms. Coastal species will be replaced by deep sea species. The projections for marine transgression, with a mere 2cm rise in sea levels, will be 25m of land lost every year. In 2009 the sea rushed in to embrace Cityplage and Sogim Cinquieme, driving families to migrate and propeties to be lost. The French did say over twenty-five yers ago not to build here. The continued over fishing of species pushes the problems faced by the coastal species up to the edge of the event horizon. Further hampered by a simple matter of economics for a poor country hammered by corruption and the inability to fully grasp the situation that they find themselves in. The sea when it covers Nouakchott will be an environmental disaster. The accumulated toxins of decades of dumping waste outside their front doors, will make the waters unsafe for the habitation of sealife and the eating of these species by humans, risky.

In the south we find the agricultural region's ability to grow crops being hammered by deforestation, mainly to supply charcoal for cooking. The locals simply remove the entire tree out of the ground and naturally the soil disappears. The poor simply cannot afford to do otherwise and add to their future difficulties by having to live now. The students in my class are of the same thought as re-planting trees as the re-introduction of the Dama gazelle. The local population will simply consume both as quickly as they did before with no thought to the future. No education is possible they tell me. There's no educational infrastructure in place that can deal with the problems the Mauritanians face.

Traditional livestock practices have also changed in the least three years or so. With less rains and subsequently there's less natural fodder for camels and goats, which need to travel respectively 20 and 30 km a day to find enough to eat. Herders have come to live nearer the water holes or at the roadside. The grasses for up to 10km on either side of the roads are of poor quality or non-existent. With ever increasing large concentrations of animals in poor health, there's the real risk of increased contagious diseases and the subsequent loss of this stock causes difficulties in the ability to feed your family as a natural course of events. We already know from my experiences here of the problems of self-medicating that goes on in animal husbandry. With the increased cost of animals it will be impossible to replace the same number of animals lost with like. With the lack of fodder, animals stop growing and lose weight. The projections for 2015 are that Mauritania will not be able to produce enough meat for its domestic market. There's already famine. Herders that are forced out of the desert, have essentially kept the Bidan in the top dog position as he rightly believes himself to be. He will not pay what is the normal price, because the weight of the animal in less than normal until he feeds it up of course.

The camel herd is fast becoming a mark of social status, kept as pets. Many of the Bidan are also changing to rearing cattle which do not need to travel huge distances and can be fed at the homestead. As A follows B and followed by C, the desert in Mauritania will soon be empty of people, until that is the seas push them back there. The fishermen and their families will simply move their cabins of course and remain in place. Unemployment already high will rocket as it is the habit of the Bidan when he is nervous around economic disturbances. He simply will not spend and sit tight and wait for someone else to rescue his ass. The projected cost in lost revenue by marine transgression by 2020 is estimated to be $3956 million and by 2050, $6330 million.

I could carry on and discuss the options available, that interested bodies have already suggested, would give Mauritania a fighting chance. The use of drought resistant crops for both man and animals, breed chickens in villages and give women the chance of some economic benefit, replant trees other than Prosopsis on a huge scale, water reclamation, desalination, wind power, the use of solar cookers that could be made from two cardboard boxes and tin foil and allow families to have other money making ventures. But nobody ain't fuckin' listenin'! They're all too busy having tea and tagine.

On the animal front, the Red fronted gazelle, gone. Barbary sheep, gone. With the gazelles gone, naturally the cheetah went too as did the lion. Harbour porpoise, the West African Manatee, gone, gone. There are ecosystems specific to regions that are under threat, that when they go, as a unique entity to the planet are gone for ever. The Bidan is entrenched in his belief that everything will stay as it always has. His approach is like that of the ostrich that once used to be a common as the sand here. Watch this space.

The following chapter brings me to the present day, Burn's Night 2011 as I commit this tale of woe to my USB in a cyber café in Bamako, Mali. You find me at present, at a cross roads in my life with my Songhay wife, Mariem, through one man I was to meet at a camel race mid-2008. He would not only devastate our plans to begin farming here in Mali in 2010 but also bring to an abrupt stop, my work on behalf of the Tamashek with Taghreft Tinariwen. This man's conduct can only be best described as being rooted in, The Big White African Hunter Syndrome. He is an entrepreneur and amateur documentary film-maker. He is the worst example of a film-maker that I've met in West Africa over the years. He is the owner of The Gershwin Hotel in NY. It is my firm and qualified belief that we, my African colleagues, the migrant subjects and their families, the various officials conducted with the migrant problem, the locals here in Mali and in RIM and the laws in these two countries, governing visas, shooting permits and the political and cultural considerations on his documentary Europe or Die, are not the first people to have been used, abused and disposed of like the weekend's cat litter.

"Mr Urs Jakob, come on down there's a bill that needs paying!"

And his most likely reply would be, "And like the duck, you can stick your bill up your ass!"

The bill he currently faces in RIM is enormous given that he, Stephane Lapierre his second cameraman, Mohamed Salem my friend, associate of Smile and Hope, a Maurtanian ONG and RIM co-ordinator and the three Malian subjects were caught around Xmas 2010, after Urs had invited the three Malians into the lounge of the five star Hotel Tyfeila, NKT for drinks. One of them gave up the entire story without as much as a how-do-you-do, when asked by police as to why he was at the hotel.

Caught illegally filming for the third fuckin' time, Urs, Stephane and Mohamed were also charged with human traffiking and espionage. I told the DSS (RIM Secret Service) through the Mauritanian Ambassador here in Bamako, that I'd be more than happy to throw his flabby ass down a deep well. In the event that he survived the 50m drop, he'd have plenty to drink. I'm not a savage man, just an angry man bent on revenge.

## CHAPTER THIRTEEN

# UNLUCKY FOR SOME

A S PREVIOUSLY MENTIONED I met Mr Urs Jakob, I'll call him Big White Hunter (BWH). He's a Swiss-German national (which will explain his racist and superior attitude to everyone around him) who has residential properties in Canada and the US, at the 2008 Inaugural Camel Race of the family Atigh, owners of the lofty Al Khaima conference centre and hotel in Nouakchott. It took place at the village of the elderly dentist chief Mohamed, some 30 km north of Boutilimit and 8 km from the road. It was arranged by Jakob and the chief's son Mohamed who has believe it or not, a Mauritanian restaurant in Montreal, serving Senegalese food. As you all know there's not a chance in hell of running a successful Mauritanian restaurant serving Mauritanian food. I heard about the race from Sidi Gratuit the night before and rushed off early the next morning to travel the 125 km by taxi in less than two hours, then a short trip out in the back of the many 4x4's going back and forth.

The sight of the huge khaima up on the short rise to the right overlooking the wide piste with several other smaller but no less large khaima dotted below was amazing to behold. People everywhere. Across the piste opposite, was the chief's homestead. Altogether there were about three thousand people, mostly members of the tribe but a fair number of esteemed guests from the large business interests in Mauritania. Mineral water, telecom, electrical, you name it the bosses from wherever were there as well as the US Ambassador who I didn't know was, which makes my piss-take of him riding a camel, a little more special. Here was I thought a well-to-do Bidan boss, in his new boubou, sirou, shirt, sandals and sunglasses being led around by his berger atop a fine white camel, with me making exaggerated chicken sounds as I walked alongside. The tribal members would later disgrace themselves by stealing everything not nailed down including my turban of three years, when camp was struck three days later. It wasn't even worn in yet.

'Je suis un rock star!'

As I approached the tent I could see familiar faces amongst the bergers, including Sidna and his brother Brahim, grinning like idiots, who had come to race and who all made sure I said hello, as would have been the case anyway. I was initially hurried up by the Gendarmes to go inside, who then realised I wasn't there specifically to see the dignitaries and actually was on very good terms with the guys and we were left to our salaam aleykums, yakamozhashee's, tarribess's and the ritual three dozen, ca va's. I then was led into the huge khaima where two hundred or more people were tucking into michui and filling their pockets with free drinks, supplied by the sponsors. No free phone credit though! The chief's son came to meet me and to my right I saw some familiar toubab faces and guides with their charges. His English is top class and I had no trouble in explaining to Mohamed Junior, that I had come to race against my former colleagues, not for the money but just for fun. He immediately took to the idea and led me to his father who had a fuckin' blue fit. I briefly gave him my CV and was eventually given permission to try out for the team. I didn't see the three man documentary team following me until I was given my mount, a fine looking white camel. I was told to get up whilst the berger held the rope. I told him no and to give me his baton. He said I didn't need it. I told him to get a blanket to fill the saddle and I'd get myself a baton. He took off laughing and I stripped a sturdy branch off of a nearby tree, surrounded by a multitude of people. A little way off in front of me was the grinning Sidna and Brahim. They and me as calm as anything in this surging sea of highly excited on-lookers. Another berger arrived on his camel and when the blanket was in place I took the camel and walked away towards the piste to mount in peace. The crowd did their best to unseat me and a few well placed whacks discouraged the more persistent imbeciles and a tight rein on the camel's nose rope, kept him firmly on the ground until I'd chased away everyone and when up on his feet, stopped him from bolting due to being pumped up. My companion for the piste arrived and tried to goad me into galloping through the tents, trees, debris and the mental masses on the way down to the piste. With my baton leveled at his face he of course drew back and we walked the camels down to the piste. On reaching it I kicked and whacked and took off with the berger in pursuit. We did a once around the race track shouldering and pushing each other and I decided afterwards when he'd had enough sport to showcase a little, nothing too spectacular, just enough to reinforce that I wasn't the virgin everyone expected. Then it was back off to the tent; with Sidna giving me a wink, and Brahim pretending yawn, to stuff my face on a large leg of beef, a loaf of bread, a full packet of Arabic custard cream biscuits (just not the same thing folks) and 2L of mineral water which I ate alongside the Gendarmes as I believe it or not I already knew one, who was more than happy to give the full details to the others of my life in the desert. It's while I'm eating that BWH finally comes over and asks if we could talk later. He was interested in interviewing me for a documentary. I had that look I expect and followed it with, "If it's about bandits, beautiful Tuareg girls, Al Qaeda and deeds of derring-do then I don't." He assured it me it wasn't, simply that I should recount a half hour ride on the back of a camel and I agreed to the interview.

After finishing my small haul of grub, I was summoned with bloated tummy to mount up and surprised, to find another strange white camel for me to ride. This was the idea of the chief's I believe to see what I was made of. No matter. I had my baton and the saddle had a blanket inside it, so all's well and I did almost as exactly as before to mount and fuck off from the madding crowd. The ride out to the start line would be our, 'getting to know you . . .' phase and pick out a return route. He was a dream. No bitchin' or moanin' or any such nonsense. I was the ninth rider and we all eventually got into a line of sorts, exactly as you'd see at Redcar, with the jockey's riding around in short circles . . . . then we're off! It's one kilometer to the finish-line and there's a large patch of tourja in the middle of the track, which other eight riders went around to the right and then swung back left to go straight onto the finish-line. I elect to go straight through and keep on a direct line to the finish. I am totally alone as the other eight riders push shove and whack their mounts asses and I see one unseated, camel and rider sent sprawling pulling down another and diverting two around the long way. My boy stumbles as we exit the field of tourja but he keeps his feet and I'm third/fourth equal until the finish and end up fifth. Four bergers walk their camels to the finish with me waiting to congratulate them. The crowd go fuckin' mental all around me but not the winner.

'Darlings, I'm a bloody star!'

I've five camera and one documentary team on me. I suddenly feel very isolated as I make my way from the finishing line, with children and young women prancing around me shrilling and wanting to touch and be touched. Mothers are winking to nod in the direction of their daughters, all of whom are now my new beautiful girlfriends and around the same age as my first.

'What a fuckin' life!'

I climb up on top of a nearby 4x4, the owner being a French girl I know who was in RIM teaching Gendarmes, who is sitting photographing everything and who is mightily impressed that I finished in the saddle. Sarcastically I ask, "Do you want to make babies with me?"

"Not particularly. Is it the custom here?" She replied.

"No, it's refreshing that you don't. I've several girls and their mothers waiting for me to join them for tea and crumpet. Can I pretend you're my wife/girlfriend?" I ask. "If you must but no tongues." She replies.

The day and my reputation are saved and the day slowly but surely winds down and the ever so excited crowd begins to melt away to leave an eerie silence behind. Then Soundguy arrives as the last of the toubab visitors mount up and drive off. I'm given the general salute by the Gendarmes and Peter takes me up the steep slope behind the big tent into the dunes above, where the tents of the chief's family are to be found. I meet up with BWH, roll a spliff and have a general chat about the race, the Bidan and other related topics until the camera team were ready to begin. Apparently it's sand that's the problem and I'm onto rolling number two before we're sat down inside the khaima. The single question previously discussed is what is asked and I begin to recount the sensation of riding my camel. The creaking of the saddle straps at each complete set of steps. The sound of the water in my 5L bidon being sloshed around. The snorting and humphing of my camel as he walks around obstacles put in his way by the desert. The annoying crunch of ancient pottery beneath his feet, being registered in the small of my back. Only because I don't like to be a vandal. The heat of the sun bearing down on the tops of my feet, head and shoulders. The sight of a bead 30m away spotted in an instant. There's just time enough to pluck a few Acacia flowers; small frail balls of pollen excellent for their vitamin C content as we negotiate around it's welcoming spread of shade. Two lime green flies buzz around my head for 5 fuckin' km, thank god for my mp3. The smell of females on the wind as Topographic Oceans plays inside my turban. The distant sound of a 4x4 which arrives in a moment of silence spoils the moment that you're totally solated from everything that is modern for it to disappear again as quickly as it arrived to prolong the fantasy. To watch in disbelief as Mwoiny crosses underneath in a moment of complete and utter madness. She's decided to make for cooler shade, sending Wahad and I, into a dressage sort of moment. He doesn't quite match the tempo of the Yes but it's a near as we'll get. The moment passes and my breathing returns. The myriad of thoughts that pass through your head, as you and your animal plod on at between 3 and 5 km/hr. There's no rush, nowhere you need to be other than where you are at this moment and if you do need to be somewhere else it doesn't matter a fuck. There's a spliff rolled and smoked in the happy knowledge that you can't be done out here for being intoxicated in charge of a camel.

In the UK as I think I previously mentioned, you'd need a man with a Red Flag walking in front of you just because it's a camel and all the relevant horse riding gear. You really do need to be barefooted on a camel you know. Boots may be sexy but your camel ain't gonna like them. Then there's all the veterinary certificates in place and the patience of a fuckin' saint in answering fifty times a fuckin' day, "Is that a camel mister?"

As we near the end of the chat, we're joined by the chief who's come to congratulate me on my good showing at the race. He's impressed and talks of inviting toubab riders to the next camel race for their own specific competition. Would I be interested? Of course I would. I had already thought of asking the Saracen Rugby team out to ride, their mascot being a camel and didn't know; obviously, that in the following year they would have their own little race on the banks of the Thames, with Astroturf, helmets, boots, kneepads, backpads and fannypads!

"Sorry chaps I didn't mean to imply that you are a team of gay boys. I know all that necessary shit is for insurance purposes. Come on down to the Sahara and race with me berger style. I know of a few soft patches of sand for you to fall onto to and not hurt yourselves. You have also read that the lovely patch of soft welcoming sand may have welcoming acacia thorns or sea shells or . . . bring your pads if you think you'll need them but be warned, the nomad girls will only laugh at you and won't believe you when you tell them what you do for a job!!" The owner of the camel asked me if I'd like to buy him, for 265 000 UM (795 euros). I told him that as I now live in town that I couldn't and he took off. It transpired later that one of the bosses present at the shindig bought the camel for

500 000UM (1500 euros) as it had been ridden by a toubab and had been filmed in action by five different TV companies!

We are brought food by the chief's cook and re-supplied with water and goodies. I am introduced to the world of the documentary and am not surprised that I too could make a few, as my life in West Africa has thrown up a hell of a lot of stories. I don't venture to tell any of them my ideas and finally everyone drifts off to sleep. Me, I take off and walk out to distant dunes to sleep alone.

'Can't be doing with that snoring shit!'

Don't have any trouble of course sleeping beside 200 ruminating camels or bleating goats. But one man snoring, no can do baby.

After breakfast the next morning in the tent of Mohamed Jnr and his lovely wife, we all climb aboard the 4x4, with me in my usual place, out beside the baggage. The trip up the road to Nouakchott is trouble free and the Gendarmes have no idea there's a nasrani out back and we arrive at the Menata in record time. It turns out that Mohamed Jnr didn't want to follow in his father's footsteps and join the family dental practice. Although a personable old man and qualified dentist, I wouldn't either. In all honesty, I cannot for the love of me describe the horror that befell my eyes, even though the photograph remains as vivid as if I were there now. Helpmaboab! He's got all the gear but I'd rather not risk a bacterial infection reaching my heart killing me and would prefer to DIY the job with pliers instead. He of course was completely oblivious to the squalor. So after a sojourn in Canada, Jnr decides to go back home for a visit and within the day he is brought to his father's study to be told that he is married! Stunned ain't how BWH described his reaction. He takes off. He has another love interest, another life and now he's married to a near stranger. Time passes and he comes around bit by bit and when I met them in their tent you'd know straight away there's love in the air. She's gentle, pretty, intelligent and head over heels in love with her husband. It's not until three days later that my status of 'rock star' arrives. There are people shouting "Rais" or "Berger" at me from passing cars, or as people pass by in the street. A troupe of Bidan girls stuffed into a car stop alongside to ask me for my autograph and drive around to pass in the opposite direction pumping the horn and their hormones. In a country of three million people it ain't hard to get noticed. I've been on Mauritanian TV twice now and yet to see myself once. When I get back to school, nearly everyone comes to congratulate me and to apologise that they didn't believe that I was ever a shepherd. As it turned out, it was a bizarre mix of fame and no fortune. To be known and respected by the West African migrant community but to be a poor as a church mouse, my life in the balance.

Four weeks or so later I get an email from BWH, Could I phone him as he hasn't my number and he needs a guide. My immediate thought is, 'How many people and how long?'

My ready reckoner is in place as I dial his number.

"How are you?" he asks.

"Fine." I reply.

"I need your services as a guide, are you available?" he asks.

"How many people are you bringing and how long would you like to go out into the desert for?" I ask.

"Ah it's not a trip. I need you as a researcher and presenter for a documentary about migrants." he says.

Amongst a shitload of things, we'd talked about my knowledge of the Malians who gravitate to RIM en route for Tenerife as well as all the other African nationals who arrive there and, the 50 000 or so sub-Saharan Africans who traverse the Sahara every year hoping to reach Fortress Europe. To say that I was thrown a curve ball and knocked for six would be mixing my sporting metaphors but what the hell, I ain't conventional. Researcher I can do standing on my head but presenter, "Yeah okay." I tell him.

I send him my demand for the salary for work that I was led to believe would be over six months, which was in actuality nearly a year and a half and would include the job of producer as well. None of which I'd be paid for! You think I'm shitting you? He'd not pay me one fuckin' cent! He'd leave me here in West Africa to hopefully wither away and die as he has done to the three Malian subjects in his film. He fucked off and abandoned them!

My first WU Red Cross Parcel arrives around August 2008 and I begin to wind up my teaching with my English students, to begin researching all that had been said and done before, on what was being said and done at present and any future intentions anyone had who was stupid enough to broadcast it. My suspicions on some of the footage on YouTube of filmmakers travelling with migrants, was that many had simply done it to fulfill their own egos, adventure borne out of too many beers perhaps. Other films I've seen are the real McCoy. This wouldn't be BWH. He'd completely ignore the cultural and political aspects of the story. His interest would simply be down to the choice of equipment, the quality of footage shot and what he could do with it in post-production, on how he could further inflate his ego as he toured the documentary film festivals off of my back and that of the team, their families and anyone he could film for free, leaving a trail of broken promises behind him. He prefers instead to be locked up in isolation trying to perfect perfection. He's on a number of psychotropics dealing with this and other vital questions in his life. He should be locked up for the liar and abuser that he is. In Dec 2010 Urs, Stephane and my good friend Mohamed Salem would spend ten days in Dar Naim Prison in NKT, through the simple belief that BWH sits beside or above God. As you all know, this isn't possible.

From the start, I knew that a sea trip in a pirogue was a distinct possibility and I offered him two safe scenarios. The third being, that I risked my life by having my throat cut and dumped over the side, not-with-standing the threat from pirates and the RIM, Moroccan and Spanish authorities. Scenario number one was to simply shoot a film. We'd present our script etc to the authorities, fill the pirogue with African actors, have a safety boat to film from and transfer to; which amongst other things he'd sent me to The Canaries to try and hire. No-one on any of the three islands, in any of the marinas I visited wanted anything to do with the project in any shape or form. The second scenario was that he buy a pirogue for 25 people and I'd fill it with a 22 hand-picked crew, two experienced captains and the migrants could contribute to their food needs. We'd have everyone rendezvous on the beach north of NKT and ship out directly into international waters on Thursday night/Friday morning when everyone knocked off for the weekend, the traditional time for the pirogues to leave RIM. Everything was itemised and costed as requested and rejected because of his first principle:

'Spending A Cent To Save A Dollar Principle.' He'd prefer the cheapest and therefore the worst case scenario for him not to miss out on his 1000 euro bottle of wine with dinner every night. His second as producer/director is: 'Not Being Able To Organise A Piss-Up In A Brewery Principle.' His third is: 'He'll Abandon You When It All Goes Tits Up Principle.' I hope everyone is getting the message here. Don't work with this guy. He'll fuck you over and then blame you for it.

He arrived for the first shoot in September 2008, with two of the three Canon 5D's he'd bought, lenses for all of the bodies, covers, a steering wheel to mount it on, walkie talkies that were to be a major pain in the ass with the RIM authorities, radio mikes and a Sony helmet cam, that I was to use later for secret filming! You simply needed a backpack just to carry the fuckin' cable! Arsehole. It was like a scenario out of a Bugs Bunny cartoon. In all honesty I'd have more faith in Bugs Bunny. The Gendarmes never found it in my possession. Le Dieu Merci. I had asked for a more discreet pen-camera that I could go into the Postes and offices with, but he said this would compromise the footage shot on the Canons. He'd prefer that I got myself arrested to spice up the story no doubt! There were unnecessary toys of every description to feed his ego and four brand spanking new Chinese extension socket sets which would cost him an extra 1 000 000 cfa in the hotel bill in Bamako because they all burned out the first night he arrived with them to charge up the batteries we needed for filming the next day! The subsequent footage of the 5D is indeed superb and cannot be opened up on anything less than Deep Thought. He made me a gift of the footage shot that I can do nothing with. Such is his overwhelming generosity and sarcasm. Cunt.

The West African trade in migrants had by 2008 dwindled to a slow trickle of pirogues leaving the shores of RIM. They continue to leave in appreciable numbers from the shores of Senegal, Guinea and Sierra Leone en route for the islands of the little yellow bird that sings. You will no doubt be surprised to find out, that it is not illegal to leave the shores of RIM in a pirogue. But detaining and arresting them is. The Spanish and RIM governments know this to be the case but it doesn't stop them from doing so. The heyday may have passed but the problems with the migrants in RIM remains and is a major headache for the Mauritanians and Spanish to deal with.

The Bidan had exploited the migrants to the point of exhaustion just over the pirogue issue. The scenario runs something like this: the African would contact a middleman. The middleman would take half of the 600 euro ticket price. The African would then be told to wait for a month and the necessary phone call for the beach rv where he'd pay the balance. He'd need to buy clothes for the trip, which naturally are the standard bright yellow waterproofs worn by the fishermen and he could recommend a shop! The day duly arrives, the Africans rv, pay up and wham bam thank you Ma'am, everyone is surrounded by the police, arrested, robbed and the money taken for the tickets divvied up. Some would be taken to the detention centre and others released back into the community. It wouldn't do to have all of your slaves locked up, who'd do the work! Of course a great many other pirogues did leave and it got to the point as it is now, that the African themselves; as a syndicate if you will, buy the pirogue, motors, fuel etc and go it alone.

Of the 18 Malian tribes it is mainly the Sarakole, from NW Mali; in the circle of Kayes, Yelimane, Nioro du Sahel and Diema, who are genetically infected with the travel bug. Certainly there are other Malians who go north but here, it is the eldest son's responsibility at the end of the harvest is to set off and seek the family's fortune. They collectively pay for him to travel to wherever and wait for him to send back the promised millions. As you and I both now know, many many thousands cross the Sahara every year. How many are robbed and left to die? How many die of hunger and thirst? In Dec 2005, 3000 African migrants were rounded up in Morocco at the behest of the Spanish government who had asked for them to be sent home. The Moroccan King being a barbarian, used his soldiers to round them up, lorry them east of Smarra into the waiting minefield. Here at gunpoint they were told to fuck off. They were given no water or food or indeed a safe route through the minefield by which they could gain entry into RIM. The Moroccans regularly dump Africans out in No Man's Land, sick, malnourished, dehydrated and dressed only in the clothes they stand in, for the RIM Red Crescent to pick them up and BE SEEN to give them assistance. The Mauritanians for their part return them to the Malian border in the same condition as the Moroccans.

At first all seemed well and the boss was pleased with my endeavours if not a little too obsessed in me going back to research old news and re-confirm known information all the time. I found it frustrating and irksome as I knew that I could have researched, shot and delivered the entire story in four months. In the course of my researches over the year and a half, I'd travel from RIM to Mali to RIM to Mali to Morocco to RIM to Mali to RIM to Morocco to the UK to The Canaries to RIM and back to Mali to finish in RIM, chasing my ass back and forth, when all he had to do was simply read what I had written. What I had done, was in effect I had written a book, which I was to lose through Gmail closing down my account?

"Thanks very much you cunts, I've lost the material I was going to write a book with!" I'd spend this year and a half travelling up and down the Route L'Espoir (20 times now—1500 km from NKT to Bamako). On the last count between the Malian border and NKT there are 20 Postes, 24 wrecked vehicles and 37 dead animals. Between NKT and NDB, 9

Postes, 9 wrecked vehicles including a brand new Gendarmerie quad bike and 4 dead animals. Urs has filmed most of them. Once I did the route in a Toyota LandCruiser and had the poor car shipped off to the mechanic after we did the 1500 km in 23 hours. I have slept on condemned buses that drive along at a 15° shift from straight-ahead, at Gendarmerie Postes, in roadside tents, up a baobab tree during the rainy season to be rescued by a Fulaani berger who'd brought a bull for me to ride as the tree was surrounded by a large lake. I'd sojourn in a myriad of Soninke and Peul villages, (killing in total six black mambas in the north and another five green one's further south,) the occasional auberge, a friend's house now and again, seven times on a plane and twice in a five star hotel for the weekend. Out in the countryside of Mali I mainly walked or begged lifts from Fulaani on their carts and animals. In the more civilized parts I have travelled in sotrama, (a white van painted green) lorries, with tourists, in pinasses, on Jakartas, taxis and even a horse. BWH was frustrating my sense of order and priorities with his misplaced mis-direction and more and more as time passed, he began to leave me unsupported for not just a day or so at a time, but days, once for ten days. He told me he was on board a sailing ship and couldn't arrange for money to be sent, that I'd have to wait. I did, not eating for three of them when I was in the hottest town in Africa during the hot season. There, on a chance Facebook encounter through the use of a French tourist's laptop, I found out that he was on a ten day bender with a burlesque dancer doing the pubs, clubs and sleezy bars in fuckin' Tokyo. I phoned him and gave him a mouthful and he cut me off for another three days as punishment, consigning me again to bread and water.

Working up close with BWH in the field, is a complete cluster fuck. He started off gently enough by finishing my interview in Atigh's village. He returned there as he wanted to do close-ups of me in race mode that he would not take at the time. Old Mohamed would charge him 300 euros for the rental of a camel for the day! We did a few Route L'Espoir shots to try out his Canon that Africa would eventually chew up and spit them out. We then went into NKT to interview migrants living in Cinqieme and an interview on the beach with a captain who has done the pirogue trip to The Canaries twice. This time around, we had the official permit and journalist in tow but was too disorganised for me, as he would constantly change from the plan he had outlined at breakfast. He did not include anyone else in his butterfly mode of decision making and we'd be constantly chasing our asses to find out what he actually wanted. He on the other hand believed he'd told us what was to befall us and gave us short thrift when we fell short, which was all the fuckin' time. In short, he is fuckin' impossible to work with. In time, I would dread his up-coming field trips and any cancellation was heartily welcomed by me, even if it were only two days. Merci Le Dieu.

The first cameraman I was to work with was a Frenchman, Mr Jedj Cassone, who I found by chance in NKT. Juge is a truly professional cameraman with a good eye. Stephane on the other hand is fine if all you want is shots in a supermarket. Juge was instrumental in teaching me Presenter 101. Fuck me but ain't it difficult! A friendly tip (number 1) is to watch as many different presenters as you can and discover the zone, man. Get a camera, write a script and get someone to film you as you walk, talk and negotiate your way through the crowds in a busy street. Watch the results and piss yourselves with laughter. We became a tight team and I and only faltered when BWH stuck his two cents worth in, which I was constantly waiting for, so upping stress levels. Footage from the initial shoot was sent to BBC Scotland for appraisal and the feedback on my performance came back as:

'A strong forceful character who stands out and would be listened to. Professional. Was he an actor?'

"No I wasn't, no I'm not and wouldn't want to be either. Not even if it meant that I could simultaneously bed Monica Bellucci and Megan Fox. Honest!"

As my year began with the documentary, life also began to get serious with Mariem, who I had met through home teaching two Bidan sisters. She worked for their older sister and was in effect a bonded slave. Her salary was in sent to her father. She therefore had no money to buy clothes or a phone or even had spoken to her mother in over a year. Her days were nearly eighteen hours long, cooking, washing clothes and child-minding and fighting off the advances of the older sister's husband and getting to eat the scraps of the meals she prepared for her employers. I gave her an Opinel No8 which she slept with and would use should it be necessary. The point in which I arrived that I'd like her to walk with me, was not long after the race when we passed each other on the spiral staircase that leads out into the garden. Mariem stopped and turned to face the wall as I passed, my large bag over my shoulder and the girl's folders in my arms. She then carried on as I did. I stopped dead when I reached the garden. It really REALLY angered me that she placed me alongside her so-called betters who were not in any shape or form better and I ran back up the stairs after her. I told her that I wasn't like the Bidan, that I didn't have slaves and that I was angry and sad that she thought me like them to insist that she bow and scrape in front of me and that she was never to do this again. She promised she wouldn't and we became closer and closer as time passed. I bought her a Nokia torch which she kept secret from her employers and the first call she made was to her mother, tears streaming down her malnourished face. This loss of contact is a big thing to an African girl as her mother and family, is the cornerstone of their existence. Throughout the year we'd keep in touch by phone, first thing in the morning and last thing at night, no matter where I was. The phone bill must have been fuckin' huge eh BWH? In between times I'd get a few snatched moments here and there as I dived in and out of NKT and in and out of her boss's radar.

As I said previously, I'd commit everything to email and pass it on. There were times when I'd need him to carry out sensitive or difficult research and most every time I'd get little more than the bare bones, which wouldn't satisfy me as I was consumed daily with the story for the year and a half. He'd be infinitely more interested in his life than actually helping me to help him. Though on one point he was up and at them with me! The Spanish had given RIM two Boeing 747's and a fleet of 12 LandCruisers to help deal with the migrant repatriation problem. The planes arrived at NKT International Airport and disappeared the next day. The fleet ghosted away too, as well as 720 million euros in aid, which was divided up between the RIM and Spanish government. I tasked an Al Jazeera journalist I know onto the story and he too was ghosted away. I have had absolutely no news of him since. An interview with the Spanish Minister never materialised and that's where the thread ends, for the moment. Like a dog with a bone, I'll find out eventually.

In the course of my wanderings I came into contact with officials at every level, NGO's and interested individuals tasked with migrants in West Africa. One incredible man, who lives and works in Kayes, is Demba Traoré. He has personal experience of losing family to the ocean. He is a father, teacher and broadcaster; at Radio Rurale Kayes, (Radio-Kaama FM: 105.30MHZ) who has dedicated his life in trying to stem the flow; like King Canute, of Soninke/Sarakole men leaving Mali. He has written nine books and uses his time on one of his two days in trying to educate and dissuade young men and their families in sending them into RIM. He is, as I am, a rebel and he's been arrested twice now. On his second time, he was imprisoned without trial and released two days later when representatives from the 192 villages who subscribe to the radio station, staged a protest outside the prison. Demba's friends who join him in the studio have heard it all before and now bring a sleeping mat to have their siesta as he rants and raves like a madman over the airwaves. He is indefatigable, defiant and alone.

In a brief sojourn in Kayes in December 2009 I was to meet a Scottish exile, Albert, who had immigrated with his parents to Rhodesia when he was four and was now living in South Africa. He had come to Mali to manage a gold processing factory, in the village of Dialafara, 160 km south of Kayes. He suggested that when I was finished with shooting that I come and visit as I had planned to survey the area in which to farm, open an auberge and raise children and goats with Mariem. We exchanged numbers and I prepared to leave but was again phoned and asked by the musician I had come to interview to wait for him. I thought it over and reluctantly agreed saying that it as his last chance. He promised he'd be there the following night. I changed my ticket and chilled out with Albert. As it turned out he didn't arrive and when I got to the bus station I was to learn that the bus I had intended to take had left the road some 100 km out of Kayes. There were 11 dead, 23 badly injured and the 18 others with major injuries. The bus had been full of mothers and their children. The buses of Sonef and Bani Transport are little more than road going coffins and packed to the gunnels with travelers and baggage. You'll find goats in the hold;

"Not me this time, eh sir?"

Small motorbikes strapped up on top, a huge mountain of assorted baggage that simply defies the laws of physics and God combined with the unsound mechanics of the bus. It simply wasn't my time.

"I have no choice but to use these buses, because I ain't a wealthy man, am I Urs?"

In Nouadibou I was to find the grim details of the life of the migrants as heart rending and as desperate as you'd expect. You in effect, walk into to a very tightly regulated and monitored town. Let me say here for anyone interested enough to go to RIM to work, 'THERE IS NOWHERE SAFE IN RIM TO FILM, EVEN IF YOU HAVE A SHOOTING PERMIT!"

"Isn't that right Alison?"

As lovely and as adoring as ever, she replies, "Yes teacher. You once told me a story about four French journalists in RIM who were put in jail even when they had a permit."

On the road up from the Malian frontier Africans are required to pay 500 UM (1.30 euros) at each and every Poste, except the Surete Poste at the frontier which hammers them for 2000 UM (5.20 euros). On arrival at NDB, choice of digs is limited to the sprawl of shacks at the back end of town, tightly packed together, next to the huge mountain of rubbish and here as in Cinqieme, the ravagers that are cholera, tuberculosis and typhoid live and do their stuff. Here you will find Africans from every country on the continent. Men sleep perhaps 7 to a room that perhaps only measures 5x5m. Their clothes and phones quite out of character with their financial state as for the first time they actually have money to spend on themselves. The phone's are a lifeline to families who send on the much needed cash by Western Union, who do very well from the migrant trade as they do from criminals. Their salary for an eight hour day, should they in fact be lucky to find work for the day is 500 UM. Here is the thing though. The Bidan boss has a ploy. Of course he fuckin' has! He waits until they have done almost six hours or so hard graft. No breaks, nothing to eat and nothing to drink. All day they are expected to lift, carry and grind. The boss will wait until the man takes a two second rest and pounces.

"Do you think you're here to chill out! Fuck off!"

The migrant has no recourse to argue his case with anyone or involve the police. He has worked hard and has no means with which to buy food when he gets home or the money for the shared taxi. This perhaps was only one day's work out of the week for him. Tonight he was going to eat grilled fish. Like me perhaps; since BWH dumped my ass, he'll have rice pudding, without the milk or sugar of course. Or perhaps his house mates have been luckier and he'll of course eat with them. Or perhaps they too have suffered the same fate.

Raids by the police are as frequent as the rain in Scotland, where it rains 300 days a year. I've experienced the hell of being dragged off so that I can't see what is going to happen. I of know what's happening and of course get to see the aftermath and to be honest it doesn't shock either me or the migrants anymore. The newbie's just about manage to keep it together. The African thing, 'Don't cry!' They lose everything just as they have done before they arrive in No Man's Land or at the RIM/Malian border. The migrants simply get on with it and work to amass the funds with which to buy: a thin sleeping mat, flip flops, fourth hand clothes, a new phone, food, water.

As you'd expect there's a heavy Surete and Garde Civile presence in NDB. The Surete carry radios that you don't see in NKT and the GC have technology to help them on the front line. They have a helicopter which patrols the inland waters, a surveillance aircraft which patrols the international waters and a coastguard cutter out in international waters too. Their house is directly across from the airport and the cutter crews are helicoptered there and back. On one occasion as I arrived in NDB in the wee small hours, a soiree could be heard from their terrace as they danced and drank the night away with their Senegalese girlfriends. It's amazing how far your voice travels when you think you're being quiet. I mention that it's a, "fuckin' bordel" and a Spaniard looks over the wall of the terrace. He says something in Spanish and I give him the finger, walking on.

As I've mentioned before to the point of boredom, that BWH had no respect for the terms of his visas in Mali and RIM, his shooting permits when he had them, his subjects, his team, the locals, officials, in fact whoever he came into contact with and could, he exploited them. He'd re-enter into negotiations keeping me remote from the process and I'd be bounced back and forward as the instigator of the contract; which I'd already negotiated and therefore the trouble-maker who'd fucked it all up. This was classic BWH. Trying to save his dollar from those who had nothing, who if they had their dollar would still have nothing and BWH wouldn't have missed it anyway but he had to do it. He had to cheat them out of it like a drug addict needs his fix. He is a bully who typically transfers his abusive behaviour onto those he bullies.

It is November 2009 and we're in northern Mali. Mariem had joined me on the road to learn a little of the documentary business as we intended to start up our own production company and film a number of documentaries I'd discovered waiting to be made here in Mali and on behalf of Taghreft Tinariwen, the Tuareg cultural association. (www.keltinariwen.org) Mariem would at least know not what to do! BWH had set me off a month or so earlier to set up a meeting with a Malian family and a German singer who had been attacked in a German town by three Malians and woke up in hospital. He'd come on a short visit to discover what had fuelled the attack and in my opinion hadn't given himself enough time to carry out the research and closure but he did need to heal his mind. This would also give his lordship another language version in which to sell his film. He'd use Stephane too for a French version. So it was with this story that I approached the mayor of Nioro Tugane Pulaar and Wolof (being a Senegalese language), though here they speak Soninke. Confused? I was too, even after it had been explained to me. Wolof was the adjoining village of one of the three Malian subjects and it was both the protocol and common courtesy for BWH and the team to visit her before filming started. Afterwards, the singer would stay with her family for the night to eat a traditional Malian meal and discuss with his translator; a true gentleman Mr Soulemayne who has some eighteen languages in his head, on what it was he needed to ask in order to help him heal. We'd then collect him the next morning. Her father was the village chief and her grandfather the village Imam. Mme Diallo is a dynamic and strong woman and she and her family are both well-known and highly respected locally.

"What window will we be looking through today? We'll be looking through the arched window. Can you guess what happened next, children?"

"A serious of cluster fucks is what happened next, teacher!"

I of course had briefed everyone on the protocol at the hotel. I briefed everyone at breakfast on the protocol before we left for the village, in our three vehicle convoy. I arrived in the last vehicle with Mariem. BWH is at the head, naturally and loses his immediately. He is completely oblivious to all that I told him and I go and sit under a tree, leaving Mariem in the car and wait for the storm to arrive. He has Soundguy, Cameraguy, Germanguy, the translator, the journalist from the National Centre of Cinematography all jumping through his hoops. He runs here and there, directing locals to do their thang, who are already doin' their thang and sets up brief meaningless interactions with Germanguy. He doesn't I see, thank them for their time and involvement. The drivers aren't pleased and they can see that I'm not fuckin' pleased either, as is Mariem. Then he's got everyone back into the cars and we're off! After a brief drive we're . . . off at the run as BWH walks into homesteads and films without a care in the world. Germanguy is paraded here and there. Our subject is then brought into the tornado and he wanders about with BWH as if he's just been shot in the head but doesn't know that he's actually dead! At this point I wished I fuckin' was. I had spent time with our subject's extended family of twelve families. I tried as best as I could to introduce Mariem and smooth the aftershocks. BWH didn't arrive, he bull-dozed his way into and out of the villages. There was no salaam aleykums, diawal or bonjour. I had helped with their livestock, given advice on growing vegetables, prayed in the mosque. I am seething but there is nothing I can do to deter BWH from acting like a pure cunt. I eventually begin to dance as the homestead of our subject is filled with women and girls, musicians and two griots.

"This'll make you laugh!"

The Pulaar griot opens his song with, "We're here to do serious work . . ."

'I'd like to seriously work on BWH's face and reduce it to a bloody mess!'

In amongst all this, is Soundguy, armed with his recording equipment, headphones and boom-mike. What a sight to behold. The compound is seething with vibrant music, energetic dancing women and children and there he is . . . he doesn't budge one fuckin' centimetre! No tapping of his feet, like a rock in a raging storm he is immovable. He only moves when he needs to record from another direction and it's the same again. I believe he did smile once, though so fleeting, it might just have been wind.

As filming begins to wind down, there's a visitor. It's Mme Diallo's secretary and he ain't fuckin' chuffed is he? He beckons me over to say that filming is to be suspended, that we are to leave the village immediately and that we are to report to the mayor's office the next morning at 06.00hrs. BWH doesn't give a fuck of course. He calmly tells me that he's got everything he needs in the can and directs Stephane who is going to stay over with Germanguy in the house of our subject, as to the shots he needs at sunset and at sunrise the next morning, adding as we leave, "We'll give the mayor her five minutes and we'll be off! No problem."

I've nothing to say and really really don't give two fucks what he does now. He's gone native as far as I'm concerned and I'd like to drop him down a deep well in the middle of the Sahara. The journalist has been writing his report of course and is highly critical of me and wants to fight with me over every little thing that BWH does wrong. He wants to give me a good kicking. I tell him that he is more than welcome to try, to phone a friend or six but that he'll go directly to hospital as I've had enough. It'll be him that I go for first; it'll be him that I will handicap for the rest of his life that he'll never again eat with his right hand. I tell him to do his job and speak with the boss. He won't, he's shit scared of him. I tell him to write up everything he has seen and report it to his boss. He doesn't talk to me again for the rest of our time together.

BWH is the worst example of all the film-makers I've met in West Africa since 2005. There are film-makers who return every year to continue their close association with their subjects, bringing real benefits to them and have become honorary members of their subject's families. Maybe not a big deal to you but to those of us that it happens to, it is. "Okay, smart ass at the back, maybe not on the same scale as Save The Children or Oxfam but their input and drive comes from the heart."

As we drive away from the village, I mention to Mariem that I really miss the desert and that I'd like to leave Mariem in Mali as I can only see the team being put in prison if BWH carries on as he does, also that he hasn't got a shooting permit for RIM. BWH had been evasive with me over the permit and had Mohamed Salem petitioning the Minister at The Direction de La Communication for over a month without success. It's no surprise as for the last six months, yours truly had been the subject of an investigation by the Counterespionage Section (DSS) and my photograph and name are obviously on the paperwork. BWH knew that they'd chased my ass, knew the danger I was in (which wasn't as bad as I first thought) and that we were going into the lion's den in a matter of two days. Mariem's adamant she's coming with me. I'm surrounded by stubborn bastards!

So we arrive late the next morning, naturally enough as BWH hasn't had enough breakfast or inflated his ego enough or something or other. From where we parked up, we're directed on foot to the Mayor's office, a km away and asked to sit outside under a bacha. As we sit under its straw roof, supported by four roughly hewn posts, I'm reminded of the phrase, "Those who are about to die, we salute you!"

The secretary duly arrives to tell us to come in to the mayor's office. With the mayor and her secretary there are another eight officials and our party is eight strong too. We are directed to sit on what can only be described as chairs for primary school children. The room is small and hot and only the mayor is sitting comfortably in her luxurious leather swivel chair. BWH sits opposite Mme Diallo and the translator beside him. I'm off on stage left. Mme Diallo then proceeds to rip into me; naturally enough, whilst looking directly at BWH and Translatorguy is calmly giving him every comma, semi-colon and full stop. She talks non-stop for twenty minutes and I'm asked to respond. But BWH steps in to save my ass. He is of course apologetic and firmly plants the responsibility of non-communication onto, my fuckin' lap.

"Quite right too Alison, eh!"

She's as unhappy as Mariem is and looking at Mariem in profile, she's as proud and as mad as hell but in perfect control. She opens up her small handbag to reveal her Opinel. I take her hand and tap my pocket to reveal mine. We are in perfect harmony. There is a two-way conversation between BWH and Mme Diallo for nearly an hour. I'm suffering from cramp, thirst and a hunger that won't be satisfied until I've cut his fuckin' throat. That hunger exists to this very day. The journalist is busy taking down each and every word and will soon run out of paper which makes me smile. We are forced to endure BWH's pompous arrogance to counter, quite rightly, Mme Diallo's displeasure at the dishonor brought upon her family and reputation. Then as the bell in my head sounds the end of round one, we're asked to wait outside. I'm next to last out and Mme Diallo smiles and asks us to remain. She and Mariem talk for what seems ages and they shake hands, a lingering handshake. She then tells me that she knew that Cameraguy and Germanguy remained behind last night and that she understands the difficulty I had in explaining the protocol to BWH. She apologised for using me as she did and I shrug it off as being necessary to calm the waters. That it would have in any case been impossible for him to have acted in any other way and also to apologise for bringing him into her life. Mariem and I walk out into the early morning sun with Mme Diallo and go off to sit away from the crowd.

The cavalcade proceeded on foot the km or so to the school complex. Mme Diallo, BWH and Translatorguy off alone in their own group the others strung out here and there in one's and two's. On arriving at the school I go to the first of the four classrooms and try out the teacher's and pupil's English, which is okay in two of the teachers and next to non-existent in the pupils. BWH is grimacing as Mme Diallo points to this and that, lingering at an empty site. Translatorguy is working hard and BWH's being hit for money, I can see it written over his face. He's nodding enthusiastically like the little plastic dog in the back of English cars. True to his nature, he promises to help with an aspect of the school building as by way of reparation. His only real intention is to get the fuck out of Dodge. As with any future call from the numbers of the contacts he made in Mali and RIM, he'd simply ignore them. This done, we go back to Wolof and he winds up by organising a few more shots and gets into the car without as much as a by-your-leave to the families of our subject. He's done his bit for the day by kowtowing to Mme Diallo and we're off to Nioro to rendezvous with the other migrants at the house, as Translatorguy, Germanguy and the journalist took off for the five hour drive to Bamako.

BWH had decided to rent a blockhouse of three rooms with a large courtyard in which to gather returning and arriving migrants. The Migrant Centre in Nioro had been closed down as the Malian government did not want to give the migrants the opportunity to stay and make their way back north. It was agreed by all, that the house was indeed necessary and although no permission was sought or given it was generally accepted. He had the Nioro co-ordinator manage the house and a migrant-in-limbo to act as guardian. He paid out monthly for a sack of rice and a few litres of oil to help feed those staying there. I would be in and out over a three/ four month period, trying to capture three subjects who would agree to be filmed as they went into the lion's den. This is the maddening thing about BWH; he loses all sense of proportion whilst trying to organise his piss up in a brewery. There was still a month to go before he arrived in Mali to film and he wanted to close the house down. This would of course disperse everyone and make interviewing a difficult and laborious process. Nioro du Sahel is a frontier town where there are special considerations involved, not in the least the heavy military and police presence. With the compound he would be free to conduct interviews. He grew increasingly angry at having to pay out for the house and food. He accused the co-ordinator, guardian and migrants of conniving to steal from him. An accusation he'd later level at me in NKT. I cautioned against closure, kept the house open and would pay for itself later, big time.

So it was to the house that we decamped after being dragged over the coals and our goodbyes to the others. When BWH got back into director's mode, he actually enjoyed it and was happy he told me, that he'd decided to keep the house open, albeit superficially. He had skimped on the rice and oil allowance, claiming difficulties with WU. Cheap bastard. Of course he enjoyed the atmosphere! He was the fuckin' king for the day, again. There were representatives from the various migrant associations of West Africa who came to be interviewed, a few returning migrants known to me and the other migrants who'd undergone the rigours of recently being thrown out of RIM. BWH directed everyone and everything to his requirements and I was sent off to buy bus tickets for the crew, taking with me Mariem and all the passports. The boys would have to buy theirs; paid for by BWH but there was a problem. The subject from Nioro Tugane hadn't an ID card! He didn't think to tell us either until the moment came to buy the tickets, as if he really hadn't intended in going. I surmised that perhaps he'd take as much money as he was given for each stage of the work. We were then sent back to the village to get his birth certificate and necessary papers to then go to the office and obtain his ID card. What a fuckin' mess. This took two days of being sent here, sent there and every fuckin' where, because our subject was nowhere to be seen on the family birth certificate. I lost it after day one, wanting to kill the subject and simply began to pay out bribes in order to get the ID card into his grubby hand. The other problem was that none of them had Yellow Fever Certificates. No problem, you buy the booklet in a local shop, take it to the local doctor who takes your blood pressure and enters the details of the injection etc and takes 2000cfa, roughly 3 euros (Banque Centrale Des Etats De L'Afrique De L'Ouest) for his troubles. BWH and the camera crew were content to hang about drinking beer and playing around with the footage in the auberge and with all the bus tickets and certificates in hand, we prepared ourselves by packing up for the trip north to NKT.

BWH begins the next day by saying that he hasn't got very many cfa left. Mariem and I buy enough for a picnic of sorts and BWH promises to change money to buy more food and water. He wouldn't and we'd suffer. I'd later tumble badly through being dehydrated and put myself on the sidelines. He'd arranged for a 4x4 to come from Atigh's travel agency in NKT to ferry him and the baggage north, whilst the 'team' travelled on the bus. He'd rendezvous with us at the rest stops and give us money for food and water. BWH thought it a good idea to give me a walkie-talkie because it would be cheaper than using the phone! I said no. He gave it to Cameraguy who then gave it to me on the fuckin' bus. It caused nothing but problems with the Gendarmes. Our cover story; through not having a permit, was that I was taking the two white men up to Chiguetti to record the Haratin singing the praises of the Prophet Mohamed, as well as exploring the five different types of Mauritanian music. Only, Atigh's driver did us in big time. He told the first Poste that we were a film crew and that was that. At each of the 20 Postes thereafter, we were subjected to a grueling question and search process that was to make the 18 hour trip around 30 hours. We met BWH only once, during the first night and he then closed his phone and fucked off to lord it up at the five star Hotel Tyfeila in NKT.

We arrived at roughly 16.00 hrs at the Sixieme Sonef bus station. Everyone is hungry, dehydrated, completely shagged out and the Cunt's phone is closed. We leave messages but to no avail. The other problem is the three Malians. My contact can't be contacted and anyhoo, we've no money to do anything or go anywhere. It's as clear as day that the Malians can't come to Hotel Tyfeila and I phone a friend. I take off to meet a friend who is holding 200 euros for me, change it and get back to the bus station and hand out fruit, water and biscuits to everyone. The 200 euros, BWH immediately refuse to pay me when asked for, instead asking me for proof and receipts! We drive around searching here and there for a suitable out of the way place and eventually due to tiredness and frustration take the three to the auberge of an associate. I pay for the night, give them money to eat dinner and breakfast and take everyone to the hotel some two hours later. There at the door is the smiley and ever so well fed BWH cunt. He welcomes us in as if nothing is wrong. I truly wanted to strangle the bastard but can only smile a smile that says, 'Say the wrong thing and you'll go directly to hospital. You will not pass Go or collect £200.'

The political life in RIM had changed dramatically since the last visit of Soundguy and BWH and as he hadn't listened to my last briefing I knew that BWH would take no notice this time either but the others had to be informed, especially as there was no permit.

"Alison, what did I say about filming in RIM?"

"You said that it was extremely difficult even if you had a permit."

At this particular time, there were four French journalists in prison who were doing a piece on slavery. They had their shooting permit, RIM journalist in tow and still ended up being banged up, their gear trashed apparently. I later heard that the price for each man the production company had to pay out in order to have them released, was 30 000 euros. This did not in any way register with BWH who I could see was simply waiting for me to shut the fuck up and for him to take over. I also cautioned on my publically being involved with the crew as it would draw attention from the DSS. I'd move the boys the next day to the last house used in Cinqieme and BWH could take it from there. I also asked that BWH change drivers as I had no trust in him whatsoever and his continued involvement would lead to a disaster. This point was agreed upon by the other two but to no avail.

"Better the devil we know." he said.

Snuggly wrapped up in bed after dinner in our five star luxury, I became aware of a tightening around my legs, then thighs and an excruciating cramp-like pain took over and I felt sick. I got up not wakening Mariem and stumbled into the bathroom to vomit the entire contents of my stomach then collapse, breaking my nose on the rim of the toilet. All done very silently. I lay there in a bloody rigour for what seemed an eternity until Mariem decided to come and investigate as she could hear no noise but could see that the bathroom light was on. I sent her off for Peter. They duly arrived, took me back to bed and he took off as cramp seemed to pervade every part of my body. He arrived with bottles of mineral water, sachets of salt, sugar and surprisingly chilli powder, not asked for but welcome and I guzzled and vomited my way through the night. BWH wasn't at all pleased the next morning and gave me little or no time in order to get my shit together to move the boys. Peter had done his best to help me with BWH but only succeeded in getting us both into trouble, as he had done on a number of occasions in Mali. It transpired that I wasn't the only person to have noticed the growing coldness and anger from BWH and explains why he never paid me. You only need to rebel once and the game's a bogey as they say in Scotland. You're fucked in other words. I took the driver with me and moved the boys, just. I was completely fucked. BWH continued to conduct himself in his normal manner as if he hadn't a care in the world. He completely disregarded the danger he was placing everyone under. It took me three days to get back on track. I chilled out with Mariem in the hotel, visited a few friends and enjoyed the break from BWH. It's on day two that it goes belly up.

BWH all on his lonesome masterminds the rental of a boat, takes the three subjects to the beach and pays some fisherman to come out on a jolly, right next to the fuckin' fishing port for a film sequence, 'The boys go to Europe.' This is the most stupid thing that he has done so far and I only know of it because a friend and associate phones to warn me. The subsequent footage is the most ridiculous I've ever seen. It has no context whatsoever in the film, has no bearing on the story whatsoever and ridicules all that I have researched and done in an effort to tell the true story of the struggle of the African migrants. It belittles both them and me. He truly is a mental cunt. The whole of NKT knows about the filming and I'm asked to have him stop before everyone goes to prison. I immediately phone BWH to stop filming warning that he could be arrested at any time. He shuts me out, telling me he'll see me at the hotel, when HE's finished! I then go to meet my friend at a beach rendezvous and discover that he fucked off not long after I'd phoned. He tells me straight off that Mariem and I are safe, that I'm an officially registered guide and that I have the protection of his uncle, a highly placed member of the Junta. We will not be going to jail under any circumstances. My friend's uncle can have the permit done within an hour or so. Commission for my friend, for this service would be in the region of 50 euros. Given the expense that BWH had gone to in order to have Mohamed Salem try was cheap. All areas access too! There'd be no need for a journalist as I was on board. But the wanton disregard for the circumstances in which BWH worked would not be tolerated. Alison knows it to be the right way to go and she's not nearly so clever as BWH, so why not BWH? This is where his massively mentally ill ego comes into play. A man who believes he sits beside or above God does not deal with ordinary mortals such as you and I or the military Junta of RIM, apparently. Oh, how the mighty will fall. "Alison, I need a little back rub, this reminiscing is particularly stressful . . . maybe a little lower down would be better . . . ahh good girl . . . ooh, that's quite low and not my back!"

I get back to the hotel and straight into a meeting. BWH has decided that it's not necessary for me to accompany the team to NDB!

'Oh, I'm definitely cut out of the equation now.'

Also, he's got himself booked on the last Air France flight outta Dodge as, "he's off to work on the Malian footage." He shit himself was all! He's abandoning us! There's an immediate mutiny in the ranks and the boys quite correctly tell him that they don't know the town or the contacts, that they'll end up in jail if I don't go with them. That they won't and can't go there without me. He immediately flies off the handle and goes into a major huff, then realizing that he's on the way out, BWH reluctantly agrees to keep me on. I then take him out into the garden where my friend is waiting. BWH is not comfortable in the slightest after the mutiny. My friend tells BWH about the reaction of the day's shoot and the possibilities that could arise from it. BWH goes on the defensive and ask immediately how much it will cost for the permit. 'The same price as normal." Which is 230 000 UM (690 euros). All he has to do is come round to his house, which is a few minutes away and over tea talk with his uncle who will give him the permit, stamped and signed there and then. BWH asks what his price is for this. My friend tells him that if he were agreeable then 50 euros would suffice. BWH goes ballistic and with spittle coming out of his fat mouth, turns on me telling me that I'm in collusion with my friend to steal from him and in any case filming has been stopped. I'm simply taking his friends on a tourist trip, which my friend knows to be a lie as I've given him the entire story of their time in RIM. BWH storms out leaving us sitting at the table. My friend warns me against getting too public with them, to shepherd them around discretely and leave them to their own devices. If it all goes down the toilet, then they're on their own. "You as their guide can say that they worked counter to what you'd advised. Do the honest thing by your clients and we'll talk with my uncle later." We say our goodbyes and I go to look for the boys. They're still in the public lounge and BWH is nowhere to be seen, he's gone off to pack. I tell them about the meeting and both are in shock. I of course miss out the bit about them being on their own if it all goes wrong. They like me can't believe that he is so fuckin' stingy as to the permit, which is a natural thing to have being a film crew and the free access without the journalist is Christmas, New Year, Tabaski and Happy Birthday all rolled into one. They go off into the bar and I go to my room to brief Mariem. She still wants to cut his throat.

The next morning we unhappy few, are all at breakfast waiting for me to arrive. There's an uneasy atmosphere, instigated only by BWH's indifference of us. Everyone is still loyal to the project, myself included. My responsibilities are clear, to counter any shit that BWH might throw in our direction from Canada. I certainly don't want Peter going to jail. BWH reinforced his need to get back to Canada as of the utmost importance as he is due to go on a round of documentary film festivals. It would be at one festival in the US that he'd meet a friend of mine and not speak to him, of me in glowing terms that would eventually come back to me. How small the world is. There was some filming for them to do in Cinqieme, street shots, which sent me off into orbit but only inside my head. I'd deal with the boys myself or try to. What is there to say to a couple of nerds who will always look like nerds, "Don't look like a nerd when you're out in the street or the bullies will pick on you."

What I said was, "Don't come over like a film-crew, please."

True to form they came over exactly, like a fuckin' film-crew. Before BWH took off, he told me that he's decided to change the driver and gives me a bundle of cash, which I count out in front of everyone. I'm no thief and don't want BWH to have any reason to say otherwise. I give them the full nerd lecture. I ask them to wait for me until I have changed drivers and get back to take them to Cinqieme. They go and do an equipment check as Mariem and I take off for the agency. There we meet Moctar, who is a retired level headed army driver and speaks very little French. I'm already very pleased. We go back to the hotel and pick up the boys. Mariem will chill out at the migrants house and I'll shadow the nerds, who in all honesty play their part to the full. It's within 10-15 minutes that all hell breaks loose as a local takes exception to the nerds and he's on the verge of phoning the police when a Pulaar friend of mine drives by in his taxi. He placates the man as I lead them away down this narrow passageway and out of the frying pan and away from the fire.

I have very dark forebodings about NDB. If there was ever a reason to grow an ulcer in record time, then it would be now and not due to the copious amounts of chilli that I have consumed over breakfast, lunch and dinner for the last 38 years. The next task is to film the Malians buying their bus tickets to NDB and as usual, the subject from NT is a twisted cunt and complicates filming. It would be he, that finally brought the project to an end; well him and BWH, in December 2010. On being asked by the police on why he was with the others in a five star hotel, he spilled the beans. He told them without pressure; without being threatened in any way, the entire sad tale.

The next day the Hilux is loaded up and we go out to wait on the boys to arrive at the bus stop and film the off. Cameraguy is being a little more reserved thank fuck and eventually the bus arrives the guys get on and we mount up. We follow them to the Poste Police sorti NDB. I'm off course known and we breeze through and are off. We drive on up the road to pick out a place on a dune overlooking the road to film the bus. Peter has his sound gear at the ready and I take off for a walk knowing that I've an hour to kill. It's good to feel the sand beneath my naked feet, my head swathed in my turban and the sun beating down on my back. I could just keep going and leave them all to it but that would make me as big a selfish cunt as BWH and I turn around and get back just in time to see the Sonef bus arrive, pass and drive on. Our journey is quick and without any problem. Moctar has a few questions which I answer honestly. He's on board and one of the team, we'll have no trouble with him and indeed when trouble did arrive he was decisive and clear headed just as you would expect from an army driver. He's taken a shine to both Mariem and I, all is well, for the moment. On arriving at the Police Poste NDB I'm treated like the rock star I truly am. I'm known here both as a shepherd and a co-ordinator of gardeners and student farmers. This is true in both cases. The crew's passports are processed quickly and efficiently and everyone gets to meet Mariem, who they had often heard about and asked after but hadn't met until this moment. We carry onto the hotel of a Bidan friend, an out of the way hotel but still very comfortable if not a little expensive. My Malian co-ordinator in NDB was on hand to meet and greet the boys and take them to their next refuge.

NDB, is a highly sensitive major port and militarized zone, crawling with Surete, Garda Civile, DSS and DST. As well as, the usual suspects looking to make a fast buck.

"Please Alison remind everyone what I have said about RIM. Sorry my dear did I waken you up?"

She's as fuckin' bored as I am repeating myself and I did again but do you think it got through? I briefed them fully en route to NDB about its inherent dangers but it would be to no avail, they simply can't come out of film-crew mode even if their lives depended on it. I added, "Don't fuck around here. Mariem and I are safe; it's you who are not!"

I went to visit my Malian co-ordinator the next morning, in a taxi, on foot and alone. I told him all that had transpired in NKT and that he was quite within his rights to resign. He refused simply because I had come. Had the crew arrived without me he would have been finished. I said that given our circumstances, he would be their real producer for the five days. I'd pass him onto the film-crew and would reinforce that he was the boss. Any shit from either of them and he was to phone me. I basically worked alone as the ghost producer co-ordinating the team and I would seem always ten paces behind but thanks to Peter I was at least kept up to date. Stephane was in commando mode and I wouldn't be the one to go for him when he went down. All this was because BWH continued to direct from afar, sending them here and there without knowing a fuckin' thing about NDB or its problems or the recent changes in regulations and access. In my opinion BWH was pushing for a confrontation and the others were oblivious to the dangers.

Aware of the last dance I had encountered in NDB, Mariem and I did the tourist thang, shopping, going for coffee and patisserie and off to the market to meet a good friend. I will decline to say which market or what it is that he does. When we weren't there, we were in his apartment or chilling out at the hotel. Then on day three, it was to be a major shoot and the boys took off with Moctar to collect, the three Malians, the co-ordinator, another migrant who was to ask the questions I was supposed to do to camera and another African just happened by for the fun of it, seemingly. What a cluster fuck of cluster fucks! BWH was driving blind on a freeway in rush hour traffic, in fog and in the wrong direction! How conspicuous, how fuckin' conspicuous can two North Americans, a Black Moor driver, four Malians, a Chadian and a Senegalese be, going into a military zone? What made matters worse was that the crew brought them back to the fuckin' hotel to conduct a filmed interview out in the street opposite!!!!! Poor Alison is staring at me in disbelief as are a lot of you I expect. And true to form our NT subject plays up and fucks up filming, again. I'm in the hotel watching every move and want to cut his fuckin' throat. He's oblivious to the danger or well aware that he'll fuck us all up, only he won't. Not me. Not Mariem. He'll go to prison and rot I tell him. No-one will come for him. Ever! He tells me he is sorry. I tell him to fuck off. If I hear that you have stepped out of line I will come and get you and take you to the police myself! To make matters worse my stand-in is now demanding to be paid more than was agreed and he wants to prolong my agony by negotiating me to a point of tiredness so that I will pay up. No fuckin' way. I cut it short by explaining that what he was given is it. If he would like to go to the police and register a complaint then do so by all means. The Bank of Africa is closed. The week was conducted in a manner of driving to out of the way places which there aren't, running the risk of being pulled over at any time due to the carnival atmosphere of the 4x4 and me not knowing a fucking thing until no-one comes back to the hotel. Stressed to fuck would be an understatement and surprisingly no ulcers arrived. Thanks to my friend I was able to dine out on best quality Moroccan hashish and smoke myself into oblivion, every single fuckin' night.

As the week wore on, Stephane became the French-Canadian version of James Fuckin' Bond.

"Find me an out of the way place to film Mohamed, BWH needs some town shots." He asks me one morning at breakfast.

"Alison please, help me my dear."

"I think someone needs to be shot teacher." She answers smiling.

"Later my dear."

Please folks for the last time, **"THERE IS NOWHERE, NOWHERE TO FILM QUIETLY OUT OF THE WAY IN AFRICA! NO FUCKIN'**

## WHERE! THE BIDAN DOES NOT LIKE CAMERAS WIELDED BY STRANGERS IN HIS COUNTRY!"

So anyhoo, off we trot, Moctar at the wheel, me beside Moctar and the two children in the back playing with their toys. I tell JFB, "If I say put the camera away, then put it away."

He assures me that he will. We drive up and down the main street that brings you into NDB from NKT and JFB gets out to go for a walk, with his trusty 5D. We park up, buy some snacks and hang back, waiting about ten minutes then drive off to find the boy. There is he crouched down between a pile of bricks and some wood filming in secret. He's shitting himself and the look of relief on his face is a picture in itself. JFB isn't so fuckin' James Bond after all and he gushed his thanks at coming to rescue him, something James Bond would never do. Then again he's French-Canadian and not Scots. I'm then asked to find an out of the way place to continue filming, so I direct Moctar towards Robinet Deux and we eventually park up. JFB is filming fuck knows what exactly when a car approaches slowly at first and then makes straight for us, the driver's head swathed in a black turban. I tell Moctar to move and JFB cries out that he's not finished. Having a 4x4 I direct Moctar into taking the rough pistes but as the car following is a 190D he naturally follows too, albeit at a reduced pace but keeps up. His car isn't so precious when there's money or an arrest to be made. Same difference really. I have to tell JFB twice to stow the gear or he's out in the street. It's no use talking to him now, BWH has filled his head with all sorts of shit as well as the shit he brought with him that he thought he could use and the shit in the belief that he's JFB. No, not fuckin' possible.

We take off into rush hour traffic and I head in the opposite direction of the hotel. We go left right back on ourselves and then right and left and all the time he keeps up. I then direct Moctar towards a big roundabout and we double back up towards him, pass him and leave him blocked in traffic to take the most direct and therefore difficult route back to the hotel. You can tell that I've trundled all the clandestine routes here in NDB and Moctar's surprisingly pleased at my navigation and we're back indoors, safe and sound.

As a last moment thing, BWH wants the boys to go out to Cap Blanc to do a 'boys looking back towards the port shot and then looking out to sea shot.' This is a military zone and again, the white/black passenger thing. It's not just that. There's the obvious difference in quality of clothes that the NA's are sporting and the poorer Africans are wearing. The Hilux is brand fuckin' new. The equipment bags are expensive. There's an obvious, 'What the fuck's going on here thing?' That seemingly everyone but me misses out on but off they go and Mariem and I sit by the phone waiting for news from the co-ordinator. More to the point they have the Chadian on board again. I hope to fuck that he doesn't come back to the hotel but he does and I cut him short by giving him his money and instructing the co-ordinator to get him into a taxi and fuck off toute de suite, which he does. My patience is exhausted and what's even more frustrating is that I didn't benefit financially from the shit. I know I'm repeating myself here but in all honesty folks, as it pours out from the recesses of my tortured mind, I really want to maim BWH bad. Is there at least one person who's with me on this? Contact me on Facebook: Mohamed Ibrahim Ould Daoud, I'd seriously like to know of your opinion. Am I justified in wanting to maim the bastard?

The last two evening meals in NDB were spent in a Chinese restaurant, which also doubles as a whore house with the oldest and ugliest whores I have ever seen. With one exception, a very beautiful 22 year old Chinese girl, who probably works around the clock. The food's not bad and it was Mariem's first experience of the two worlds. Mariem declines at first to order any Chinese food and orders steak and chips, the European standard in such cases. As the dishes began to arrive, she had a taste and a mouthful and then a plateful and ate just about everything there was to be had. The boys had several beers and I slipped out to have a small spliff, whilst the whores played mah jongg. Wouldn't have minded a game myself but I hastened quickly back to a time when I played with Chinese waiters in a small restaurant such as this in the UK on a regular basis and lost a small fortune. The evening's jollity came to an abrupt halt when BWH phoned to say that I was stealing from him, that I was to go over exactly what we needed with Peter and to contact him as soon as possible. I had sent a reply to his sms, "How much do you need?" with, "We need $2011."

He went ballistic and Peter and I sat down and itemised everything and how much did it come to? Exactly the same amount I had previously calculated in my head, $2011. We send the reply back using Peter's phone. The cunt sent $600 so kept us in NDB for another day kicking our heels. Peter tried frantically to have him send the money sooner but the stroppy bastard closed his phone, again.

"Nothing new there for me Peter, I've had a year and a half of this shit." Peter declined to comment but his face said it all.

Eventually it was time to go and Mariem and I said our goodbyes to my friends. The crew did a little shopping and Moctar fuelled up. We went off to see the subjects in their new digs. Peter wanted to give them a housewarming present and bought a sack of rice. BWH had phoned me the previous night to say that he'd pay 50% of their 'pirogue ticket' if they'd earn the other half. I was to tell the co-ordinator but not the boys and I was there to also pay the subjects too but not the co-ordinator, who was apparently going to be paid by WU. To say that he wasn't pleased was an understatement as he'd worked hard for his money. He'd declined work and therefore money. I knew BWH. I knew it could go bad for my friend and later on it did. We then drove back towards NKT with JFB out back with the baggage and a 5D, no turban and a sleeveless T-shirt, stupid cunt. At the first Gendarmerie Poste I banged on the rear window to warn him to put it away and JFB didn't, surprise surprise. The sergeant wasn't too chuffed and a lengthy conversation took place. I got out to see if I could hurry things along.

"Why can't I take photographs of the dunes and lizards?" asks JFB.

"It's forbidden." says the sergeant.

"Why is it forbidden?" I ask.

"It's the law." replies the sergeant.

"Thank you." I tell him.

"Go now." he says.

I thank him and as we mount up I warn JFB going against my advice again or we'll be here all fuckin' day! He take this on board as but not the fact that he's exposed to the sun and duly falls asleep. Moctar asks me if he should pull over and have JFB come inside, I shake my head and tell him that I'll wait until he's a nice colour of rosy red and then have Moctar pull over. When he becomes well done, I waken him up and he shrugs off the sunburn. I give him his turban and get back inside. I leave him to it. I take everyone to the Menata and JFB slinks off to his room to collapse from sun-stroke and Mariem and I see Moctar off, giving him an extra large tip that I had calculated for. Everyone had a day off mainly spent sleeping and eating. Then it was JFB's time to go. Surprisingly he tells me that he has to pay for his own air ticket to Canada. I don't care if he has to fuckin' swim home!

Sidi Gratuit had given me a loan of his 190D in order to take JFB to the airport as most if not all of the flights take off in the wee small hours. It being a hot country of course. We have a late meal, the boys a few expensive Chinese beers and I a few spliffs and then load up JFB's bags and off to the airport. It's check point time after 21.00hrs and we have two to pass through to get to the airport. I shout out, "Check point!"

There the waiting policeman with the whistle sees our approaching car, 'Ah, three white men and an African whore, loads of money!'

There's a cadet poking through the turret of a crappy armoured car his AK in his childlike hands to the right, parked up on the pavement. The pig signals that I should pull over, which I don't. I drive on to his furious whistling. There's a shriek from the back. It's JFB again and I look back to see the two getting down as low as they can. Miss Moneypenny has more balls than this guy. Mariem laughs and JFB asks her in French why didn't I stop? I reply that, the car doesn't have any papers, my driving license is in Mali and I don't do check points or baksheesh, ever! You know different. There's a muted howl from the back and I don't know where it came from. Ten minutes later I shout out, "Checkpoint!"

It's the same scenario as before, the two silent waiting for a fusillade of rounds hitting the car. Five minutes later we're at the airport and JFB's off to sit inside for two hours. On the return journey, Peter's lying down on the backseat as if expecting WWIII to break out. We pass through the same checkpoints and arrive in one piece at the Menata, having gone through the same scenarios, twice. There's a party atmosphere in the Magic Garden and some old friends have arrived during our absence with real fuckin' beer which Peter helps them drink. I'm spliffing out and everyone's happy. I have a call.

"Meet me outside."

It's my friend who had tried to negotiate the shooting permit with BWH. I tell Mariem that I'm going to the toilet and walk out the front door to see my friend in a rather posh LandCruiser, gold crash bars and bumpers and dark smoke coloured windows. I get in the back and there's a stout elderly well-dressed gentleman sitting in the passenger seat. His uncle speaks in Hassaniya and although translated for me I get the drift. We do a once around the block, less than three minutes and in less than four I'm back in the Magic Garden negotiating a very large bong which adds to my state of euphoria.

Next morning we take Peter to the Tuareg Taxi; in Sidi's 190D again, that is to take him to Tomboctou in more or less than five days. For 54 euros it is certainly the safest way to get there given that it's full of Tuareg. On this particular day it was mainly women and children, which is good for Peter as he'll get to eat well! There is another Taxi which goes off-piste, costs a little bit more and is used by businessmen, traffickers and Tuareg chiefs. I'd like to do that one day. Peter is sad to leave us but happy that's he's off on another adventure. We make for the Sonef ticket office to book our seats for the following day. In the early evening we go to visit an uncle of Mariem's, a marabout, who tells us that we have to sacrifice a sheep, who has a black neckerchief that will ensure a happy and safe journey. I don't have the money and we would get on the bus at 05.00 the next morning, simply glad to be leaving RIM behind, to begin our new life in Mali.

We chill out for an hour at the auberge and make our way to Malcolm's for a going away party of sorts; it is for us anyway as I don't know when we'll be back. Our co-host Sidi Boyu is in fine form and there's lobster, real coffee, chocolate and cake. Malcolm's working hard trying to impress a pretty Spanish girl, who takes us back to the auberge at midnight. A quick spliff and off to bed, bags already packed and waiting. We've not much anyway. I like to travel light.

The journey south, from the standpoint with the Gendarmerie Postes, as I had expected, went without a problem. Mariem was amused to hear them wishing us a happy holiday and bemused further by them not asking for our passports. She let it pass, happy she was en route for her family. Only we broke down three fuckin' times and spent a total of 69 hours on the road south before we reached Bamako!

"If only we'd done the sacrifice eh uncle!"

I asked Mariem to walk the km between the RIM and Malian frontier, as we had been processed in record time and the others would be ages yet. I found a tree to sit under and told Mariem what had transpired between me and my friend's uncle.

"The night before Peter left there was a soiree in the garden and I went to the toilet." Mariem nods.

"I didn't. I met my friend and his uncle out in their car at the front door and went for a very short drive."

She's looking directly in my eyes.

"He told me to phone his nephew in six months time and see how things stand. That I was to take my Malian wife back to Mali and have a well earned rest."

We laughed, really laughed. All those Gendarmes who'd said Bon Vacances!

At the Malian frontier we're met by Mariem's cousin, Maiga, who's the Chef Des Douanes. The Police Chief knows me by my work on the documentary and welcomes me home like a hero returning from the war. Everyone we saw, waiting migrants known to me, Phonecreditguy, Michuiguy, Donkeycartboy, everyone seemed to be shaking our hands. They all knew how risky it was to go north as I had done time and time again and this time, I had an extra responsibility with me, a Malian girl, a Songhay from Dire of a very distinctive family. Her grandfather's younger brother, 'Le Pere' is the Sous-Chef Des Douanes at Nioro du Sahel. Her grandfather is a marabout of some renown and known word-wide. This of course is all a major surprise to me as we have been so engrossed in getting the job done and have really had no time at all in getting to know each—others intimate details. It seems that in the blink of an eye at 0500, we are at the auberge Djamila, with Nico asking me if I'd like a beer! So fuckin' relieved was I to be in Mali I can't describe it.